PUBLICATION
OF THE
AMERICAN
DIALECT
SOCIETY

NUMBER 78

PUBLISHED FOR
THE SOCIETY BY
THE UNIVERSITY
OF ALABAMA PRESS
TUSCALOOSA AND LONDON

**CENTENNIAL
USAGE STUDIES**

Edited by Greta D. Little
and Michael Montgomery

This book is a publication in the Centennial Series of the American Dialect Society in celebration of the beginning of its second century of research into language variation in America.

Copyright © 1994
American Dialect Society
ISBN 0-8173-0739-7

Library of Congress Cataloging-in-Publication Data

Centennial usage studies / edited by Greta D. Little and Michael Montgomery.
    p.   cm. — (Publication of the American Dialect Society : no. 78)
    Includes bibliographical references and index.
    ISBN 0-8173-0739-7
    1. English language—United States—Usage. 2. English language—Spoken English—United States. 3. Americanisms.
I. Little, Greta D. II. Montgomery, Michael, 1950– . III. Series.
PE1702.A5 no. 78
[PE2827]
428'.00973—dc20   94-31291

British Library Cataloguing-in-Publication Data available

CONTENTS

Acknowledgments   v

1. Whose Usage? Fred Newton Scott and the Standard of Speech, *Richard W. Bailey*   1
2. Terminology and Usage, *Boyd H. Davis*   10
3. Slang and Usage, *Connie C. Eble*   15
4. The Linguistic Autobiography of an American, *Richard Gunter*   19
5. The Expression of Changing Social Values in Dictionaries: Focus on Family Relationships, *Sidney I. Landau*   32
6. Visual Style, *Greta D. Little*   40
7. The Language of Electronic Mail: Written Speech? *Natalie Maynor*   48
8. Studying Usage in Computer Corpora, *Charles F. Meyer*   55
9. Explaining Usage to the Public, *Michael Montgomery*   62
10. Social Uses of Possessive Adjectives in English, *John J. Staczek*   71
11. The Capitalization of Color Names and Other Terms for Ethnic Groups, *Robert S. Wachal*   81
12. The Spread of Nonsexist Language: Planning for Usage That Includes Us All, *Keith Walters*   91
13. Pan-Atlantic Usage Guidance, *John Algeo*   101
14. Prescriptive Versus Descriptive: The Role of Reference Books, *Lynn M. Berk*   108
15. "Broad Reference" in Pronouns: Handbooks Versus Professional Writers, *Charlotte C. Crittenden*   115
16. A Comparison of Usage Panel Judgments in the *American Heritage Dictionary 2* and Usage Conclusions and Recommendations in *Webster's Dictionary of English Usage*, *Virginia G. McDavid*   123

17. Usage Items in Current Handbooks of Composition,
    Walter E. Meyers — 129

18. *Drug* Usage among High-School Students in Silsbee, Texas: A Study of the Preterite, *Cynthia Bernstein* — 138

19. Dictionary Recognition of Developing Forms: The Case of *snuck*, *Thomas J. Creswell* — 144

20. The Suffix *-ee*, *Michael R. Dressman* — 155

21. More on Proximity Concord, *W. N. Francis* — 162

22. The Lawyer's *imply*, *Bryan A. Garner* — 165

23. *Vice president* and *president*: Syntax and Semantics, *James B. McMillan* — 169

24. Current Generic Pronoun Usage: Evidence from the Writing of Two Generations, *Miriam Meyers* — 174

25. The Unmarked Plural Noun Following Compound Adjective Phrases, *Avis Kuwahara Payne* — 182

26. Is *between you and I* Good English? *Richard K. Redfern* — 187

27. *Absent* 'without': A New American English Preposition, *Alan R. Slotkin* — 194

List of Abbreviations — 203

References — 205

Index of Words Cited — 223

ACKNOWLEDGMENTS

The editors first wish to thank the contributors to this volume, all of them members of the American Dialect Society. They share the view that a collection of essays on usage was important to commemorate the centennial of the Society and to demonstrate the continuing vitality of research on American English usage and its prominent and continuing role in the Society's work. The editors are grateful to each of them for quickly and patiently responding to queries and suggestions. It was a pleasure to work with them all.

For administrative support at the University of South Carolina as this volume was being edited, our appreciation goes to Joel Myerson, Chair of the Department of English, and to Ted Rathbun and Stanton Green, Chairs of the Department of Anthropology.

For assisting with innumerable editorial tasks, especially copyediting, we thank Valerie Daniel, a research assistant in the USC Linguistics Program.

For inspiration, ideas, and a healthy push early on, we are much obliged to Boyd H. Davis of the University of North Carolina at Charlotte.

We trust that this collection will testify that work on American usage is alive and very well. Congratulations to the American Dialect Society.

Greta D. Little
Michael Montgomery

1. Whose Usage? Fred Newton Scott and the Standard of Speech

RICHARD W. BAILEY
University of Michigan

The Centennial of the American Dialect Society offers an occasion to reflect on what has been accomplished in documenting usage and in determining what teachers ought to do with the information that scholars have compiled. In accumulating and assessing usage, the work of the last hundred years provides much in which we can take considerable pride. In 1889, Whitney's great *Century Dictionary* had only begun to appear; few scholars regarded the contemporary American vernacular as worthy of serious study; almost no one had thought through the schism between democratic ideals and notions of "correct" English. Today, we have shelf upon shelf of excellent reference works—usage surveys, comprehensive dictionaries, dialect atlases—all of them based upon meticulously gathered data from English in use. In employing knowledge about usage, however, the century of progress offers a more muddled picture. What we know is wonderful; what we do with that knowledge remains less certain.

In the most recent of the Society's periodic reviews of needed research, John Algeo declares:

A necessary, although unsexy, preliminary to considering needed research in the field of usage study is to define what is meant by *usage*. The definition is not obvious or automatic, yet it influences what sort of research we think should be done ("Usage" 37).

As elsewhere in this volume, *usage* here will be given its usual American definition: the choice among apparent synonyms, particularly when the alternatives have acquired distinct social meanings in which "correctness" is invoked to explain differences. For research, a definition of this sort contains its own implicit method: (1) listing variant forms with a description of the contexts in which they appear, and (2) seeking "acceptability" judgments from informed users of the language. In one way or another, that is the research program that we have followed over the last century. Does it adequately mirror the linguistic reality we are committed to describe? Some options are universally stigmatized in the late twentieth century—most notoriously *ain't*—and are acknowledged as nonstandard both by those who use them and by those who don't. Others, the majority, are regarded as unremarkable by some (for instance, *anymore* 'nowadays') yet as a source of "consternation and perplexity" for others (*Webster's Dictionary of English Usage* 106). Hence the invocation of *informed users* begs the question: Which "users" count as "informed"? The addition of the terms *informed users, stigmatized,* and *nonstandard* to the definition of *usage* only complicates the problem of definition; their indeterminacy suggests that the definition of *usage* is by no means an easy matter, nor, as I argue here, one that has been adequately treated in the century during which we have accumulated so much data.

Those who have attempted to explain linguistic variety have seldom found terminology to match a coherent theory of social ideals. Put simply, the issue resolves itself in answer to the question: "Why should the *ain't*-sayers get all the hard knocks?" In the name of describing English, language specialists have often created an elaborate, scientific disguise for our own prejudices and preferences, claiming that *we*, rather than the "pop grammarians," have the only claim to an informed view.

Usage disputes almost always presume deterministic choices—*right* or *wrong*—in a probabilistic world. Used bookstores abound in works that discriminate usage on precisely that basis. A typical example is W. H. P. Phyfe's *Eighteen Thousand Words Often Mispronounced*; another is *Well-Bred English* by Lillian Eichler, author of *The Book of Etiquette*. Even matchbooks advertise courses through which Americans can improve themselves linguistically, and books like Walton Burgess's *Five Hundred Mistakes Corrected* (1856) continue to be reissued in modern guise with their easy ascription of what constitutes a "mistake." At the same time, our best linguistic models are predicated on theories of *markedness* in which one variant is *unmarked* (for instance, the English singular noun) and another *marked* (noun plurals); labeling systems in usage guides are built around similar presumptions. Thus terms like *argot, euphemism, hypercorrection, jargon,* and *slang* presume that there are "normal," or unmarked, choices and "deviant" ones to which these labels apply. Yet such categories cannot apply unequivocally to individual usages. Are *passed away* 'died' and *aren't I?* 'am I not' really examples of euphemism or hypercorrection? Is it reasonable to assume that when educated persons employ *ain't* they inevitably intend to be "humorous" (as the usage note in the second edition of the *Random House Dictionary* invites its consulters to think)? Only if we are able to penetrate a speaker's motives can we discover if euphemisms arise from delicacy of sentiment (as if *passed away* were not a "normal" way of speaking) or hypercorrections from motives of gentility (as if the *aren't I*-user were consciously avoiding *am I not* or *ain't I*). These categories presume conscious *substitution* of unmarked forms or deliberate *avoidance* of marked ones even though there can be no evidence to ascertain substituting or avoiding (except in very rare cases of audible [or visible] self-correction). Thus our avowedly empirical inquiry is founded upon distinctly idealistic assumptions.

These issues animated discussions at the time the Dialect Society was founded, and they should continue as the basis of lively debate today. In order to see what has been accomplished—and what remains to be done—it is useful to turn attention to a progressive theoretician of usage whose ideas reflect the best thinking of the founders of the Society, Fred Newton Scott (1860–1931).

A native of Terre Haute, Indiana, Scott's university education was completed at the University of Michigan (B.A. 1884; M.A. 1888; Ph.D. 1889); he rose rapidly through the ranks of the faculty and was named professor in his fortieth year, then a remarkably youthful age for that distinction. Though not one of the pioneers of the Dialect Society (his name does not appear in the list of members until 1901), he was a founder of the Linguistic Society of America, President of the Modern Language Association in 1907, and President of the National Council of Teachers of English from 1911 to 1913 (the only person ever to have served two terms in that office). Unlike most others who joined the Dialect Society in its first decade, Scott was a public figure and an articulate expounder of new ideas about language variety. Donald C. Stewart concludes his appreciation of Scott's career with this judgment:

When one scans, even cursorily, Scott's long career and the range of topics that interested him, it becomes apparent quickly that here was the Renaissance man of his era. He brought to the field of English the intellectual equipment, knowledge, and curiosity that have always distinguished first-rate minds... (43).

A student of George Hempl's—the latter a founding member of the Dialect Society and the first to conduct a national dialect survey (Bailey, "The First")—and an influential teacher of Charles C.

Fries (author of the descriptively based *American English Grammar*) and of Fred Wolcott (co-author with Albert H. Marckwardt of *Facts about Current English Usage*), Scott was an important influence on usage study in this century.

For detailed consideration, I have chosen Scott's "The Standard of Speech in American English," read to the NCTE meeting on December 1, 1916, and published in *English Journal* in January 1917. Scott felt this essay to be of such importance that he gave it first place in and adopted its title for the collection of his papers he published in 1926. For all his modernity, Scott remained very much a nineteenth-century intellectual. His ideas of the foundation of good speech show Emerson's transcendentalism projected through Whitman: "the charm of the beautiful pronunciation of all words, of all tongues, is in perfect flexible vocal organs and in a developed harmonious soul" (quoted approvingly by Scott from Whitman's *American Primer*):

> If this doctrine is sound the stuff out of which a great national language is created is the simple, homely expression of sincere feeling and sturdy thinking. Live nobly, think good thoughts, have right feelings, be genuine, do not scream or strain to make pretense, cultivate a harmonious soul—follow these injunctions, and you are laying the foundation of a standard of American speech. Whence the speech comes does not matter. It may be the language of [Montague Glass's] Potash and Perlmutter. It may be composed of all the dialects spoken in Chicago or in San Francisco. It may be the speech of Boston, of Texas, or of Montana. No matter. If it is the voice of high wisdom, of moderation, of human nature at its best, the words will take on that power and charm which is the test of a great national speech (Scott 12–13; see Berlin 81, for further discussion).

As this extract shows, Scott was a linguistic democrat in a literary republic. Rejecting any source of authority other than "the simple, homely expression of sincere feeling and sturdy thinking," he anticipated supporters of the *rights* of students to "their own language," a position that the NCTE found painfully controversial when it was introduced in modern guise in 1972 and re-evaluated in 1984.

Where, then, are we to seek for the "standard of American speech"? Scott offers this answer:

> If any considerable body of educated Americans in any part of the country is using seriously a peculiar form of English for transacting the business of life, that form of English is good American and has a chance of becoming our national speech. Its chances are specially good if it is racy, rich in vocabulary, and is used by a large number of representative and gifted citizens (8).

What Scott does not address clearly is how we are to settle points of dispute. Who are these "representative and gifted citizens"?

Scott approaches this question when he quotes a letter he received "not long ago from a Western business man." Recognizing an expert in Scott, the correspondent wonders about the variety of vowels in *hot* and *hog*, the stress placement in *combine*, and the pronunciation of the initial syllable of *isolate* (a word he has ceased to use because "so many persons nowadays say 'ice-olate'"). The businessman's letter concludes with these sentences:

> Then there is "Chicago." Half the people I meet in the cars are going to "Chicawgo" and the other half to "Chicahgo." Now what I want to know is whether there is any right or wrong about this matter of pronunciation. If one way is right, why don't we all pronounce that way and compel the other fellow to do the same? If there isn't any right or wrong, why do some persons make so much fuss about it? (6).

In the case of *Chicago*, we have the answer. "Chicawgo" is the form preferred by Chicago-born and -bred speakers of English. Chicagoans whose parents were born "elsewhere" are only "somewhat less likely" to say "Chicawgo" than the offspring of long-time residents. "Chicahgo" is thus the pronunciation of "elsewhere," and had Scott had the benefit of Creswell's research ("Great Vowel Shift," from which I have drawn this information), he would have told the "Western businessman" that the people he met on the cars who said "Chicawgo" were likely to be returning home and the others were tourists and outside salespeople.

But like much else in usage, this answer turns out to be complicated in an interesting way. Broadcasters in Chicago are sometimes from "elsewhere," and a majority of them use "Chicahgo." Does their usage give a cachet of prestige to the out-of-town pronunciation? The question is further vexed by the rapidly spreading merger of "ah" and "aw" in a series of formerly distinct pairs: *cot/caught, don/dawn, hock/hawk, stock/stalk*, and so on. This innovation is spreading geographically and by age; at the present moment, westerners and the young almost everywhere are not likely to distinguish these pairs. The result of the merger thus promotes and favors homely "Chicawgo" as more and more speakers from "elsewhere" participate in the drift of "ah" to "aw" in these and other words with Northeastern "ah"—*pond, frog, holly*, and so on.

So how should Scott have replied to his correspondent? To go with the likely winner of this linguistic combat, "Chicawgo"? Or to tell him not to attempt to alter his pronunciation since his efforts would almost inevitably be unsuccessful and the thin guise of his pretense would expose him to ridicule? Or not to bother about the matter at all? Scott was, after all, eager that Whitman's "developed harmonious soul" not be trammeled in its expression by restraint. Yet the businessman wanted an answer. Though he had given up the word "iss-olate" altogether without much loss of expressive power, he might have found it vexing to have to work his way around *Chicago* by circumlocution and periphrasis.

Perhaps it is not entirely fair to say that Scott ducks the question, since it is pretty clear that he sides with the businessman in thinking that "persons who make so much fuss about pronunciation" are wasting their time.

In thinking seriously about English usage, however, we need to examine more difficult cases. As far as I know, the pronunciation of *Chicago* is not a distinct "marker" of social class or regional origin—that is, in Labov's sense of *marker,* a variant about which there is an articulate consensus on its status. It is, instead, an "indicator" of *Chicago-ness,* and the people who use one or the other of the variants probably rarely gain or lose esteem on the basis of the pronunciation they select. Grammatical variants, however, are much more likely to be "markers" and to rise to a level where choice does make a difference.

For my example, I turn to an incident from October 1983 when, on a slow news day, the *Detroit Free Press* reported that a substitute janitor had been assigned, mistakenly, to teach social studies classes at a Detroit high school. Instead of pointing out the mistake, the janitor went ahead and taught the classes. Commenting on this turn of events, one of the English teachers at the school allegedly "joked" by commenting, "I heard he did real good." Once this episode had been reported in the paper, the teacher was vilified and, thanks to wire-service distribution, found herself receiving letters from distant parts of the country. "Shame on you, Wanda," wrote a Clifton, New Jersey, man, "you have a chance to show your expertise and you commit a very basic grammatical error." In response, the teacher complained that she had been misquoted: "When I was asked by the reporter how the janitor did, I replied 'I understand that he did a rather decent job; he did rather well.'" To a follow-up question she says she responded, "Yes, he did a good job." The reporter said the original quotation was accurate. The follow-up to the original story (from which I have drawn this quotation) leaves unsettled the dispute about what she initially said.

In Scott's view, this English teacher must be counted among the "representative and gifted citizens" whose usage constitutes the foundation for the standard of American speech. A teacher for eighteen years and the proud holder of a master's degree from a major university, she was forced to defend her competence on the basis of, allegedly, having used *real* as an intensifier—a usage widespread since the seventeenth-century and parallel in grammar to the unexceptionable *very*. Further, she was patronized by the younger and less-well-educated reporter who had the effrontery to conclude his story with this paragraph: "'Grammar is a very important thing,' she said, and in a 45-minute interview with a Free Press reporter Tuesday, everything [she] said was grammatically correct."[1] The headline inviting attention to the story was: "Infamy not funny."

This story illustrates the importance of *usage* in American life and shows that the social consequences of using some grammatical variants can be painful and even destructive.

The status of *real good* in adverbial constructions is well-documented. It is widely used by educated and respected Americans. In *Webster's Second New International* it was described as "loose and uncultivated," but in *Webster's Third* only as "not often in formal use." Other recent dictionaries agree. The avowedly puristic *American Heritage Dictionary* calls it merely "informal." The same description appears in the most recent of the guides, *Webster's Dictionary of English Usage*: "*real* is informal and more suitable to speech than to writing." Suppose the Detroit teacher *had* said what the paper reported: "I heard he did real good." These various "authorities" make it clear that she was using respectable colloquial English, the language of informal talk among educated people who feel comfortable with each other—a much less stilted usage than "I understand that he did a rather decent job; he did rather well."

How should enlightened teachers in possession of all the information just quoted approach this usage? Should they feel obliged to pass along the socially important information that *real good* is an invitation to infamy? Should they provide the sort of background information collected from these various sources and *then* warn that *real good* is a marker that allows letter-writers to address an experienced, respected teacher by her first name and cry "shame on you"?

What are the "values of the standard dialect" as they apply to this Detroit high school teacher? These values are apparent to everyone. Detroit schools, like other urban school systems, are thought to be failing in their attempts to provide a high-quality education for their students. The newspaper story about a harried administrator confusing a substitute janitor for a substitute social studies teacher was an explicit illustration of that failure just at the time that a national commission had identified a "rising tide of mediocrity" in education and compared the alleged erosion of school quality to a fifth-column effort by a foreign power to destroy our society. The teacher is African-American and, however well educated and punctilious in her English, unlikely to persuade racially biased newspaper readers to share her self-image as a "perfectionist," "a stickler for details." The reporter drew the correct inference from these events: "As a news item, the story was excellent, but the English teacher's ungrammatical remark made it perfect, dramatically illustrating just what was wrong with the nation's schools." Talk like Scott's about "simple, homely expression of sincere feeling and sturdy thinking" is not only old-fashioned but nearly useless, even if phrased in terms of categories unknown to him like "cultural level" and "functional variety."

What we have identified through this example is the "land-mine theory of usage." Unwittingly, even the most "representative and gifted citizens" may find themselves under attack even if they are acknowledged users of "standard English." This lesson is by no means lost on students, and it is no wonder that many of them prefer silence to talk or shrink from the opportunity to write for a public beyond their circle of acquaintance. For many Americans, the road to effective speech and writing is mined with hidden explosives.

Our difficulty is that we have failed to concoct a theory of usage that finds a place for widely held prejudices. For most Americans, there is no dispute about "standards for English." There is only the monolithic collection of rules and lore "to which distracted Americans may resort for chastening and absolution." The "pleasing hallucination"—a Utopian standard English—to which Scott alluded seventy-five years ago is still very much the American dream.

Linguists who pretend that there is no consensus about the elite forms of English confuse their egalitarian ideals with the social reality that surrounds them.

Linguistic variety is, in Scott's view, a good thing, the source of the vitality and vigor of effective usage. He expressed this view forcefully in an era when optimism was rife that schools could launder English and create a uniform, "correct" national speech:

> A world in which everybody used the same words and language forms would be a much more monotonous, a much less interesting world, than the one we live in. ... It is the essence of language to change. No power can stay it. If by some miraculous intervention all the inhabitants of the world could at four o'clock tomorrow afternoon be made to speak exactly alike, it would not be twenty-four hours before differences would begin to make themselves apparent. Variations in types of character, in daily needs, in attitudes toward life and nature and society would bring about rapid variations in the mode of expression, and unless we are to conceive of the whole world as drowned in sloth or in brotherly love, competition and rivalry would soon give one set of variations precedence over the others, so that after a few generations the one language would break up into divergent dialects and ultimately into diverging languages (10).

Scott repudiates a world "drowned in sloth or in brotherly love," and he was glad that the spread of a world language (fervently anticipated in his day and ours) had not yet obliterated that variety. Yet it is worth reflecting on the idea that our ways of talking about usage—and its social consequences—have hardly evolved since he expressed this modern idea.

Note

[1] See *The Detroit Free Press*, 20 October 1983, pp. 1A, 12A.

2. Terminology and Usage

BOYD H. DAVIS
University of North Carolina, Charlotte

American English speakers create terms, surround them with synonyms, lardoon them with rhetorical conceits and flourishes, clip them and blend them, and stretch them out of recognition with a perverse pride in the creative potential of their language. Lexicographers and terminologists, the two groups of scholars most usually concerned with collecting, describing and standardizing terms, can barely keep up with the explosion, particularly since the expansion of telecommunications and computer-based technology into international marketplaces makes their spread all the more rapid.

Theoretically, at least, a term is a word with a fence around it. It is an appellation with a specific and restricted point of reference for its primary group of users, who make up a specialized group and use the term among themselves. Except that isn't really the situation at all.

The primary users may have chosen to use a specific sense of an already existing word or name, perhaps reviving an older usage. Or, given new information, new technology, new situations, they may decide to create a term, either formally, with the imprimatur of committees and organizations, or informally, by convention. Here they coin what begin as neologisms and, like crabgrass or a runaway puppy, the terms proliferate within the body of primary users, creating confusion by their multiplicity and shades of meaning. Almost at once, the terms spill over into common usage, borrowed from a specialized lexicon into new contexts. Here, as commentators from Cratylus to Garland Cannon have noted, the terms become ambiguous or euphemistic, resulting in what de Sola calls "bureaucratese, cover-up death-disease-sex-and-the-toilet terms, goody-goody garble, mellowspeak, nice-nellyisms, or officialese" (1057).

While courses in technical writing have sprung up across the country, and recognized authorities, who write clearly, plead in the pages of every professional journal for attention to precision in communicating a complex concept, there is no ground-swell to eliminate or simplify the strings of words with which technologically oriented writers try to communicate their vision of new products and new functions. Compound terms, the name usually given to such strings, have several varieties, unitary, sentential, hierarchic and categoric, according to Strehlow, who exemplifies two of them as follows (28, 30):

> two-inch intermittently stirred chemical reactor (sentential)
> precision octave-band sound pressure level meter (hierarchic)

People creating terms today apparently have just as many problems as those half a century ago, to judge from the frequent articles in *American Speech*. Since the first volume of the journal, contributors have presented lists and commentaries on special lexicons and lingos, from every type of job or profession, legal or not. Problems existed for the original compilers of the 1933 *Standard Classified Nomenclature of Disease*: its reviewer noted that figurative names were a problem as they were based on partial knowledge. Was a disease to be named for the ways it showed itself, in terms cued to physiology, or for the structural, hence anatomically cued terms based on the changes the disease produced? (Logie 17–21).

The same problem can be seen nearly fifty years later in the listing of "Legionnaire's disease terms," taken from *American Speech*'s regular column, "Among the New Words." Was the mysterious disease, affecting celebrants at an American Legion convention, to be called *Legionella pneumophila, Legionellosis,* or *Legion epidemic*? Prominent newspapers and scientific magazines used these and at least five other names until *Legionnaire's disease* became the generally accepted appellation (Russell and Porter 114–15).

Where do the terms come from, and where do they go? When Barber surveyed an earlier period, 1500–1700, to look at the explosion of new words and terms developed in early modern English, he based his study on the major historical dictionary of English, the *Oxford English Dictionary*. Mencken drew on contemporary works to discuss "The Making of New Nouns" during the Jacksonian period, another explosion in technological innovation. More recently, Cannon has been drawing on a host of other dictionaries to chart the recent productivity and processes in word-formation. All agree that people make them up, to present their notion or understanding of whatever they see as new; today, however, terminologists strive to build fences around the terms, trying to keep them out of everyday conversation.

Terminologists are rare in America, as are texts describing the electronic term banks, or on-line lexicons, which are often multilingual. International conferences, journals, networks, and the discussions of how to pin down a term, are more frequently written and published in Europe (Sager and Picht are in English, and relatively accessible). Translators and interpreters for international companies and government ministries do the bulk of the work with classifying and interpreting terms; Canadian law schools, such as the one at Moncton, employ terminologists to aid the publication of translated or bilingual statutes. The UN and the World Bank each has terminologists on the staff; the U.S. State Department is moving in that direction. Meanwhile, American English speakers daily use all the processes of word-formation to create more and more terms. There are so many new terms in the international field of telecommunications and information technology, that American dictionaries for these terms—a recent phenomenon—have begun updating nearly every year. There may even be an American accent for such terms, when we compare British and American dictionaries.

Remember the sentential and hierarchic terms? English speakers have moved to shorten those tricky strings into acronyms and initialisms. I recently spot-checked the 346 entries under the letter "B" in the British *Dictionary of New Information Technology Acronyms*, second edition (Gordon et al.), and found that 61, or nearly one in five entries, had more than three separate meanings. A few of these could be pronounced as a one-syllable word (BAMS), a few more scanned into two syllables (BIAS, BC); most were three-letter combinations that we probably speak as three syllables, sounding each letter: are you going to the BCP today? send this file to the BFL. What bemused me was the set of 61, however: each of their three to six glosses represents a different term, phrase or organization. The British dictionary cannot fairly be compared with the current American dictionary, *Computer and Telecommunications Acronyms* (Towell), because the American volume lists terms pulled from the even larger *Acronyms, Abbreviations and Initialisms Dictionary*, which is updated annually and includes all previous entries. However, a quick glance at the American entries corresponding to the British set of 61 suggests that there is very little agreement between the glosses for the entries in the two publications.

Take BASIC, for example; the British dictionary gives seven glosses—a Swiss organization, an abstracting service, a military string, and four different glosses keyed to variant terms in programming:

> basic algebraic symbolic interpretive compiler
> basic automatic stored instruction computer
> beginners algebraic symbolic interpretive compiler
> beginners all-purpose symbolic interaction code
> (Gordon et al. 27)

The American dictionary lists four separate glosses, one of which is a publication, capitalizes the three programming-related terms, and gives further information about them:

> Basic Algebraic Symbolic Intepretive Compiler (IEEE)
> Basic Automatic Stored Instruction Computer (BUR)
> Beginner's All-Purpose Symbolic Instruction Code [Programing language invented by T. E. Kurtz and J. G. Kemeny at Dartmouth College in 1963–64] (Towell 35)

IEEE is listed only once (104), and represents the "Institute of Electrical and Electronics Engineers [New York, NY] [Document publisher]." BUR has two listings (40), with the glosses "Back Up Register (CAA)" and "Buried." CAA has three glosses (41), and one is cross-referenced to BUR, with the meaning of "Computer-Assisted Accounting." Those of us who use the term BASIC to mean a language in which we sometimes write a few simple commands will find additional senses for the term listed (225) in which the terms are listed by meaning and cross-referenced to these and to other acronyms (BAL, BAP).

I have been using this term, BASIC, as both a name and a word, and using it far too loosely, slipping unwittingly into what H. W. Fowler calls "popularised technicality." Let's try another example: BCS. The British dictionary offers five glosses, the American, twelve; they share only two glosses in common, and both are the names of British societies. I recognize two American glosses as referring to technical processes, both involving Block Control. But the references to a block, or blocking, in the British glosses are keyed to different acronyms, and they may refer to different phenomena or processes (see BMC, BORAM, BTMF, in Gordon et al.).

We may be able to examine the history of science and technology by monitoring terms, just as we look to the lingoes in other professions to reveal or underscore historical change. At the moment, when there are this many terms, and this many acronyms, we can expect another Inkhorn controversy to arise. This time, however, the discussion of terms and their uses will have to be an international conversation.

3. Slang and Usage

CONNIE C. EBLE
University of North Carolina, Chapel Hill

Although expressions like *bubblegum machine* 'police car,' *crumbing* 'feeling dejected,' *five-finger discount* 'theft,' *lunchbox* 'person who is unaware of what is going on,' or *toxic waste dump* 'habitual abuser of alcohol or drugs' may be enjoyed and admired for their novelty, cleverness, humor, or even poetic qualities, such expressions are usually excluded from language use with a serious purpose because they are slang.

Educated users of English have been taught in school and by the example of most published writing that slang is not suitable in situations in which the aim of language use is to inform a general and often unknown audience. The reason for this familiar proscription is that slang is generally highly informal, confined to subgroups of users, short-lived, and often flippant; i.e., a slang term has built into it a set of connotations which are not neutral. Thus, in a courtroom or in a newspaper account—where dispassionate objectivity is prized—it would be unsuitable to say *Three bubblegum machines were blocking the exits of the parking lot.* Yet the same sentence may be entirely appropriate in recounting the event to a neighbor.

As with many usage issues, the choice of whether or not to use a slang item is governed almost entirely by rhetorical not grammatical considerations. In the hypothetical sentence above, the phrase *bubblegum machines* is a noun phrase in the plural and fits the structure of the sentence with no violation of grammar. Most slang items substitute in syntactically regular ways for words and phrases already in the language. For example, a parent's admonition *Don't belittle your sister* might be expressed by a schoolmate as *Don't diss your sister.* The grammar of the two sentences is the same. Likewise, an examination of the word-building processes entailed in slang shows them to be identical to those that give rise to the general vocabulary. Thus the proscription against the use of slang is not founded on formal linguistic grounds.

The objections to the use of slang have to do with the relationships between speaker, hearer, and subject matter. All speakers draw on a variety of styles to respond to different occasions and speech situations. The same American speaker of English may use different styles, for example, when talking about a football game to a six-year old, to a Brazilian, to a coach, to a fan, to someone hostile to the sport, etc. Vocabulary choice plays a large part in characterizing various styles. Two friends *hug*, but heads of state *ritually embrace*. A child *claps* in glee, but an audience bursts into *applause*. A pregnant woman *vomits* in the mornings, but a teen-ager *barfs* from imprudent drinking. Slang vocabulary is always associated with informal styles of speaking and writing: *rip off* is less formal than *steal* in the sentence *Somebody ripped off/ stole my bike*; *veg out* and *tube* are less formal than *relax* and *television* in *We just vegged out/ relaxed in front of the tube/ television*. Slang often implies a flippant attitude towards outsiders, authority, or propriety—as in *japscrap* 'appliance made in Japan'; *county mounty* 'local police'; and *go for sushi* 'kiss passionately.' In addition, the use of slang signals some type of bond between speaker and hearer—friendship, membership in the same group, or espousal of the same values. The implications of slang, then, can be at odds with styles primarily aimed at informing a general audience in as detached a manner as possible. Because most guidelines for the effective use of English concern exactly such neutral styles, i.e., standard written English, the proscription *Avoid slang* is generally good advice.

However, an isolated slang expression or two can be used with rhetorical effectiveness without making the entire discourse overly casual, trendy, or laughable and without undermining its serious purpose. Cartoonists and political writers are often sensitive to the attention-getting potential of the well-chosen and occasional slangy expression. During President Ronald Reagan's administration, they popularized the slang *sleaze-factor* for the quality of many political appointees and *wimp* for the uncharismatic Vice President. In the 1984 presidential campaign, unsuccessful Democratic nominee Walter Mondale borrowed Wendy's slogan "Where's the beef?" with the slang meaning of *beef* as 'strength, substance.'

The biggest usage problem with regard to slang is knowing whether or not a given expression will strike the listener or reader as slang. Some instances are clear. The current campus expression *chilly* 'relaxed' is not generally used throughout the population and can be classified as slang. In a letter of recommendation, for instance ("John Smith has a chilly management style."), the use of *chilly* will most likely be misinterpreted as referring to a cold and distant style, or if it is a slang expression to the reader, it may cast doubt on the judgment of the letter-writer. Yet the synonymous but unambiguous *laid back* has expanded its distribution to the extent that it is no longer perceived as having the same slangy flavor, and the phrase "*laid back* management style," while more informal than "*relaxed* management style," may not call attention to itself. The differences in effect between *chilly*, *laid back*, and *relaxed* are subject to individual variation and dispute. The language user who wants a definitive answer as to whether or not *laid back* is slang is destined for disappointment.

Dictionaries, the ordinary repositories of information about words, are ill-equipped to record slang. For the most part, slang is slippery in meaning, short-lived, restricted to marginalized groups, and oral—all characteristics that militate against slang's showing up frequently and consistently in the files on which dictionaries are based. Nevertheless, *slang* is a label in almost all contemporary American dictionaries of English, although just what the label means and its relationship to other usage labels can vary widely. In the dictionaries published by the Merriam Company of Springfield, Massachusetts, *slang* is one of three stylistic labels, along with *substandard* and *nonstandard*; the Merriam dictionaries more readily classify lexical items as belonging to the general, unremarkable vocabulary of English than do other dictionaries. In the Second College Edition of the *American Heritage Dictionary*, the label *slang* indicates "a style of language rather than a level of formality or cultivation" and is one of six stylistic labels along with *nonstandard, informal, vulgar, obscene,* and *offensive*. The Second Edition of the *Random House Dictionary of the English Language*, edited by Stuart Berg Flexner, co-editor of the *Dictionary of American Slang*, has a good discussion of slang in the prefatory essay "Usage: Change and Variation," which distinguishes *slang* from ten other "Labels of Style" used in the dictionary.

The labeling of specific lexical items as *slang* varies from dictionary to dictionary, as shown in a check of fifty items in five desk dictionaries published 1975-83 (Eble "Slang: Variations"). Only *bread* 'money' and *schmo* 'oaf' bear the label *slang* in all five dictionaries and also in the more recent *Random House* of 1987. *Boss* 'excellent,' *ice* 'diamonds,' *ralph* 'vomit,' and *toke* 'drag on a marijuana cigarette' are reported as *slang* in all the sources in which they occur, but *ralph,* for example, is an entry in only one of the dictionaries examined. The greatest range of variation is shown by the labels attached to *booze* 'alcohol'—which carries no label in one, is marked *colloquial* in one, *slang* in one, and *informal* in two. *Laid back* has no entry in two, is unmarked in one, and is marked *slang* and *informal* in the other two. *Random House* labels *booze* as *informal* and *laid back* as *slang.*

Slang is part of the linguistic behavior unregulated by the larger society: it is not taught in school and is learned by observation, often with little effort or awareness. Slang gives its users freedom from outside regulation while at the same time providing a powerful tool for regulation within the group of users. In the social situations in which slang naturally arises and is cultivated, issues of whether a vocabulary item is slang or not simply do not apply—nor do notions of correctness.

4. The Linguistic Autobiography of an American

RICHARD GUNTER
University of South Carolina, Columbia

Part I: Introduction

This is the life story of one American as seen in his linguistic development. The story consists of little adventures in dialect, usage, and style. With those words the writer hopes to sum up the things that a person does as a language-using animal dwelling in a land like the USA, where there is much variation in the sounds and words and grammar of the language. Such an adventure may be a single, isolated little drama; or it may be a sudden flash of insight into many such past dramas. All these adventures—we may call them *linguistic epiphanies*—give understanding of the self and of the surrounding social world. Through such epiphanies a member of the American nation learns how his language depicts him to others; he learns to use language to get what he wants. In the end he may settle upon some habitual use of his language as the one variety that he finds most comfortable—the style that he regards as his best and most genuine self.

After these introductory words, we go on to Part II, where we get a look at how the writer came to know, through his speech, something about the loyalties that he was born to; in Part III we see how he went out into the larger world beyond the bounds of family and intimates; in Part IV we see how he became an academic in the field of linguistics, which changed and shaped him; finally, in Part V, we learn a bit about what the writer makes of his present linguistic attitudes.

The story is told mostly in little vignettes: first a few prefatory words and then the adventure. To each vignette is appended a MORAL. These little tags attempt to distill out the significance of each adventure; but also, in part, they allow the writer to poke fun at himself: he hopes that by putting a MORAL after each story, in the manner of the Duchess in *Alice's Adventures in Wonderland*, he may seem less self-absorbed. It is difficult to write about one's own life without appearing to be obsessed with self.

The writer also has adopted a third-person sort of reference: he will speak in the following sentences of the *Subject*. But he knows that nobody will be fooled by any of this appearance of modesty; for the subject of all that follows is the man who is writing. In fact, the Subject's greatest fear is that he may actually stray from his core of reality-remembered. He knows that he tends to edit his past. He knows very well that in using these anecdotes many times in classes he has embellished things and made them more dramatically simple. Some of these events happened decades ago. The tendency to misremember is real. The Subject knows that he may seduce himself into dramatic fiction; yet he also knows one important countervailing fact: this notion of a linguistic autobiography is an important one—it is a story where nothing can serve the Subject as well as the plain truth.

Part II: Beginnings

The Subject was born in a little town in the northwest quarter of Alabama. From the hour of his birth he was entangled in language variation, for the family and the town were by no means homogenous. The Subject began his days with a complex set of identities: he was born male, white, and Protestant, and fate plopped him down in a social class rather difficult to name: it was, in a loose sense, urban; it was Anglo-Saxon by usurpation and by courtesy, for we assumed (if we thought about the matter at all) that we were WASP, and nobody contradicted that assumption, though a little research would show we were mostly Scotch-Irish who had absorbed here and there some wandering Welshman or Choctaw; it was middle class for want of a more precise category. The Subject was second of three sons. He was more drawn to his father than to his mother. The former was not long off the farm; the latter had a taste for literature and music and flowers.

These identities supplied the Subject with a complicated set of values, with a range of hopes and fears, with fields in which he might legitimately take interest, and with great blocks of the world that he was licensed to ignore. All of these things worked in so intricate a way that the finest team of psycho-socio-savants could not have explained them to the Subject. And all of these identities were marked by their shibboleths of sound, word and syntax. It would be decades (and a PhD in linguistics) before the Subject felt that he understood these things well enough to dare commit his conclusions to paper.

The Subject's mother and father, though born only about fifteen miles apart, spoke related but palpably different dialects. His father, like most Americans, said *They're sick* and *We're fine*; his mother omitted the *are* in such expressions, saying *They sick* and *We fine*.

Mother always said *I'm gon try* (with the vowel in *gon* heavily nasalized and the consonant *n* missing altogether); Father, on the other hand, said *I'm aimed to try*. The children said neither of these things, but went forth into the world saying, with the larger American community, *I'm gonna try*.

For a third illustration, Mother had the diphthong /ay/ in the first syllable of the words below; Father had the more expectable /æw/: *towel, power, tower, Howell*.

The two older sons went forth saying this series as their father said them; the baby boy copied his mother, and to this day, in his late middle age, says those words as his mother said them.

MORAL: In the silent contest in the house for the dialect fealty of the three sons, Father won most of the chips.

But not all was disharmony, for most of the Subject's usages were the same as his parents' and passed without comment or even notice by his fellows, so that he remained quite unconscious of them until years later when, among unloving strangers in the U.S. Navy or at Indiana University or elsewhere in the great world, somebody giggled or scoffed at his speech.

The Subject had double modals in such sentences as these: *We might could find it* and *She may can get her mother to do it*. He had a distinction between the vowels /ɛ/ and /ɪ/ in most ordinary words: *let, lit; bed, bid*. But he had no such distinction in pairs of words where the vowel occurs before a nasal. The following pairs were exactly the same for him: *dint, dent; pin, pen*. On the other hand, he had vowel distinctions before /r/ that many Americans do not have, cannot hear, and in fact do not believe: *merry, marry; boarder, border*. He had the sequence /tyuw/ and /dyuw/ and /nyuw/ in words like these: *tune, dew, new*.

He was astounded to learn later in life, in other parts of the USA, that these pronunciations were considered unacceptably hifalutin by many.

MORAL: We are utterly unconscious of most of the features of our normal, ordinary speech; it is only when the features differ from someone else's that they come to our attention.

But just outside the house more complexities were to set in.

Meg was the Subject's favorite cousin. (She was one of a mass of cousins.) Meg was sweet, helpful, supportive; she was universally loved by her kinsmen. It was this esteem that made her linguistic defection all the more painful: she went away to the University of Chicago to get a graduate degree—the first of us to go so far away for schooling. (Chicago was rumored to be even farther north than Nashville.)

When Meg came home for Christmas that first time, we noted, with instant dismay, that she had picked up a YANKEE ACCENT. Probably this amounted to nothing more than some slight shifting in vowel coloring, perhaps a centralizing of the unstressed /ɨ/ in words like *roses* or *bushes,* plus a few new and academic words, but we all felt a tremendous letdown. Our nearest and most trusted had turned her back on us.

MORAL: Southern small-town people have a kind of solidarity in manner and values and speech that would be hard to exaggerate. We feel a special kind of disappointment when one of our most esteemed breaks the solidarity.

In the fourteenth year of the Subject's life, a Martian appeared as a new teacher in English at the beginning of the school year. (Or if she was not actually a Martian, she was at least from some very alien and distant place such as Europe or Wisconsin.) She had heard our speech and instantly set herself to cleaning it up.

One goal she set for herself was to root out of our speech the sound /ǰ/ at the end of words like *garage* and *rouge,* having us use instead the sound /ž/.

Now it was to be many years before the Subject saw clearly what this odd person was meddling in. No doubt he understood down deep, but not consciously. The fact is that we had in our town and surrounding outback a sexual division in speech. In this, as in many other matters, there was some kind of convergence of urban and female things, and convergence of rural and manly things. Everything the Subject wanted to avoid was associated with girls; all things good and wholesome, on the other hand, were associated with the woods and waters and fields—with hunting implements and fishing equipment and man-type *gear and tackle and trim.*

Now comes this person who wants us to say /gəraž/. She had pretty good luck with the town girls of higher social station, for they talked that way already and were happy to have their predilections ratified by official persons; girls of lower social station were quite ready to go along (for these were the girls who aspired to set a more elegant table than their mothers and grandmothers had dreamed of doing); the country girls offered more resistance, perhaps, but could be bullied or coaxed into conformity—at least as long as they were in the safety of the classroom; but the country boys merely guffawed. We town boys were the ones on the hot seat: here was a clean, upstanding Christian lady in a position of authority who wanted us to say things that would have imperiled all that we held dear. We wanted to be he-men; this Martian wanted us to put on lace panties.

MORAL: It is useless to preach to persons who see no gain for themselves in the doctrine preached—who, indeed, see only the gravest danger to what they treasure most. Whenever, in subsequent years, the Subject's mind has turned to the thought of hopeless tasks and lost causes, he has recalled that Martian and her program for improving southern boys in their fourteenth year.

The Subject's best friend and rambling buddy was H. Now H. was somewhat more "of the people" than was the Subject. But H. was superior in knowledge of firearms and fishing tackle; he knew where squirrels were soonest found; he knew which logs in the Sipsy River were most attractive to turtles that wanted to sun themselves on a July day.

H. had a peculiar linguistic habit concerning the major city of our state. All the rest of us pronounced it /bərminhæm/ but H.

said /bərginhæm/. One day, perhaps in the summer of 1936, the Subject pondered whether to correct him, but held back.

MORAL: Some of us (all of us?) misapprehend some details of our native tongue. Our fellows, maybe knowing that correction might wound us, refrain from calling our attention to these eccentricities, so we are never aware of them.

Thus the Subject lived the first eighteen years of his life. Powerful forces, he now understands, were always pulling at him in those years—pulling him to favor what was male, what was rural, what was rough-and-tumble; the things to avoid like leprosy were the girlish, the sissified, the hifalutin. To be a male, competent at manly things—that was the most attractive goal in the world.

Yet not all was rigid and marked out: the Subject had his complex loyalties and the converse of loyalties—whatever the word for that notion is. He was most emphatically not an *old girl*! (For the first thirteen years of his life he said that expression with curling lip.) And he was not black. And he was not a sissy with clean fingernails. But he was not exactly a Redneck either. He could never have said girl-words like *lovely* and *delicious*; he would have chosen death rather than say 'proper' past participles like *fallen* or *ridden*; yet he would have stopped short of *I haven't saw him* or *This watch was give to me*. Chameleon-like, he could say *isn't* to members of his mother's garden club; but he would never have permitted himself anything but *ain't* in the locker room with the football squad. To behave otherwise would have been too costly.

Perhaps all of these things sound as if they made a very uncomfortable setting in which to spend a boyhood. From the outside it may seem that the Subject was a very small planet tugged this way and that by massive stars in a game of capture unutterably complex; but the Subject has no memory at all of feeling cramped and confined in bonds of usage.

Part III: Into a Wider World

The Subject graduated from high school in 1941 and immediately entered the University of Alabama. This move was ill-advised: under the pressure of family to imitate a cousin, who had become a chemical engineer and was very successful and admired in his new profession, the Subject drifted into the same path. He quickly discovered that he had little talent for math and chemistry and mechanical drawing, and he felt ill-at-ease from the first day. Not only had he drifted passively into uncongenial things, but he had drifted away from what he was best at—language. Before the first semester ended, the Subject had joined the U.S. Navy.

> The world is wide: at the Pensacola Naval Air Station in about the Summer of 1942, the Subject witnessed a conversation between a Brooklyn type and an Arkansas type. They were trying to be friendly, trying to surmount the frictions and difficulties that arise between two people who come from circumstances so different that much good will is called for. There followed an exchange of sentences of this sort: "Up home we do so-and-so." "Really? Well, down home we do such-and-such." It was all very comradely with good intentions showing in the manner and attitudes of both parties. But at length the whole production ground to a sudden halt when the Arkansas type said, "You'uns have a right smart of taxis up there, don't ye?" This language was very familiar to the Subject, who knew it from the playgrounds of the schools he had attended in Alabama. The expressions *you'uns* and *a right smart* were as common as dirt in the Subject's hunting-fishing-football circles, though distinctly beneath his own usage. He would never have used these archaic-countrified expressions except as a jest. But the Brooklyn type had no faculties at all for handling these expressions. He could not have seemed more helpless.
>
> MORAL: Most Americans can understand each other most of the time. Rarely does one come upon native Americans with whom one cannot converse. (But it has happened to the Subject twice: once when he tried to buy a sandwich from two country women at a sandwich stand on the New Hampshire shore, and again in his own back yard in South Carolina when he tried to engage a plumber's helper in conversation and discovered that the helper spoke Gullah.)

Not everyone admired the Subject's native manner of speech. Take, for example, the New Jersey dentist on a northern Pacific island who once filled a cavity for the Subject.

> The Subject, as has been pointed out, had the /y/ glide after /t/, /d/ and /n/ before /uw/ in such words as *Tuesday*, *dew*, and *new*.

This dentist heard the Subject say a few words and began to mock and scoff at the Subject's speech. He exaggerated that /y/ glide, putting it in words where it did not belong, such as *noon* and *toot*. His purpose was to ridicule and demean. His manner suggested that he was deeply stung that people like the Subject existed and were permitted to speak that brand of speech.

MORAL: We are sometimes reacted to for speech habits of which we are entirely unaware.

Part IV: Academia

The Subject went back to college when World War II had ended. He sailed through his undergraduate study this time, taking such requirements as he could not escape and electing courses in language when he had a choice. Having some success in this curriculum, he decided to go to Indiana University to do graduate work in linguistics. With many an interruption, he finally got his PhD in 1962.

The Subject had stored away, unconsciously, many features of the speech of his native region. Sometimes these were very complicated things. Before the Subject got special training in graduate linguistics, he could not have given any general and precise account of them, though he could imitate them in a kind of mockery that we might call *phonic cartooning*. That is what the dentist from New Jersey employed in the sketch above; it is what many of us use in telling a story when we come to a colorful character and give an exaggerated mimicry of his/her speech—ordinary spelling: *Take that book, Pull this rope, Paint those boards*; transformed into a related set heard from Rednecks from the Carolinas to Texas: *Take kat book, Pull lis rope, Paint tose boards.*

Before studying linguistics, the Subjèct was unable to give any very coherent account of what is going on here. Perhaps he might have said, "The speaker doubles a consonant before a word that begins with the *th* in words like *these* and *those*." But in graduate school the Subject learned to use Trager-Smith symbols and other markings to do elegant and meaning-packed formulas like this: $/- C + ð/ \rightarrow /- C + C -/$.

MORAL: To work up complex sets of data and to formulate them with such exotic marks can bring rich satisfaction. But further questions can arise, too. For example, the Subject remembers that sometimes he himself used this sandhi rule in the locker room at school or with his hunting buddies, but in the rest of his life he did not apply it. Furthermore, once a fellow has made the formula above, he begins to notice ragged edges such as this one: some people drop the /ð-/ but don't double the /C/. How, the Subject wonders, can one capture such complications all in one formula?

In the Fall of 1961 the Subject presented himself in the English Department of a certain midwestern university, which had just hired him. He was given a 'welcome-aboard' interview by a very superior Assistant Chairman. This Assistant Chairman was not a native midwesterner, but came from a large city on the Atlantic seaboard. The Subject received the impression that this Assistant Chairman considered himself to be serving in a hardship post. He was, even in the Middle West, serving among pedestrians who barely deserved his presence. Now to be confronted with a Redneck southerner showed the Assistant Chairman the depths to which he had been obliged to sink.

The two discussed a certain course that (the Subject grants it!) the Subject was barely competent to teach; yet he was needed to teach that very course. The Assistant Chairman was querying the Subject about his knowledge of the material to be covered in the course.

In the subsequent give-and-take, the Subject used the word *harry* in some such sentence as, "I think I'll feel less harried when I actually settle down in the course and have taught a few classes."

Now the very superior Assistant Chairman did not actually respond, "You do not mean *harried*; what you mean is *harrowed*, which in your peasanthood you have mispronounced." No, he did not say that, but that is what he meant. What he actually said was, "Oh, good, you will feel less harROWED," putting plenty of emphasis on the last syllable of the word.

The Subject, who by now hated this Assistant Chairman, felt a surge of satisfaction in his heart, for he knew that there are two distinct words, *harrow* and *harry*. The Subject felt quite certain of his ground; nevertheless, he went straightway to the *OED*, rejoicing to find that, indeed, a farmer employs an implement called a *harrow* to *harrow* his fields, and a 'toad under the harrow' is a toad (or metaphorically a person) that feels much done down and done in; on the other hand, to *harry* is to chase prey with intent to catch and kill and perhaps eat it: hounds harry rabbits; a thing harried is a thing hard pressed and in fear of rout or utter defeat: brand new instructors, newly turned up in strange places, feeling under stress and being grilled by haughty Assistant Chairmen whose natural merits deserve much more than having to live among pedestrians and interview peasants, may be considered harried—and, of course, harrowed as well.

But then later when such instructors go to the *OED* and reassure themselves about these words, having been subjected to the raised eyebrow of a big-city type caught out in a splendid piece of ignorance about words and usage, they understand for the first time the full meaning of Mark Twain's remark about *the calm confidence of a Christian with four aces.*

"Boy," the Subject said to himself, "will it ever be fun to deal with this guy again when the conversation turns to usage questions, especially *harrow* and *harry*!" For the Subject fully intended to engineer such a happenstance very soon, whereupon he would drop on this very superior Assistant Chairman the full weight of the *Oxford English Dictionary*—thirteen volumes plus supplements!

MORAL: Rednecks with a bit of learning do not take kindly to being corrected in their usage by slick, big-city types.

Few things have ever seized the Subject's mind with as much force as the notion called *cultural relativism*: the idea that something might have a particular meaning in one culture, but quite another meaning in a second culture. The Subject devoured the reading that came his way on this and kindred topics. He especially enjoyed Veblen's chapter "Archaism and Waste" from *The Theory of the Leisure Class* and Wilson's *To the Finland Station* and Edward Hall's *The Silent Language* and William James's great essay *On a Certain Blindness in Human Beings.*

The Subject had long chafed under the tyranny of manners and beliefs in the southern tribe in which he had been brought up. He welcomed the notion that there is no absolute, universal standard of values for mankind, for he wished to disbelieve much of the cultural baggage that he had inherited. He relished propagating this liberating doctrine in his classes, illustrating his thesis with such variants as *I saw him* and *I seen him*. There is no scientific procedure, he loved to explain, that allows us to tell which of these variants is "correct." The judgment that one is better than the other is a social truth, not a scientific one. Such variant forms call up associations in the mind—details of manner and clothing and habit. These variants are in a kind of social-political-erotic struggle for dominance. That struggle will be decided by real people like ourselves and our children—real people living real lives and deciding each day what they want and how they wish to appear.

Actually the competition between *I saw him* and *I seen him* is already decided, for almost everyone knows that the former is widespread and vigorous, while the latter is a dying remnant of older, rustic corners of the USA. *I seen him* is a poor, battered contender; *I saw him* is the champ. This pair is an extreme case.

At the other extreme we have pairs in which the competition is mild—variants such as *pled* and *pleaded* in a sentence like *She (plead) with him not to go*. The variant *pled* is a shade more professional, maybe, being common in courts of law, while *pleaded* is rather colorless and arouses no very powerful feeling.

But the cases that fall between the two extremes are very interesting. Take, for example, the pair *dived* and *dove*. This pair is not loaded with feeling for most Americans, who perhaps feel that *dove* is a bit 'down home' and *dived* a trifle more 'uptown'. But some Americans have extremely hostile reactions to one or the other of these variants.

The Subject gave much attention to these notions in his classes. He devised tests and experiments to determine what the students really felt about such usage variants. He saw himself as bringing enlightenment and at the same time lessening tensions about usage. But by revealing that students often have wildly different and sometimes hostile reactions to some variant or other, perhaps the Subject only heightened tensions, if anything.

One day the Subject's thoughts were given a new twist when he heard a radio interview with Walter Mondale, who was then running for president.

> The interview was held on the run, as the candidate and his entourage were leaving one hotel for another. Mondale, telling

some bit about his routine that morning, used a certain preterit that is normally irregular, giving it the regular preterit form; but then, suddenly doubtful, he chose another variant of it; finally, obviously flustered, he gave up and recast his sentence.

MORAL: Really to find what tendencies are in the soul of an American when he comes to some usage pitfall, we must somehow put into the scene some source of real tension, like the tension that Mondale was feeling as his words went out to the world by radio at a crucial moment of his life. How can we seine through the American psyche and discover what each heart, under stress, would choose to say at some critical moment? The Subject pictures a helpless young woman having to choose some tricky preterit when she knows that her prospective mother-in-law is watching and listening.

Part V: Summary and Conclusion

It has been a long voyage—the Subject's trip through the great sea of the American Language. Early he discovered his own interest in, and modest talent for, style and usage and dialect. These things have been his life.

Now in his Emeritus years, he does not cease to review the whole matter with deep interest and strong feelings. In language as in many things, he finds within himself a conservative turn. He wonders whether justice has actually been done to the more conservative side of the argument for a stable, standard usage. Let us grant that most of the attempts to argue the conservative case have flown in the face of all evidence from the last fifteen hundred years of English history, simply ignoring the fact that earlier doctrines about 'correctness' have, one after another, fallen to the victorious insurgent expressions that those doctrines denounced.

Have we perhaps missed the point? Is it possible that at every moment in American life there *is* a standard usage, whether linguistic scholars wish to see it or not? That standard varies from place to place and person to person; it is vague about the edges and it may change from year to year. But for all that it exists, because most people *think* it exists. The political feelings of the American people are no less fluid; but who would want to doubt the existence of a political mood at every moment in the USA?

We must never stop thinking about this difficult question. We need much more information: we need to know what people really feel about this and that variant. But we also need to face the fact that a perfectly normal American is capable of carrying about in one and the same head two rather different sets of feelings about something—two sets of notions that are actually in great conflict. The Subject, for example, still believes in the doctrine of cultural relativism; but at the same time he has oddly hostile feelings about many new variants that are creeping into the American Language. He cannot quite accept the people in the American 80's and 90's who bypass the first two expressions below in favor of the third: *As far as Fascism is concerned, I hate it. As for Fascism, I hate it. *As far as Fascism, I hate it.*

The Subject freely confesses that as far as that usage is concerned, he hates it. And while he is confessing, he might as well tell all: in those classes where he used to preach the cultural relativism doctrine, when he came to *dove* and *dived*, the Subject never expressed his own reaction; but the fact is that he has always said *dived* and is unfriendly in the extreme toward *dove*. At that point, his belief in cultural relativism seemed unable to work upon him with its usual soothing magic. During those sessions when the Subject was pushing his students to bare their psyches about some pair of variants, he suppressed his own very hostile feelings about *dove*.

A guy who would say *dove* is not to be trusted. He is not the sort of person that would do things in an orderly manner. For example, he would not squeeze the toothpaste out of the tube in a neat way, first systematically emptying the tail end of it and rolling up the empty part in seemly fashion. No, a *dove* speaker would go at the thing like a vandal, attacking the tube with random violence, simply squeezing and denting it here and there: he is a barbarian who just wants his way instantly, and never mind what destruction he wreaks upon the tribe and its harmonious working. The Subject wouldn't want a granddaughter of *his* to marry a guy like that.

5. The Expression of Changing Social Values in Dictionaries: Focus on Family Relationships[1]

SIDNEY I. LANDAU
Cambridge University Press

The manner in which dictionaries reflect shifts in prevailing social sentiment can tell us a great deal about how far and fast attitudes, and possibly behavior as well, have changed over time. The social values embedded in dictionaries are perhaps most accessible in children's dictionaries, where the abundance of invented illustrative sentences in support of definition betrays as few other contemporary sources can the prevailing attitudes toward family relationships, particularly the roles of mother and father. This study was suggested by "An Evaluation of the 1952 and 1962 Editions of the Thorndike Barnhart Beginning Dictionary," by Ann Ediger Baehr. By compiling a list of the illustrative sentences in the 1952 edition, Baehr convincingly demonstrated, among other things, that boys were presented routinely as mischievous or wicked and girls as tender and dutiful. This paper is an elaboration of her method and represents an attempt to analyze in a systematic way the corresponding illustrative sentences of two different editions of the same work.

Let us make our assumptions clear at the outset. Commercial lexicographers, like other people engaged in business, are mindful of their market. The values their products express must be designed, whether consciously or not, to appeal to those who are likely to buy dictionaries. (In this they are no different from textbook publishers, producers of movies, or manufacturers of swimsuits.) Their customers may not actually observe the values expressed any more than they really look the way they think they do in the swimsuits they buy, but the question here is one of self-image, not behavior. Or rather, of buying behavior, not the coincidence or lack of it between ethical standard and moral behavior. The Thorndike Barnhart dictionaries, published for the school market by Scott, Foresman, are the most successful school dictionaries ever published. There can be no question of their appeal to large numbers of educators and teachers over many years. One can assume, therefore, that the social values expressed in the Thorndike Barnhart dictionaries succeed in reflecting the prevailing social values of their market.

This study compares two editions of the *Thorndike Barnhart Beginning Dictionary* published twenty years apart, 1968 and 1988.[2] The 1988 edition, called the *Scott, Foresman Beginning Dictionary*, contains about 25,000 entries and, like the earlier edition, is designed for children in grades 3–5, that is, for children of ages 8 to 10 or 11 years. The focus of my attention is references to family members in illustrative sentences: references to mothers, fathers, sons and daughters, grandparents, uncles and aunts, etc. For example, "Mother clipped the recipe and pasted it in her cookbook" (1968) is a family reference, changed in 1988 to "She clipped the cartoon and passed it around the class." Specific references to mothers, fathers, and other family members are tabulated separately.

This study was based on three samples of twenty-three pages each from widely separated sections of the alphabet—*ceaseless–compartment, hideous–infuse,* and *run–settle* (first entry) representing together more than ten percent of the entire 650-page A–Z section of the 1968 edition. Within these three sections, every illustrative sentence was examined to see whether it included reference to a family member. If it did, it was recorded and compared to the corresponding definition in the 1988 edition to see whether and how it had been altered. If reference to mother was changed to that of another family member or was deleted entirely, this fact was noted. The three alphabetic sections in the 1988 edition were also examined to see whether new references to family members had been added to definitions not having such references in the 1968 edition, and these too were noted.

A comparison of the two editions shows that the 1988 edition contains almost exactly half the number of references to family members as the 1968 edition. Family relationships today are apparently of much less immediate interest to this age group, at least in the view of the editors, than they were twenty years ago. However, the deletions of references to all family members are not uniform, and we shall be repaid by taking a more detailed look at which family members have been hit hardest and which have been spared suppression.

TABLE 5.1

	ceaseless/ compartment	hideous/ infuse	run/ settle	*Total for Sample*	*Total Projected for A–Z*
mother					
1968	16	9	14	39	368
1988	1	2	2	5	47
father					
1968	9	3	4	16	151
1988	1	0	0	1	9
parents					
1968	0	3	1	4	38
1988	4	6	0	10	93
family					
1968	5	4	1	10	94
1988	4	3	2	9	84
sister					
1968	3	1	1	5	47
1988	4	2	1	7	65
brother					
1968	6	1	3	10	94
1988	2	4	2	8	75
grandmother					
1968	2	0 (1)*	1	3 (4)	—
1988	1	1	0	2	—
grandfather					
1968	1	0	0	1	—
1988	0	0	0	0	—
grandparents					
1968	0	0	0	0	—
1988	3	0	0 (1)†	3 (4)	—
daughter					
1968	0	0	0	0	—
1988	0	0	0	0	—
son					
1968	1	0	1	2	—
1988	0	0	0	0	—
others (aunts, uncles, cousins, relatives, twins, etc.)					
1968	6	1	2	9	—
1988	4	2	1	7	—
Total					
1968	49	22 (23)	28	99 (100)	934
1988	24	20	8 (9)	52 (53)	486

* great-grandmother
† great-grandparents

Most of us would approve of many of the changes made. Few would disagree with the decision to delete the 1968 illustration for *scour*. "Mother scours the frying pan with cleanser and the floor with a mop and soap," especially when the same dictionary consistently represents father in terms of authority and power. Up-to-dateness is the mark of a good dictionary, and I mean to imply no criticism of the editors by my remarks. My point is that up-to-dateness involves more than modernizing the hair styles and clothing fashions in pictorial illustrations. It involves more than recasting definitions to exclude old-fashioned diction. It involves cultural adaptations influenced in part by the changing mores of the dominant culture and by the publisher's perception of what those values are. The trends we see reflected by this study have of course been underway for much longer than twenty years, but it is instructive to see how dictionaries change to reflect changes in middle-class values and specifically in the public perception of the roles and importance of family members.

The changes are of staggering dimensions. Ninety percent of all references to mother and father have been deleted from the 1988 edition. In 1968, mother was referred to more than twice as frequently as father (39 to 16), but references to both have been cut back drastically in 1988, to 5 for mother and to a single reference for father. As noted, the three alphabetic sections sampled in the 1968 edition totaled 69 pages of 650 A–Z pages overall, or 10.6%. The same three alphabetic sections in the 1988 edition totaled 79 pages of 732 A–Z pages, or 10.7%. These are substantial samples from three widely scattered sections, and may be taken to be representative of the book as a whole. To extrapolate from these findings, we can estimate that there were 368 references to mother in 1968, reduced to 47 in 1988, and that there were 151 references to father in 1968, reduced to 9 in 1988. On the other hand, an estimated 38 references to parents without specification of gender in 1968 have grown to 93 overall in 1988.

Let's take a closer look at how some of the family references have been altered, since the subtle way in which they have been changed can tell us a great deal about the attitudes governing modern life.

In 1968 the illustration for *check* was, "When we finished eating, Father asked the waitress for the check." In 1988 it is, "After we finished eating, the waiter brought the check to our table." Not content with excising Father, who initiated the action described, the editors have been so sensitive to the relationship between Father and the waitress and about feminine-ending words in general that they have substituted *waiter* (now like most *-er* words usually defined as neutral in gender). Moreover, it is the waiter who now performs the action, apparently unsolicited by anyone.

In 1968 mother was associated in many illustrative sentences with nurturing, love of children, and household obligations:

> "Mother has taught me always to say 'Please' and 'Thank you.'"
> "Mother cut the pie into equal sections."
> "The care of the baby claims much of Mother's time."
> "The cleanness of the boys' rooms pleased Mother."
> "Mother sensed that Father was tired."
> "One of Mother's plates has a chip on the edge."

Father was associated with the support of family, parental discipline and business affairs:

> "My father has an income of $8000 a year."
> "My father pays most of his bills by check."
> "After the guests left, the boy got a sermon on table manners from his father."
> "She coaxed her father to let her go to the dance."
> "The running of Father's bath water early in the morning woke up the children."

The role of mother in 1988 has been sharply reduced, whereas father has been almost completely extirpated. When any family reference is retained, as a rule "mother" and "father" have been changed to "parents," thus merging parental roles and suppressing identification of gender. To the extent that anyone other than children is now part of a family, it is simply a parent, with grandparents hovering in the background, more important than mother (counting together grandmother and grandparents, they edge mother, 6 to 5). Even brothers and sisters outnumber mother, whereas in 1968 there were more than twice as many references to mother than to brothers and sisters combined. Not surprisingly, the ratio between references to brothers and to sisters almost reached parity in the 1988 edition, whereas in 1968 there were exactly twice as many references to brothers as to sisters.

Another noticeable trend is the increasing use of animals as genderless objects of concern or affection. For example, "Give Mother a hug" (1968) has been changed to "She gave the puppy a hug" (1988). Tied in with this trend is the more significant one of introducing peer-group members in preference to family members. To illustrate *humiliate*, the 1968 edition had, "The boys humiliated their parents by behaving badly in front of their guests." In 1988 this is, "They humiliated me by criticizing me in front of my friends." "She was in a hurry to see her father" (1968) has become "She was in a hurry to meet her friends" (1988).

Allied to the new role of peers is the changed relationship between children and adults and particularly between children and their parents. Whereas in 1968 parents told children what to do, in 1988 children tell parents what they want. Thus "The lazy boy's parents hounded him to do his homework" (1968) has been changed to "The children hounded their parents to buy a color TV." In the 1990s we can be sure the color TV will become a VCR or personal computer. Or, to take another example, *choice* was illustrated in 1968 by "His father gave him a choice between a bicycle and a pony." In 1988 this had become "I have my choice between a radio and a camera for my birthday." No parent necessary. The illustration for *indifference* in 1968 was, "The boy's indifference to his homework worried his parents." This has been changed in 1988 to "The child's indifference to food worried his parents." Although both sentences refer to parental responsibility, the former implies a responsibility on the child's part as well—namely, to do homework—whereas the latter implies none. Interest in food is not a responsibility but an appetite. The first implies the need for discipline, the second concern for a possible emotional or physical disability for which the child cannot be held responsible. The first case expresses a condition of the child's will, the second a state of health to which the child is passively subject. One should not read too much into a single instance, but this change symbolizes many others that suggest a much diminished sense of personal responsibility and a picture of ourselves as more often being acted upon by others (as by the waiter who brings our bill) than initiating action ourselves.

The altered representations of fathers and mothers may indeed be an accurate reflection of social roles in many American homes; my purpose is neither to question nor confirm the accuracy of the changes but to show how they illuminate altered perceptions of family relationships, perceptions moreover that suggest certain assumptions of class and status. Just as dictionaries describe words, not things, so they may be said to represent in their illustrative examples common attitudes and perceptions (rather than the actual circumstances) about the class of people to whom they are addressed. For example, the 1968 edition illustrated a sense of *club* with: "The children clubbed together to buy their mother a plant for her birthday." This sense was deleted from the 1988 edition and a new illustrative example inserted for the noun sense: "My parents belong to a tennis club." Many children (and not just those living in inner-city ghettos) come from backgrounds in which tennis clubs are altogether foreign. This does not make the example good or bad, but it does suggest that it is intended for people who know what a tennis club is. Another example illustrates the same point. Although as a rule the editors have decided to change the status of mother not by showing her in situations of authority but by deleting all mention of her, one of the few exceptions, a reference added in 1988, is "My mother is in charge of her company's art department." It promotes mother but at the same time presumes knowledge of what a company's art department is. Children who have no familiarity with advertising or publishing companies may find themselves baffled. These few examples cannot establish any prevalent bias, but they suggest that more systematic study of this feature might confirm our feeling that the dictionary is addressed to children of a particular class.

The method employed in this paper for close textual analysis of two different editions of the same dictionary might be used profitably to examine cultural presumptions and the treatment of other specified social relationships. Dictionaries are comparable to archeological sites waiting to be excavated, except that instead of unearthing artifacts or bones one can uncover the refuse of discarded social attitudes.

Many of the illustrative quotations in children's dictionaries twenty years ago assumed that Christian values, exemplified by the Protestant work ethic and the deification of motherhood, were universally held. Although there are very few overt examples of racial or religious prejudice, the quotations suggest that the intended audience was perceived as white, Protestant, and middle-class. Since then the roles of men and women, of children and the elderly (indeed, in the very definition of being old), of the handicapped and of those stigmatized by a physical attribute (such as obesity or short stature) have changed, in some cases radically. By systematically exploring a single subject over time, one could trace the direction and extent of the perception of change and perhaps be able to date, as lexicographers now date the earliest recorded examples of a particular sense, the earliest record of predominance of a particular social attitude, such as the equality in ability of women and men, the capacity of the handicapped to be productive and independent, or the ability of the old to think, read, and vote.

One can no more pretend that dictionaries are culturally neutral than one can pretend that any other utilitarian object such as a doorknob or clothes hanger is culturally neutral and without any particular design. Our familiarity with such objects should not blind us to the truth that all such objects are designed in the context of a social history, whether we are ignorant of that history or not. Although dictionary treatment of social attitudes necessarily lags behind the present, dictionaries, in choosing to recognize one set of values over other possible sets of values, give the values they select stability and authority, and by subtly representing those values (i.e., in their illustrative examples), they can be a progressive influence in furthering social change, especially when social behavior has not kept pace with predominant social values. On the other hand, if the social changes they represent do not affect all social classes equally, they may find themselves trapped between unwelcome alternatives: either they faithfully reflect social changes at the expense of the groups left behind or they resist recognizing those changes and alienate the more affluent groups who constitute the major market for their dictionaries.

Notes

1. This paper is an adaptation of the author's "The Expression of Changing Social Values in Dictionaries" (*Dictionaries* 7 [1985]: 261–69; used with permission).

2. *Thorndike Barnhart Beginning Dictionary*, 6th ed., ed. E. L. Thorndike and Clarence L. Barnhart (Garden City, NY: Doubleday, 1968). The copyright was held by Scott, Foresman and Company, which published the school edition, identical to the trade edition published by Doubleday except for the introductory matter. *Scott, Foresman Beginning Dictionary*, ed. E. L. Thorndike and Clarence L. Barnhart (Glenview, IL: Scott, 1988).

6. Visual Style

GRETA D. LITTLE
University of South Carolina, Columbia

Most of the usage and punctuation which characterizes so-called standard edited English is dictated by handbooks or publishers' style manuals. It is to these handbooks and manuals that we refer in our efforts to teach students the conventions of written English. These students, however, belong more and more to a generation of casual readers whose encounters with written English are primarily with very casual varieties, those not governed by these conventions. One example of these casual varieties is found in the written language appearing on television screens. Ted Koppel named it "Visual Style" in response to a former English teacher who had written in to complain about ABC's failure to use a comma in the date which introduces their evening news. Koppel was solicitous and sympathetic as he explained that such graphics were subject to rules of visual style, which dictated that the comma should be omitted in order to give a clean, uncluttered, and balanced picture. Koppel confessed to believe that the usage was "wrong" and even promised to work on the network to change its practice—apparently to no effect since the commaless date (as in *13 December 1990*) continues to introduce ABC news.

The incident, however, serves to bring to light a set of usage conventions based on vastly different principles from those believed to govern standard edited English. In visual style the goals are to achieve symmetry and balance, not to clarify structure. In an effort to discover exactly what differences might exist between visual style and AP or MLA style, I began to give more serious attention to texts that appeared on the television screen, enlisting my English grammar classes to assist me. What we discovered was that visual style varies a great deal from station to station. Yet for all their differences, stations clearly shared common goals. The major networks provide makeshift style sheets for affiliate stations setting forth their priorities. In a xeroxed booklet for affiliate stations, ABC lists its goals this way:

1. Direct the Viewer's attention
2. Clarify or amplify information
3. Reinforce the positive image of the Newscasters and News Organization
4. Add visual interest
5. Provide visual transitions.

These goals are a dramatic departure from the grammar-driven goals of ordinary handbooks and style manuals. Four of the five specifically mention visual impact; only the second addresses a conventional concern of usage rules.

Why should television style require such different focus? First of all, what makes television a special medium is its capability to integrate words and pictures. The picture is central; the words, both written and spoken, are incidental. When TV news directors make decisions about what is to appear on the screen, they consider graphic labels a visual accompaniment to the picture, parallel to the announcer's commentary. According to the advice ABC gives to its affiliate stations, "The challenge of graphics, just as with words, is to use them with precision and clarity. All too often the end result is a visual cacophony; a competition of images so strong none is intelligible."[1] ABC's over-riding concern is to simplify— having too many characters on the screen is visual garbage. Punctuation marks contribute to video tear, that is, they mess up the picture, so most punctuation is omitted from ABC graphics in order to achieve a cleaner look. The concept of "correct" or "standard" English is almost irrelevant. Since graphics and supers (TV jargon for the identifying captions under or over pictures) are on screen for only about five seconds, there is little concern for error. Although other networks do not share the details of ABC's approach to visual clarity, they too are more concerned with the image than with correctness of their written messages. The product is information and broadcasters are concerned about the form of written language only insofar as it affects the communication of that information.

What has this strong orientation to visual impact meant in terms of format and style? On ABC-TV and ABC affiliates, visual style has meant simplifying and reducing redundancy. Dates do not include commas to separate the items of information:

13 December 1989

Placenames have no comma between the city or town and the state or country:

> Morton Grove Illinois

Abbreviations are given without periods:

> Brian Gibbes
> ASST ST ATTY GEN

Compound noun patterns are preferred over prepositional phrases:

> COLEMAN YOUNG   vs.   COLEMAN YOUNG
> DETROIT MAYOR   MAYOR OF DETROIT

This preference for compounds leads to limited use of possessive apostrophes. In some instances the result is questionable in terms of normal usage practices. If the modifying noun is plural, the -s appears to be possessive even though the apostrophe is missing:

> JAYS GENERAL MANAGER

This practice is especially common in sports captions:

> ANDREW TONEY
> 76ers 1st draft pick in 1980 (ESPN)

One reason that confusion so easily arises over the function of the -s is that the first, modifying noun in noun compounds is not usually marked for number. Thus 'keeper of rabbits' is *rabbit keeper*, not *rabbits keeper. Following this pattern, the form should be *Jay general manager*. However, with human nouns problems of ambiguity can arise. For example, the Atlanta Braves would represented by the **Brave general manager* if compounding were formed consistently.

ABC is not alone in advocating compound nouns, nor is it only ABC that reinterprets possessives as compound nouns:

> BAKERS DOZEN (CBS)

> NEW KNICKS HEAD COACH (CNN)

Another approach employed by television networks to reduce the number of characters on the screen is the use of colons as substitutes for other words—usually prepositions or verbs. Again, the goal is to simplify, to take less space and attention away from the picture:

> Courtesy: CBS (local NBC affiliate)

> B Mullen: 3 assists (ESPN)

These are logical strategies for emphasizing the visual aspects of communication demanded by television. However, they are not the only strategies to be found. NBC and CNN, for example, have concentrated on the first goal articulated above—directing viewers' attention. They, in fact, do not reduce redundancy. They retain all the punctuation marks usually omitted by ABC. Furthermore, their concern for directing viewers' attention has led them to insert colons in several places where they are not ordinarily found:

> Voice of: [speaker's name] (CBS, CNN, NBC)

> SUNRISE AT: 7:15 am (local affiliate)

Nevertheless, on the whole, punctuation is used rather sparsely in television graphics and supers. These captions almost never provide truly new information and are used to reinforce the verbal and pictorial message. Consequently, complete, well-formed sentences are rare. When they do occur, they are treated as newspaper headlines are, and periods are seldom used. Many of these sentences resemble headlines also in that they employ a telegraphic style without articles, copulas, and so on:

> BANKS HIKE PRIME (CNN)

> BILL CARTWRIGHT SENDS GAME INTO OVERTIME (ESPN)

The information may or may not reiterate what the commentator is saying.

Other marks of punctuation are used infrequently in television graphics. Some stations place an ellipsis following the tease line: "Coming up. . ." (CBS affiliate). Hyphens can occur in identifying labels:

> Sen. Strom Thurmond
> R–South Carolina (CBS)

Donald Regan – Treasury Secretary (NBC)

Question marks are used if circumstances demand them, and exclamations points are found occasionally, usually as special features:

WILL COONEY FIGHT? (ABC)

SUGAR LOOKS AHEAD! (ABC)

Both the above examples are tease lines indicating what will follow the commercial. On some stations, quotation marks may signal a nickname or movie title. They are also used for direct quotes in supers.

As with all other forms of language, variation is prominent in visual style. The format for city-state designations illustrates three of the four possible variants—with and without commas, with and without periods:

CHARLOTTE NC

CHARLOTTE, N.C.

CHARLOTTE, NC

Even on a single station, inconsistencies are evident. In fact, variation frequently occurs within the same half-hour broadcast. Local news programs usually consist of four parts: actual news stories and interviews, business reports, sports, and the weather. Each part may have its own set of conventions. For instance, the business report lists "NYSE Volume" without periods to separate the letters representing New York Stock Exchange while periods are used in news and sports stories. In weather forecasts the periods are almost always eliminated from abbreviations:

DECR CLOUDINESS TONIGHT

Sports seems to suffer the greatest inconsistency, often because of the creative nicknames teams carry. CBS and its affiliates used five different labels in referring to San Francisco during Super Bowl week of 1982:

49 er's

49 ers

San Francisco 49er's

49ers Coach Bill Walsh

49'ers

They had no such problems with the Cincinnati Bengals.

Who decides the shape and form of the graphics shown on television screens and how is the decision made? A survey of local stations revealed that personnel in the graphics department use their own judgment or a popular dictionary. Although networks do have guidelines, in many stations they are not readily available. Even where they are available, affiliates are under no obligation to abide by them. For example, the sample supers in the ABC guidelines are nothing like what appears on the screen. All the abbreviations have periods, and commas are included in all the dates. More contradictory yet is the advice on the use of abbreviations:

> Use common sense in making Chyron abbreviations. Avoid them whenever possible. Remember that abbreviations tend to confuse the Viewer.... If you end up using more than one abbreviation in a super, something is wrong.... Instead of listening to the interview, the viewer will spend a few seconds trying to decipher the cryptic abbreviations.[2]

This advice is thoroughly consistent with that given by handbooks. Why then are the actual data so diverse? Obviously, in the hierarchy of principles governing style, space is a very important component. Even at the price of possible confusion, cluttering the screen is to be avoided.

Visual impact is the crucial factor. According to the news director of the Columbia (SC) ABC affiliate, viewers hardly notice the details of the text: "The supers are only up for five seconds; nobody pays attention. It's the picture that's important."[3] I can certainly provide personal testimony to the accuracy of his statement that no one pays attention. I had been completely unaware of the ABC's stylistic innovations until they were brought to my attention by the Ted Koppel viewer. Even when consciously trying to collect data, I find myself responding to the content of the label, not its form. Because the supers appear for such a brief time, I process the information first and then when I begin to notice something remarkable about a form, the super disappears.

If the punctuation and style are so easy to overlook on television, do they operate differently in conventional written English? Since the text does not disappear after five seconds, readers, unlike viewers, have the leisure to digest not only the message but the form as well. Consequently, inconsistencies are more likely to distract readers. But what about the special concerns of visual style? Although the goals are stated in terms of viewers (even spelled with a capital V in the ABC guidelines), there is no empirical evidence available to indicate that viewers in fact respond as predicted. There are glaring contradictions in their assumptions. On the one hand, viewers pay no attention to graphics and punctuation, and on the other, the chief purpose of such marks is to get the viewers' attention. Even when the graphics on the screen do attract attention, it is unclear whether it distracts viewers or guides them.

What does television indicate about possible changes in punctuation practices? If students trying to master the written language constantly encounter examples which contradict the rules they are taught at school, can we be surprised at their failure to learn? Since our children have grown up watching TV day in and day out, the written language they find there will surely have an impact on their own ideas about written English. They may learn more from watching the TV screen than from their English teachers and usage manuals. Indeed, they may encounter new ideas about the purpose of punctuation. Current schoolbooks adhere primarily to grammatical explanations for punctuation following a tradition which stretches all the way back to the 1800s when grammatical considerations replaced rhetorical ones in punctuating on effect rather than structure. Recent studies at the New Hampshire Writing Process Laboratory under the direction of Donald Graves have turned to a more rhetorical focus in teaching children to punctuate. They work on the association between what is written and how it affects the reader by having children read each other's work aloud. Reader response criticism, too, is renewing the rhetorical orientation by calling attention to the effect of punctuation. Consequently, television usage may be one of several factors contributing to a change in punctuation practices. The visual style of today may have an unexpected impact on the standard edited English of tomorrow. We tend to believe that usage practices in written English, especially in punctuation, are fairly stable. Yet the few studies which have been done show that the stability is an illusion (Summey; Little and Johnson; Crittenden, Redfern, and others in the current volume). Handbook decrees may be stable, but actual usage is not. The visual style of commercial television is a striking example of how much variation can confront us everyday without our being distracted or even noticing.

Notes

1. ABC provides its affiliates a xeroxed booklet of guidelines, including some ten pages addressing supers and other graphics.
2. ABC xeroxed booklet.
3. Personal communication—news director, ABC affiliate.

7. The Language of Electronic Mail: Written Speech?[1]

NATALIE MAYNOR
Mississippi State University

During the past few years electronic notes have begun to replace ordinary letters in the lives of many people. Why bother to put a piece of paper in an envelope, address and stamp the envelope, carry it to the post office, and then wait several days for the letter to reach its destination, when it is so easy to turn on the computer, log onto a network like BITNET, and watch the message arrive at its destination a few minutes later? BITNET, one of several networks electronically linking universities and other education-related organizations throughout the world, provides a quick, easy, and free way to correspond with people locally or at great distances. In addition, BITNET supports electronic journals, special-interest discussion groups (called lists), and RELAY, a forum for interactive chatting among multiple users. While electronic networks clearly offer valuable resources to all members of the academic community, they offer even more to linguists: They offer an opportunity to witness the emergence of a new style of writing.

As early as 1984 Naomi Baron published an essay exploring the linguistic implications of electronic mail. In it she says, "Linguistic studies of computer mediated communication are still in their infancy, barely reaching beyond the realm of anecdotal observation" (128). Although Michael Spitzer has addressed the topic of language in electronic conferencing, and several other studies have examined e-mail from sociological and psychological perspectives (e.g., Kiesler, Siegel, and McGuire; Hiltz and Turoff), it appears that linguistic research on the topic of e-mail is still in its infancy. Yet it is a medium inviting linguistic analysis.

Note the following short excerpt from a "conversation" on RELAY:

User A: i'm about to eat leftover pizza
. . . .
User B: but watch out for your keyboard ;-)
User A: i'm an expert pizza-eater\keyboarder now!!

48

User B: you have done well young grasshoppah
User A: thanx!

User A, an associate professor of English at a state university, has for many years marked spelling and capitalization errors in student papers and warned students to avoid the use of exclamation points. Yet she types "i'm," "thanx," and "!!." User B, who lives many miles away and has never met User A, assumes that she will understand that ;-) represents a wink.

Here are excerpts from a local one-to-one BITNET "conversation":

User A: i think i just got mail thru a gateway that wouldn't work last summer
            . . . .
User B: a coupla answers to questions . . .
User A: ok
User A: waiting . . .
User B: 1. i ain't mad
            . . . .
User B: write it like a hemingway novel
User A: :-) well said!
User B: short and punchy :-)
User A: i think my kermit prob is with procomm, btw

User A is the same English professor quoted in the previous example. User B in this example is a well-educated, literate systems programmer in a university computing center. Both users violate the conventions of traditional writing: they omit capitalization; they employ the icon :-) to represent a smile; they use simplified or phonetic spellings ("thru," "coupla"). User A writes "prob" for "problem" and "btw" for "by the way."

The most apparent features of what may be thought of as "e-style" are probably the lack of capital letters, the simplified spellings, the clippings, and the icons (see table 7.1 for a list of icons.) With the exception of clippings, these are features which would not show up in speech. Yet they seem to be attempts to make writing more like speech. Since capitalization, for example, does not exist in speech, it is often stripped from computer conversations. When it is used in e-style, it is most likely all caps, referred to as "screaming." Occasionally a word or two will be written in all caps for emphasis, although a more common way to indicate emphasis is to enclose the emphasized word or phrase in asterisks.

TABLE 7.1
Examples of E-Mail Icons

:-)	=	smile
:-(	=	frown
B-)	=	masked smile (wearing sunglasses)
>-C	=	anger
(-_-)	=	secret smile
:-o	=	oh, nooooooooo!
:-]	=	small smile
:-★	=	kiss
;-)	=	wink
:-))))	=	emphatic smile

Punctuation also serves to add conversational touches to e-style: exclamation points are used more often in e-mail than in other kinds of writing; trailing dots signal that more is coming or at least that the topic is still open; dashes represent the less clearly defined sentence-endings that are often the norm in conversation; parentheses enclose conversational asides. Icons add non-verbal marking like smiles and frowns. Traditional writing, of course, has methods for indicating tone. E-style, however, is more direct—closer to the methods used in speech. As for the simplified spelling, obviously phonetic spelling is more like speech. Since "night" has three phonemes, why bother with five letters? And since people say "gotta" and "gonna," why not represent that pronunciation in e-mail? "Hmmm" is often spelled out in e-mail to indicate thinking in progress, as a substitute for spoken "hmmm" or a gesture like scratching the head. Some of these features are not unique to e-style, of course. They are sometimes used in chatty tabloids or informal letters. It is interesting, however, that BITNET is a network used by people associated with universities, not the typical readers of tabloids and not people who are likely to write "gonna" and "gotta" even in letters to friends.

Syntactical features of e-style sometimes reflect informal habits of speech and sometimes are even more simplified than informal speech. Pronoun subjects are often omitted, with context indicating the intended subject, e.g., "guess i need to do a few things here anyway," "don't know," "must have," "depends on where you are." Sometimes both subject and verbal auxiliary, copula, or modal are omitted: "glad it hasn't," "be back in a minute." In questions, the subject is usually included, but parts of the verb phrase are frequently deleted: "you still hanging in?" "we gonna party before school starts back?" "what you been up to?" Articles are commonly omitted: "link die on you?" "he's not on list."

E-style also has its own lexicon. In addition to acronyms and to jargon (see tables 7.2 and 7.3), there is a tendency in e-style to use informal words like "nope" and "yep" while also using Latin-based words like "via" and "re." The reason for the prevalence of "nope" and "yep" is unclear. Perhaps this is another example of informality extended beyond that of ordinary conversation. I, for example, never use "nope" and "yep" in conversation, yet I use them in e-mail. Probably words like "via" and "re" are used both because they are short and clear and because they are associated with computer communication. For example, when someone new signs

TABLE 7.2
Examples of E-Mail Acronyms [2]

BTW	=	by the way
OTOH	=	on the other hand
WYSIWYG	=	what you see is what you get
PITA	=	pain in the ass
TSR	=	terminate-and-stay-resident program
OIC	=	oh, I see

TABLE 7.3
Examples of E-Mail Jargon

flaming	=	verbal attacks
ghost	=	someone who has turned off the computer without signing off of a chat mode like RELAY and whose name therefore still appears on the list of current users
lurker	=	someone who reads discussions on a list but does not contribute
rehi	=	a greeting to someone who has left a chat mode like RELAY briefly and then returned
screaming	=	a message written in all caps
snail-mail	=	traditional mail

onto RELAY, the other users see on the screen something like "Sign on jdoe @ moou via Atlanta," indicating that the RELAY link of the newcomer is Atlanta. And when the "reply" command is used to answer a BITNET note with the subject header "Dogs," the reply will have as its subject header "re: Dogs." The use of "re" in subject headers is, of course, an e-mail borrowing from memo style. But how often is the word "re" used in the body of a memo?

Most of these examples are from informal exchanges like those on RELAY. Traces of e-style are, however, present in more formal exchanges. Icons appear in electronic mail at all levels of formality; capitalization is sometimes absent in lengthy, well-written postings on lists; exclamation points and parentheses abound in postings and in notes. In examining the style of electronic notes, I have run a very limited, very crude test on a few samples of my own writing. Obviously it is not appropriate to compare electronic notes with serious scholarly writing, although I have done so out of curiosity. Using parse.com, a simple style-checker that is included in volume 2 of *PC Magazine*'s Utilities, I noticed grade-level discrepancies of seven to fourteen years between my BITNET notes and documents like papers and course descriptions. A more appropriate comparison would be between BITNET notes and personal letters. Based on very limited data, I found grade-level discrepancies of four to seven years. The few personal letters that I had copies of on disk checked out at college level, the BITNET notes at junior-high level. One especially appropriate comparison was between a letter I wrote to a friend in Australia before he had an e-mail address there and two BITNET notes I wrote to him with similar subject matter after he had gotten an e-mail account. My "snail-mail" letter to him was at a grade level of 14.8; my BITNET notes to him were at 9.6 and 7.3.

What is it about electronic mail that leads to e-style? One answer is probably related to speed at the keyboard. Since interactive BITNET exchanges transmit a line at a time, the sender must hurriedly reach the end of the line and hit <enter> in order to keep the "conversation" moving. Not all of the features of e-style lead to a reduced number of keystrokes, however. Extra punctuation, for example, adds keystrokes; "nope" takes twice as many keystrokes as "no." I believe that we are witnessing something more than reduced keystrokes. We are witnessing the emergence of a writing style that is closer to speech.[3] Interactive exchanges are obviously very much like conversation, and even in the exchange of notes or the posting of comments on lists the rapid turn-around time gives a sense of immediacy. Many of the differences between speech and writing are a result of the immediacy of speech. E-mail represents a sort of convergence of the two media. E-mail obviously employs many features of traditional writing; after all, it is in fact a written medium. Yet it also resembles transcribed speech, with facial gestures added. In addition to approaching the speed of exchange found in conversation, e-mail can be almost as ephemeral as speech. Just as the spoken word disappears immediately after being uttered, most e-mail vanishes after it crosses the computer screen.[4] In this respect it differs from the rapid communication of FAX machines, which normally involve hard copy.

Let me emphasize that I have not collected enough data to make definitive statements about e-style. Nor have I applied any sophisticated stylometric tests. This essay is intended to be introductory rather than conclusive. It is intended as a suggestion that perhaps the language of e-mail is worthy of our attention as linguists.

Is it possible that as more people rely on electronic correspondence, e-style will influence traditional writing? As we all realize, writing tends to be more conservative than speech, slowing the rate of language change. If electronic writing is in fact different from traditional writing, and if the new style influences traditional writing or becomes the dominant form of writing, will it perhaps replace traditional writing as a kind of arbiter of language?

These are questions without easy answers. Predictions about a "paperless society" in the future or about major linguistic changes as a result of e-style can be no more than speculation. But even if e-style is a temporary oddity of limited influence, its evolution is interesting. Because underlining, for example, cannot travel through most networks, e-mailers are moving toward a codified substitute for it, with enclosure in asterisks seeming to edge slightly ahead of all caps right now. Simplifications that result in fewer keystrokes are also indications of adapting communication to a new medium. Whatever else its significance may be, electronic style is another indicator of the flexibility of language and the adaptability of human beings.

Notes

1. I wish to thank the many BITNET correspondents who have offered suggestions for this paper. Special thanks go to Greta Little, Michael Montgomery, Rose Norman, and Dana Paramskas for commenting on an earlier draft of this paper, although I have stubbornly ignored some of their advice.

2. WYSIWYG and TSR are not unique to e-mail. They are probably e-mail borrowings from more general computer jargon.

3. Most of my observations about e-style have been restricted to BITNET and to the English language. E-style is also evident on commercial networks and is not an English phenomenon. Features of e-style are immediately apparent in the interactive areas of networks like CompuServe; a few minutes logged on to Minitel in France is all that it takes to realize that the electronic exchanges are not in textbook French.

4. Michael Spitzer makes the same point about computer conferencing: "Words on paper are permanent and palpable; words in a conference can disappear with a flick of the on/off switch" (19).

8. Studying Usage in Computer Corpora

CHARLES F. MEYER
University of Massachusetts at Boston

In his survey of treatments of usage in dictionaries and usage guides, Thomas Creswell demonstrates quite convincingly that so-called "authorities" on English are the least reliable source of information on usage: not only do they disagree about what constitutes good usage but their disagreements are so extensive that Creswell (122) describes his survey of their opinions as "the orderly documentation of chaos." A much more reliable way to study usage, Creswell maintains, is to base one's judgments of good usage on empirical studies of actual language, and an excellent way to study actual usage, he observes, is to study the language of computer corpora—large collections of written and spoken English that have been computerized and made available for use on either mainframe or personal computers. To illustrate to readers the kinds of valuable information on usage that can be obtained from computer corpora, I will describe in this essay the major computer corpora now available for study, briefly summarize some important studies of usage that have been conducted on them, and discuss one large-scale study of usage that I have undertaken: a study of punctuation practice in a computer corpus of edited written American English.

Computer Corpora Presently Available

Currently, there are four major corpora of modern-day English available to researchers: the Brown University Standard Corpus of Present-Day American English (in short, the Brown Corpus), the London-Oslo-Bergen (LOB) Corpus, the Kolhapur Corpus, and the London-Lund Corpus.[1] The Brown Corpus (Francis, "A Tagged Corpus"), the oldest computer corpus of English, consists of a million words of edited written American English published in 1961; the corpus is divided into 2,000 word samples representing a variety of different genres: press reportage, public documents, technical reports, fictional prose, and so forth. The LOB Corpus is parallel to the Brown Corpus, except that it contains samples of edited written British English (cf. Johansson and Hofland, "The Tagged LOB Corpus"). The Kolhapur Corpus is a million-word corpus of edited written Indian English that is comparable to both the Brown and LOB Corpora but that is based on texts published in 1978 (cf. Shastri). The London-Lund Corpus consists of approximately 435,000 words of spoken British English recorded between 1958 and 1976 (cf. Quirk and Svartvik).

These corpora have been used as the basis of many important studies of usage. There are, for instance, detailed studies of vocabulary frequencies in the Brown Corpus (Francis and Ku era) and the LOB Corpus (Hofland and Johansson, *Word Frequencies*, and Johansson and Hofland, *Frequency Analysis*). Other studies have used computer corpora for information on more specific matters of usage: disputed usages in American English (Meyers, "A Study of Usage Items"), the use of the subjunctive in British and American English (Johansson and Norheim), differences between speech and writing in British English (Biber), the use in American English of verbs ending in the suffix *-alize* (Francis and Ku era), the kinds of vocabulary characteristic of learned and scientific English (Johansson), appositions in British and American English (Meyer, "Apposition in English," "Restrictive Apposition," and *Apposition in Contemporary English*), and differences in the use of *shall* and *will* in British and American English (Krogvig and Johansson).

These are but a few of the many works that have used computer corpora to study usage.[2] To give readers a more detailed overview of how usage can be studied in corpora, I turn my attention now to a study of American punctuation that I recently conducted.

American Punctuation

Most discussions of American punctuation are based not on actual punctuation practice but on the opinions of the authors of style manuals or handbooks.[3] Because, as mentioned earlier, opinions are often in conflict with practice, I undertook a study whose purpose was to determine whether prescriptive rules of punctuation were in accordance with actual punctuation practice in three genres of the Brown Corpus: journalism, learned writing, and fiction. I focused on one type of punctuation in my study, structural punctuation: the use of commas, periods, dashes, parentheses, semicolons, colons, question marks, and exclamation marks to set off units of structure. Below is a brief discussion of some of the more interesting facts about American punctuation practice that I found, followed by a discussion of the extent to which practice mirrors prescription.[4]

First of all, the Brown Corpus contained a very skewed distribution of structural marks of punctuation. The vast majority of marks in the corpus (over 90%) were commas (47%) and periods (45%). The other marks occurred only sporadically: dashes (2%), parentheses (2%), semicolons (2%), question marks (1%), colons (1%), and exclamation marks (1%). As these figures indicate quite dramatically, structural punctuation is a system in which two marks—the comma and the period—fulfill most needs for punctuation: the other marks occur so infrequently that it is tempting to characterize them as "esoteric."

The individual marks of punctuation occurred with varying frequency in the various genres of the corpus. Fewer commas and periods occurred in the learned styles of the corpus than in the other styles, a reflection of the fact that the learned style contained lengthier, more complex, and therefore fewer sentences than the other styles. Certain marks occurred with greater frequency in certain styles than in others. Most of the exclamation marks occurred in the fictional style, largely because the exclamation mark is an informal mark that would be distracting in learned or journalistic styles. Most of the semicolons and colons occurred in the learned style of the corpus, suggesting that these marks are indicators of formal style. And while dashes are normally thought of as emphatic and therefore somewhat informal marks of punctuation, the learned style—the style that most associate with formality—contained the most frequent occurrence of dashes. This finding suggests that the dash is not necessarily an informal mark of punctuation but a mark whose emphatic characteristics are appropriate in a variety of different contexts.

Because handbooks and style manuals discuss the marks of punctuation individually, they obscure the systematic nature of structural punctuation. Structural marks of punctuation are related and their uses are governed by a complex interaction of syntactic, semantic, and prosodic considerations. As an illustration of the systematic nature of punctuation, consider the punctuation of coordinated constructions: constructions joined either explicitly or implicitly by a coordinator such as *and* or *but*. In the Brown Corpus, coordinated constructions were either unpunctuated or punctuated with a variety of different marks: commas, semicolons, periods, or dashes. Just which of these marks was used depended on a variety of linguistic considerations.

The structure of the units being coordinated was one factor that affected their punctuation. In the example below, because the conjoins of the compound sentence are lengthy and complex, they are separated by a heavy mark of punctuation, in this case a period:[5]

> Their world, again, was a still simple, traditional age which was only slowly beginning to appreciate the complexity of life. And perhaps an observer of the vases will not go too far in deducing that the outlook of their makers and users was basically stable and secure. [J54 90–130]

In contrast, in the example below, the conjoins are two noun phrases (*haunts* and *joints*) that are short, non-complex, and therefore separated by no mark of punctuation:

> Also on the bill at the Fifty-fifth Street is a nice ten-minute color film called "Sunday in Greenwich Village," a tour of the haunts and joints. [C01 1930–60]

The semantic structure of the conjoins was a second factor that affected their punctuation. If the conjoins were closely related, they were generally unpunctuated. In the example below, the clauses of the compound sentence are unpunctuated because they are joined by the coordinator *and*, a coordinator indicating a close semantic relationship between clauses.

> "Melodious birds sing madrigals" said the Poet and no better description of the madrigaling of the Deller Consort could be imagined. [C07 680–700]

On the other hand, if the conjoins were distantly related, they were generally punctuated. In the following example, the units are punctuated because they are joined by the coordinator *but*, a coordinator indicating a contrast in meaning between clauses.

> The visceral brain as well as the neocortex is known to contribute to memory, but this topic is beyond the scope of this paper. [J17 300–20]

Prosodic considerations affected the punctuation of compound sentences in instances where neither syntactic nor semantic considerations were important. Short compound phrases were sometimes set off by punctuation to impose a prose rhythm on the written text for purposes of emphasis. In the example below, the conjoins of the short phrase ending the example would not ordinarily be punctuated, because they are short and semantically related. However, the conjoins are punctuated with a comma to create an abrupt pause that emphasizes the fact that the farm mother tolerated nonsense from no one.

There were several fairly good minor portraits in the play, including William Hansen's impersonation of a stubborn, rather pathetic father, and Katherine Squire's vigorous characterization of a farm mother who brooked no hifalutin nonsense from her daughter, or anyone else. [C13 1562–66]

To convey to writers the manner in which marks of punctuation set off linguistic boundaries such as those detailed in the previous examples, handbooks and style manuals set forth a series of rules of punctuation. For the most part, the rules of punctuation I surveyed in handbooks and style manuals corresponded to the actual boundaries I found punctuated in the Brown Corpus. However, there were a few notable exceptions. A number of nonrestrictive modifiers (10%) were not punctuated if without punctuation their meanings would be clear from the contexts in which they occurred. In the example below, the reference of *These Women* is clear from the context. Consequently, the relative clause following *These women* will be interpreted as nonrestrictive, even though the clause is unpunctuated:

The League of Women Voters, 40 and now admitting it proudly, is inviting financial contributions in the windup of its fund drive . . . These women *whose organization grew out of the old suffrage movement* are dedicated to Thomas' dictum that one must cherish the people's spirit but "keep alive their attention." [B01 340–400; emphasis mine]

A large number of adjectives premodifying nouns (37%) were punctuated, despite the fact that they were not in a series (i.e., could not have their orders reversed or be separated by the conjunction *and*):

Then epistolatory me was a foreign correspondent dispatching exciting cables and communiques, quoting from the books I read, imitating the grand styles of the authors recommended by a teacher in whose *special, after-school* class I was enrolled. [K29 300–40; emphasis mine]

In the fictional style, some marks were used to punctuate boundaries not sanctioned in style manuals or usage guides. In the example below, a semicolon is used to separate the middle part of a short series, a usage not mentioned in any source I surveyed:

He felt cheerful again, refreshed; presentable in the wide-cut brown suit, the well-made riding boots. [K16 1600–10]

It must be emphasized, however, that usages such as the above were the exception rather than the norm, and that practice was overwhelmingly in accord with prescription.

Conclusions

Because computer corpora have until recently been available for use only on mainframe computers, they have been somewhat inaccessible sources of information. However, with recent improvements in computer hardware, most major corpora are now available for use on personal computers.[6] In addition, a number of software programs have been developed that have ended the drudgery of analyzing a corpus by hand and made automatic analysis much easier (Kaye and Jones). Consequently, researchers interested in studying usage ought to give serious consideration to studying the language of computer corpora.

Notes

1. Shorter corpora of written Australian English and spoken British English have also been computerized and made available to interested researchers. In addition, an International Corpus of English is now under development (Greenbaum, "A Proposal"). This corpus will permit the study of the many varieties of English that have developed in such countries as Canada, Australia, New Zealand, Nigeria, and India.

2. For additional references, readers should consult the 1986 issue of *ICAME News* (now the *ICAME Journal*), which contains an extensive bibliography of research conducted on computer corpora.

3. The only empirical study of punctuation was conducted in 1949 by George Summey.

4. The results of the study are discussed in detail in Meyer (*A Linguistic Study of American Punctuation*).

5. The numbers following example sentences identify the section of the Brown Corpus the example is from.

6. For more information on purchasing corpora, interested researchers should contact the Norwegian Computing Centre for the Humanities (which sells copies of the corpora at cost): The Norwegian Computing Centre for the Humanities, P.O. Box 53, Universitetet, N-5027 Bergen, Norway.

9. Explaining Usage to the Public

MICHAEL MONTGOMERY
University of South Carolina, Columbia

Where does the American public get its information on English usage these days? Certainly the traditional sources are still around, in abundance. Dictionaries provide it. Since the first edition of the *American Heritage Dictionary* was published in 1969, American dictionaries have been less shy about providing usage information than they were a generation earlier. Providing it as well are widely available usage glossaries and guides of various orientations, including the recently published, nearly 1000-page descriptivist *Webster's Dictionary of English Usage* (ed. E. Ward Gilman). But however useful and dependable these sources may be for language professionals, for many Americans they are cumbersome, impersonal, and just not very satisfying. If our day is one which prizes and increasingly demands instantaneous access to information, especially if it is "individualized" for the consumer, how is advice on using the English language to be provided? One possible source might be computer software which leads the individual user through a series of questions in addressing a specific usage query. One source that has already been meeting the demand for over a decade is the Writer's Hotline, a type of telephone answering service. Nothing addresses more quickly, easily, directly, or personally the variety of usage questions from punctuation and subject-verb agreement to word choice and sentence construction. Relying on the Writer's Hotline is not unlike having one's own consulting service on call.

Since the fall of 1978, this writer has fielded questions for three telephone services, two of them called the Writer's Hotline, at the University of Arkansas at Little Rock, at Memphis State University, and since 1981 at the University of South Carolina.[1] Although people have long phoned the local university's English department for answers to questions about the English language, it was at the University of Arkansas at Little Rock in February 1978 that the department's practice of doing this first received a name and drew enough media attention to catch the awareness of the larger public. This awareness quickly transformed into public demand, as the hotline became an immediate success, attracting local and national publicity and inspiring similar services at many other institutions.[2] The callership at Arkansas-Little Rock quickly increased to two dozen a day, mainly from out of state, to take advantage of the quick, easy, personal, and authoritative assistance we offered. This demand spread to other institutions and has never slackened, with an average of nearly 1,500 calls a year to the University of South Carolina Writer's Hotline in the period 1985–90. All along callers have with few exceptions been neither students nor professional writers, but rather writers on the job—such as in local businesses and public service agencies—with specific, "real-life" situations of writing the English language and trying to choose between two or three ways to do so. While the majority of hotline calls involve well-known issues like pronoun case, subject-verb agreement, comma placement, and distinguishing wordpairs like *affect* and *effect,* others involve unusual issues that reflect the quandaries that on-the-job writers get themselves into. Distinctive to hotline usage calls is the very personal stake that callers have in their questions, which requires individual attention and flexibility in response. It is about these calls that have come in and the usual approaches taken by the hotline, and particularly this writer, in dealing with them that will concern us here.

First, a further word is warranted about typical hotline callers and the large segment of the general public I believe they represent. In answering perhaps three thousand questions over the years, I have developed a profound respect for the general public's conscientiousness in using the English language. Despite a current fashionable dismay that the American public knows little and cares less about writing English, a view often expressed by English teachers and the media alike, my experience is quite different—that the public is often well informed and determined to write the language as carefully as possible.[3] Most Writer's Hotline callers know their choices, whatever the issue is, and they call primarily to confirm the one they have already made.

If at all representative, hotline callers reveal a public that is curious about how the language is changing and why it varies (as indicated by such questions as "Can *disco* be used as a verb?—it's not in the dictionary"; "Why is *could care less* replacing *couldn't care less*?"; and "How does one form the plural of *Ms.*?"). The public, I believe, knows at least one thing that student writers often have not yet realized: that linguistic choices have important consequences.

Hotline questions are invariably serious, even if occasionally naive (as when a Little Rock furniture dealer wanted to pluralize *ottoman* as *ottomen,* or when a caller wanted to know how to represent "silent e" in phonetic notation).

For my part, I have often been in a position to learn the public's attitudes and sensitivities about usage and the implications of making various linguistic choices. I have learned, for a case in point, that reflexive pronouns such as *myself* and *himself* are used not so much as "escape hatches" to avoid choosing between *I* and *me* or between *he* and *him,* but rather are employed by a writer who wishes to mitigate his or her role in writing with respect to the addressee. The pronoun-avoidance explanation doesn't account for why more than half the questions I have answered on this matter concern the first person singular (as *John and myself* or *one of my friends and myself*) or why most of the rest concern second person (as in *it was a pleasure to have a person such as yourself on our program,* where there is no pronoun to avoid). Writers on the job base their usage choices on tone more commonly than I suspected. Another example of a usage issue that has frequently come up, one not dealt with in any usage manual which I am aware of, is which relative pronoun should a writer use (i.e., *who, that,* or *which*) to refer to their company or business, if they are trying to "personalize" it (as in *Nelson's is the company who cares*).

Obviously, many hotline callers have a very personal stake in the usage choices facing them. In tailoring answers and advice to individual situations, I have had to assume many different roles. I have frequently arbitrated disputes, most often between secretaries and their bosses and between wives and husbands. A couple from Boston phoned one day, saying they had argued over a question of subject-verb agreement for fifteen years and asking me to render a decision. The sentence was *Jane is one of the girls who work* (or *works*) *in the office,* where the "right" answer (*work*) violates the idiom of most speakers. I have sometimes found myself consoling callers who have already lost a dispute. A member of the Arkansas Parks and Recreation Department asked one day about the correct spelling for a roadsign. His department had already decided on *Marks Mill,* sparing the apostrophe, as was its policy, but the caller was convinced that the mill at one time belonged either to a man named *Mark* or to a family named *Marks.* But his reasoning that an apostrophe was necessary was to no avail.

I have tried to help callers conquer their hobgoblins, as for instance a second-grade teacher on Long Island who complained about a Xerox Corporation advertisement saying *Drive slow* and had to be persuaded that *slow* could sometimes be used as an adverb. I have often had to decipher cases of overwriting, as for a New York insurance firm that received a letter from a lawyer which closed with the sentence *I hope this letter is dispossessive of your fears.* (Translation: *I hope this letter disposes of your fears.*) For the most part, though, my time has been spent either in reassuring writers who have already made an intelligent and appropriate linguistic decision or in reviewing the options for callers in a descriptive manner, that is, of course, within the limits of a telephone call.

The Desire for Prescriptions

Nevertheless, as one might expect, many callers are interested only in knowing what the "correct" answer is. Their desire for a prescription is very strong and to the point. They write by rules and try to apply a rule whenever possible, from whatever source. They frequently begin their questions with "Isn't there supposed to be a rule that . . ." Many of the rules they employ are phantoms, half-remembered or mis-remembered from their schooldays, such as the "rule" for using *speak* and *talk*. The many calls I have received about the use of these two verbs, primarily from the New York City area, are a mystery to me. My surmise is that the "rule" concerns which preposition to use with which verb, but I have never found it in any handbook or usage glossary. Nor have callers enlightened me on this matter.[4]

Writers-by-rule seem to have a firm predisposition that, if there are competing forms or usages in a context, only one must be correct and the other(s) must not be. Such writers become uneasy when told that some usage choices apply to the level of usage (e.g., *can* and *may* to express permission), or that others are interchangeable (e.g., *that* and *which* in restrictive clauses, or the use of the comma before a conjunction in a series, the latter being considered optional by even the fiercest prescriptivists).

Further, the writer-by-rule tends to want prescriptions in inverse proportion to the gravity of the usage issue. That is, the narrower, the less consequential (for clarity and comprehension), and the more nearly an either-or matter the usage issue is, the more likely a writer will be to want, even insist on, a prescription. The disputes I have arbitrated have always concerned single word choices, isolated punctuation, or aspects of the written code (see the next section). By the same token, the more general the matter (e.g., rules for subject-verb agreement), the less prescriptive writers tend to be.

Such a writer frequently falls prey to hypercorrection, using some forms in certain contexts (e.g. *whom, badly, fewer,* subject case pronouns as objects of prepositions) out of a sense of insecurity. Hypercorrection or overuse of such forms is nearly as common a problem for hotline callers as the underuse of forms where they are traditionally prescribed. Such a writer may thus apply logic at the complete expense of idiom, as did the caller who was determined to recruit hotline support for her letter writing campaign against the television networks about their "subject-verb agreement errors" in the program titles *Three's Company* and *Eight Is Enough.*

Because writers create problems by overapplying rules, part of the hotline's approach is to show writers how to avoid having to make their choice entirely. Most, if not all, writers already employ avoidance strategies for those aspects of writing which give them qualms and thus understand their usefulness. A writer can more often than not choose a third variant (*that* or Ø in questions of *who* versus *whom, if* in questions of *providing* versus *provided,* and so on), or the writer can recast part of a sentence to sharpen and clarify it, as in rephrasing the subject of a sentence containing subject-verb-agreement or pronoun-agreement difficulties, to avoid a choice of verbs, or in choosing for instance between *different than* and *different from* by finding a more specific comparative than *different.*

Rules of the Written Code

Almost as numerous as the questions about word choice, phrasing, and grammar combined are those concerning aspects of written English (capitalization, punctuation—especially the comma and the apostrophe, some spelling) that have no reflex in spoken English. Such aspects of language, it is usually said, are governed by largely invariable conventions and not to any apparent extent by educated usage. Because writers cannot rely on the sound of the language to punctuate, capitalize, and spell, these matters are especially subject to the overapplication of rules and to become points about which on-the-job writers call the hotline. No doubt this is the motivation behind the old rule of thumb for commas: "when in doubt, leave it out." Uncertainties and disagreements arise particularly frequently with the apostrophe; recall the question about *Marks Mill* mentioned earlier.

I stated above that the conventionalized aspects of the written code are "largely invariable." This is certainly the customary view. One significant factor bringing this into question in actual usage choices is what I would term something like "on-the-job considerations." The desire of writers to achieve a certain tone or emphasis often overrides conventions of punctuation and capitalization. That is, they violate conventions in understandable ways because of their conceptions of their tasks and audiences. Nowhere is this clearer or more intriguing than in the capitalization of political and administrative terms, about which I have answered many dozens of calls. Does one capitalize terms such as *federal* (in *federal government*), *state* (as in *the state of Illinois*), *president* (as of a company, used descriptively, not as a title), and *legislature* (as in *the Arkansas legislature*)? In discussing this at some length with callers, I find it not at all hard to appreciate their inclination to capitalize such words when they refer to the writers' own state, company, or agency. But here's the rub: Many callers admit to being more reluctant to capitalize these words when they refer to another state, company, or agency, and they are resentful if these words referring to their own are not capitalized by other writers. Thus, there is a thoroughgoing double standard in the workplace for using capital letters and, most likely, for other areas of language usage as well.

Levels of Usage

Concerning the desires and tendencies of the writers who call the Writer's Hotline, much has already been said of how I as one member of the answering staff have handled the gamut of questions that come in. Certainly the most important consideration is to fit the advice to the call, to do what works for the individual caller. In the remainder of this paper, I will discuss the approach to describing usage variants and the distinctions of usage levels that I developed during the early days of working for the Writer's Hotline.

The Writer's Hotline draws a broad distinction between two levels of writing—formal and general. This distinction isn't new (Porter Perrin made it years ago in his *An Index to English*), but it is an accurate and important one that most workaday writers can appreciate. In *The Writer's Hotline Handbook*, the handbook based on the questions the Writer's Hotline received, we explain this distinction in the following manner:

> Although many of our writer-callers may not think about it, there are two basic levels of writing—formal and general. These are two different styles of standard English. Formal writing—the writing of legal documents, some scholarly journals, and "official" publications—gives utmost importance to form. Its grammar is conservative, and it adheres to many distinctions (e.g., *shall/ will* and *may/ can*) for the special effect they seem to create. Formal writing does not need to be dull and pompous, although it often is; it can be graceful and precise.
>
> General writing is the writing that most writers write and most readers read. It is the writing found in annual reports and in interdepartmental memos, in magazines and newspapers. It is the only style of writing that most writers ever use. It is less formal in tone, usually livelier, and more varied in texture. It usually contains fewer abstractions and more concrete examples. It may contain contractions and first- and second-person pronouns. Writers of general writing may use formal writing for a special effect; they may make occasional use of slang and colloquialisms and may bend rules for dramatic effect. Thus, in general writing, a writer has more choices and more possibilities for expression than in formal writing. General writing should be lively and brisk, but it need be no less precise, nor are there any fewer possibilities for expressing complex, abstract thoughts in general writing than in formal writing. [Montgomery and Stratton xiii]

The Writer's Hotline makes many further distinctions, of course, but this one is basic to all others and offers a number of advantages. First, the formal vs. general distinction allows the hotline to give realistic and common-sense usage advice to writers on the job about the level of writing they are comfortable with most. General writing is closer to speech; general usage is therefore a surer basis on which writers can make decisions. Second, the distinction allows us to counteract one of the basic on-the-job problems of writing—overwriting. Since many writers are not in secure command of the diction and phrasing of formal writing, they often tend to misuse it and to overapply the rules of that level of usage.

Third, because formal vs. general is a more accurate and descriptive distinction than formal vs. informal, found in many college handbooks, it allows us to transcend a one-dimensional continuum which creates artificial either-or distinctions of usage. Formal vs. general allows us to use three types of judgments in characterizing usage choices: 1) relative judgments such as "acceptable," "unacceptable," and "preferred"; 2) stylistic judgments such as "vague," "confusing," and "wordy"; and 3) sociolinguistic judgments such as "specialized" (as with reference to the plurals of originally Latin and Greek words such as *antenna*; the specialized plural is *antennae*, the general one is *antennas*) and even "prejudiced." We term a usage "prejudiced" if it may meet the disapproval of critical readers, even if it is justified by history and general practice and is listed in all dictionaries (e.g., *hopefully* as a sentence adverb and *like* as a conjunction). In short, we rarely use the label "correct."

The Writer's Hotline takes this multifaceted approach because of the nature of the callers and their calls and because this is what seems to work, not because its staff has training in linguistics. Hotline callers—ordinary, everyday writers on the job—are much more sensitive and broadminded about using the language than usually given credit for. They often see the artificiality of writing according to prescribed formal rules and are frequently interested in discussing the pros and cons of the usage choices facing them. Generally they are more concerned with appropriateness than correctness, wanting to know not what is right so much as what works. Their sensitivity to their audience is great. They know, this writer believes, much about using the English language, much, in fact, that usage professionals should pay attention to.

Notes

1. At Memphis State, where I taught from 1979 to 1981, the service was designated the "Cool Line."

2. During the first year of the Writer's Hotline at UALR, media interest was nothing less than astounding, with stories of the service appearing in such periodicals as *Time* and *People,* with nearly one hundred radio interviews being conducted with stations throughout North America, and

with long distance calls from reporters in London, England, and Sydney, Australia.

3. This experience differs quite markedly from that described for the Illinois State University hotline by Neuleib and Scharton, who claim that "no one, however, wants to know that many questions have two or more right answers, that often usage is relative to audience and occasion, . . . if we try to give a full, accurate answer to a question, the responses vary from anger to dismay" (414).

4. For a possible explanation I am indebted Lois Rauch Gibson, who grew up in New York City and who recalls English teachers correcting usages like *He talks Spanish* to *He speaks Spanish*. Thus the usage rule that Hotline callers tried to remember may well involve which verb can take a direct object, not which preposition is appropriate with which verb.

10. Social Uses of Possessive Adjectives in English

JOHN J. STACZEK
Georgetown University

Most recent accounts of the possessive adjective or possessive pronoun in its determinative or genitive function (Huddleston; Leech and Svartvik; Quirk and Greenbaum; and Quirk, Greenbaum, Leech and Svartvik *A Comprehensive Grammar*) discuss the distributional characteristics of such forms as *my, your,* and *our* in terms of their prenominal position; further, these same accounts discuss the semantic features in terms of *alienable* and *inalienable possession,* or *attribution* and *non-attribution.* No account yet appears to provide information on the distinctive uses of at least two of the forms—*your* and *our*—from the perspective of their more unusual social functions in spoken and written English. Malinowski (1923), in his early work on primitive languages, makes the claim that "in its primitive uses, language functions as a link in concerted human activity, as a piece of human behaviour. It is a mode of action and not an instrument of reflection." According to Hudson:

Another use of speech is simply to establish or reinforce social relations—what Malinowski called PHATIC COMMUNION, the kind of chit-chat that people engage in simply in order to show that they recognise each other's presence. We might add many other uses of speech to this list—speech to obtain . . . information . . . for expressing emotions . . . for its own sake . . . and so on. [109–10]

The point of Hudson's interpretation of Malinowski is that speech in social interaction has more than a single function. We will see that possessive pronouns in English are excellent examples of this.

I propose to describe four distinctive social settings that seem to trigger at least five social functions of the possessive adjective in English, referring also to some written historical data as well as to a recent advertising-copy formula.

The data analyzed in this essay are, for the most part, natural and spontaneous; the scripted tokens are almost as authentic as the natural data. At present, the corpus consists of 143 tokens. There are more than four types of settings but I will refer only to four for the principal illustrative examples. For the majority of items, the source is provided in the corpus. Among the data to be analyzed are the following:

1. On your average evening, you can fire a cannon from one end of the wall to the other and not worry about hitting a soul. [TV, interview]
2. What are we going to do with our Certificate of Deposit? [transaction, bank officer]
3. Put it into the oven and then pull out your beautiful buns. [PBS, cooking program]
4. We used to have, for your major, the comprehensive exam. . . . [meeting]
5. You'll notice we've got your door opening laid out. [*This Old House*]
6. They're not your standard shingle. [*This Old House*]
7. First we make our marks on the railing cap. Next we use the saw to make our cuts for the biscuits. [*This Old House*]
8. Now they can really play your perimeter game. [TV sportscaster]
9. You got your fan, your temperature gauge . . . Those are your fog lamps in the front. [Volvo salesman]

The principal data come from four different types of sources: the instructional format of the 'how-to' public broadcasting program; the sales/marketing setting; the scripted television situation-comedy, be it a 'sit-com' such as *Cheers* or a 'skit-com' (to use a phrase from a recent *New York Times Magazine* article about Tracey Ullman) such as *Saturday Night Live*; and national/local weather broadcasts. The corpus reveals that *your* and *our* have a number of social interactional uses with regard to the following characteristics of discourse: impersonality, intimacy, audience engagement, status determination, and social deixis.

A look at possible contexts for the following sentences reveals that the prosodic features are different and that the conversational implicatures are also very different:

10. You got your checkbook. [falling intonation]
11. You got your checkbook. [rising intonation]

The stress on *your* is different to indicate contrast in 10 and a demonstrative deixis in 11. The interpretation of *got* may also be different, either 'have', 'receive', or 'obtain' (in sentence 10 with falling intonation) and 'have' as a copula for 'there be' (in sentence 11 with rising intonation).

In the first grouping of tokens, sentences 12 through 14, the setting is demonstrative/instructional, to some extent, deictic.

The speaker is the host of a show, in this case, *This Old House*, who moves about showing the progress of renovation and remodeling. In tokens 12 and 13, the host is carrying on a conversation with either the carpenter or some other craftsman. Neither member of the dyad is the owner of the house and, for that reason, the possessive forms cannot convey the usual attributive meaning, that the stove and the door opening belong to the members of the dyad. In both cases, the possessive form can be replaced with a definite or indefinite article. We might argue that this function of the possessive, at least in (12), is not unrelated to the royal *we*.

> 12. We'll have an island with our stove there. [Bob Vila, *This Old House*, talking to the carpenter but also describing to the TV audience the finished design of a kitchen]
> 13. You'll notice we've got your door opening laid out. [*This Old House*]

The host and carpenter are interacting with each other. Neither use of *our* and *your* indicates possession of the object but rather a kind of oblique attribution that is more demonstrative and deictic. In both cases, the genitive form is easily replaced by the definite article with no significant change in meaning. What these two tokens and others like them have in common is their instructional format, one in which the speaker demonstrates something by pointing it out or referring to it for the viewer. Because these data are derived from radio and television formats, they are somehow scripted but not in the same way as, for example, a situation comedy. Post-performance production notes would help to confirm the detail of the scripted formulas. However, since the formula is also common in conversation, the familiarity suggested by the formula is quite possibly one writers recognize and consider appropriate for such an instructional setting. Without seeing the working script, it is not unlikely that the host's language is spontaneous for the setting. He is, after all, moving about a house, inside and out, without cue cards. The segments are clearly taped on site and edited at the studio for splicing into a 30-minute program.

In sentence 14, the host is addressing the owner while using a non-contrastive genitive form:

> 14. Your beautifully remodeled kitchen that you did yourself. [*This Old House*]

This is a way of pointing, of demonstrating.

In 15 the radio show host is giving advice, again suggesting and demonstrating, trying to achieve a level of informality, even chumminess with the listener, as if he were at the listener's side reviewing the steps of a procedure.

> 15. We're gonna go ahead and put our fertilizer down. [radio gardening show]

Since this is a phone-in radio advice program, there are neither cue cards nor rehearsals. The interaction is conversational and informal. In 16 the saleswoman instructs and demonstrates using the same formula, in which *your* can also be equated to a simple definite article.

> 16. That's your lighter finish. [saleswoman in furniture gallery]

The interaction represents an attempt to be informal and instructive at the same time. The use of *your* implies no type of possession but instead functions as a deictic marker.

The next sequence of items, sentences 17 through 21, clearly reaffirms the instructional intent of the setting. Since speech plays a role in social interaction, these possessives or genitives can establish or reinforce social roles and relationships (Malinowski 1923 in Huddleston 1984, 109). In the instructional setting before a studio camera, the speaker can establish a bond with listeners by referring to instruments or objects in the setting as if they, in fact, belonged to the listeners in their kitchens. This is a way of engaging listeners in the act of the speaker, of establishing an informal context, of building a coziness, a chumminess, a level of intimacy. The setting almost allows this to be done very impersonally but with a personal touch and a personal form.

> 17. The smell is not too hot. The chicken is not your real hot Mexican food. [PBS cooking program]
> 18. Reduce the wine by half, then add your chicken stock, then your heavy cream; then place it in your broiler. [PBS cooking program]
> 19. Pecan Pie: I'm first starting with my flour...There you are. You have your pecan pie. [PBS cooking program]
> 20. You preheat your oven to 350. [PBS cooking program]
> 21. We preheated our oven to 350. [PBS cooking program]

Sentences 22 and 23 verify the instructional formula in a basket-weaving instructional setting:

22. Taking my long piece of cane and turning my basket . . . [TV, instructional]
23. With my finger, I'm going to be holding on to my basket. [TV, instructional]

In surveying a handful of native speakers about the usage, I have received comments such as the following: "I react logically by establishing that I am not in possession of such an article or object" or "The tone of the usage suggests some condescension much as the parent-child instructional/demonstrative format does" in, for example, the teaching of the nearly extinct art of shoelace tying.

Related to the above tokens extracted from the radio and television format is the next set of tokens, 24–26, that are produced in spontaneous conversation. They verify the usage as instructional, demonstrative, deictic.

24. See what you can do. Type in your number 4. [KC to M in lesson on NBI word-processor]
25. You got your east-west roads running at one-mile intervals and your north-south roads the same. [PK, conversation, 30 Apr. 88]
26. If you need stronger power, you get down to your little loops. [optician, Birmingham, MI, 29 Apr. 88]

Sentences 27 through 30 support the conclusions for the use of *your* and *our* as a deictic marker that demonstrates, distinguishes, or focuses on an object within the instructional/demonstrative setting.

27. This is some of your choices for sinks. [*This Old House*]
28. Before we do that, we prenotch our post. [*This Old House*]
29. We are ready for our rough plumbing inspection. [*This Old House*]
30. We're gonna cut this miter with our miter saw. [*New Yankee Carpenter*]

Only 27 is attributable to Vila on *This Old House*; 28–30 are attributable to the carpenter, Norm Abrams, from the same program and from his own new program.

A second setting is the sales/marketing situation in which a salesman attempts to establish an informal, yet still impersonal, relationship. He tries to draw the client into his confidence by using a personal possessive marker that has an overt attributive function and a covert deictic function. Examples 31 through 34 occur as part of a rehearsed sales pitch which, because of the frequency of *your*, has become quite formulaic for a particular

Volvo salesman. The usage suggests a strategy of the salesman to establish familiarity, intimacy, and chumminess through the *your* form. Its function is also deictic in nature.

>   31. Under your hood you find . . . [Volvo salesman]
>   32. You got your fan, your temperature gauge . . . [Volvo salesman]
>   33. Let me just check my inventory. [Volvo salesman]
>   34. You've got your basic car with dealer prep . . . [Volvo salesman]

In sentences 31–32 and 34, there is also a syntactic trigger, namely, the *you + got/have* construction. An adequate paraphrase might be *there's your X* or *there's the X . . .* , both of which are too impersonal for building confidence and engaging the listeners in the interaction.

In sentence 35, a spontaneous setting in a men's haberdashery, what is inappropriate about the indefinite article that allows the salesman to choose *your*? If the salesman had sold the customer such a shirt, it would be logical for him to remember having done so. However, it's not logic that prevails in these settings. It is interactive social function such as the authority to judge and advise or to build confidence that will lead to the obvious conclusion of the speech act, a sale.

>   35. Customer, admiring his suit and tie selection:
>   What color shirt would I wear?
>   Salesman: I'd wear your cream color. [men's haberdashery]

A third setting is the scripted sitcom or skitcom in which the same forms and social functions occur with regularity. Refer to tokens 36-38.

>   36. Talk about your corporate office in the sky. [*Cheers*]
>   37. I see we got our new issue of Cosmo today. [*Kate and Allie*, male lead]
>   38. Hey, this is your real big-time corporate office. [*Cheers*]

Cheers, Kate and Allie, and *Saturday Night Live* have been excellent sources for the data, most certainly because of the comedic nature of the setting. *Cheers* was taped in front of a studio audience. It achieved some of its authenticity through the spontaneity and creativity of its performers. *Kate and Allie* enjoyed the same good writing and authenticity and naturalness of spoken text. *Saturday Night Live* is performed live in the studio as a series of short skits and is dependent on the creative interpretation and sense of timing of each of its performers, whose scriptwriters have captured the essence of form and function in the expression of social register for theme and role within the theme. In all three cases, scriptwriter as observer and performer as interpreter are the key ingredients to making the forms and functions work naturally to convey attitude, status, distance, intimacy, formality and informality, all the elements of Malinowski's phatic communion.

The final major setting is local and national weather forecasts where the *your* form appears with uncommon frequency, on the NOAA (National Oceanographic and Atmospheric Administration) sponsored All-Weather Channel, as well as in local forecasts and even transitions to forecasts. In addition, transitions from one program to another take advantage of the same form and function with *your*.

39. It's very cold on your eastern side of the country. [TV, weather, NOAA]
40. So there's your six-day outlook. [TV, local weatherman, completing report]
41. Here's a look at your local weather. [All-Weather Channel]
42. Now stay tuned for your local news. [CBS network announcer after *West 57th*]
43. Let's look what's going on for your holiday weekend. [*NBC Sunday Show*]
44. Let's take a look at your weather for the week. [*NBC News*]
45. The big problem on your island side will be flooding. [TV weather re Hurricane Hugo, in response to question from local weatherman]
46. 91 degrees for your high in Miami. [NOAA]

In tokens 39, 41, 44 and 46, the NOAA announcer, in conveying information about national weather patterns, portrays a general aloofness but then switches to the more socially intimate *your* form when addressing views by region or city. The switch, because of its regularity, has to be more than simply fortuitous. Using the pronoun has become a formula for decreasing distance and for engaging the listener in a description of the weather in a particular locale. Weather reports on local television stations support this claim, as tokens 40 and 45 demonstrate. This exhibits the same demonstrative/instructional format in which the *your* form is used as a deictic marker that helps to engage the listener/viewer and to establish a level of informality and social intimacy. Tokens 42 and 43 show the use of the same formula in the same type of setting transition on two different networks.

The next three tokens come from a historical source in the 15th century. Because of the instructional or deictic format that appears almost universally in the tokens so far described and because of some examples from a cooking setting, the question arises if there might be reason to look into some very old recipes to determine whether the form and function of *your* and *our* could be established in other settings and at other times. The Harleian manuscripts confirm one of the earliest written sources for the phenomenon, and if we acknowledge that speech does, in fact, precede writing, then we can tentatively conclude that the writing is a reflection of the oral tradition.

Thanks to the careful eye of a colleague, David Harris, with whom I have been discussing this topic for several years, I was led to Austin's (1888) edition of *Two Fifteenth-Century Cookery-Books*, 'cookeries' edited from Harleian MSS. 279 and 4016 in the British Museum. The manuscripts, dating 1430–50, contain a number of recipes and menus of banquet fare. At this point in my research, these manuscripts, extracts of which are found in tokens 48 through 50, represent the earliest occurrences of the use of *thy* in contexts similar to those already described as instructional settings. Harris' help in locating Old English texts revealed that in "several collections of recipes and magical cures [that] have been preserved from Old English, the usual construction [was] the singular imperative, e.g., *nim* 'take'." What he found in the sampling was that these recipes revealed no instances where *thy* was used to modify ingredients, the usual modifier being the *se*-demonstrative, which we could translate either *that*, or less strongly, *the*, as in

47. Work the plants to dust, mingle with soap, and the juice of an apple.

This is perhaps a type of deixis. In these same texts were found instances of inalienable possession with body parts in such expression as *take with thy two hands* as well as instances of alienable possession such as *stick thy knife [or: dagger] into the plant*, which also have similar reflections in the Middle English Harleian manuscripts of 1430–50, shown in tokens 48 through 50.

48. Take almond milk and egg yolks mixed together, saffron, salt, and honey; dry thy pie crust and lay thy marrowbones thereon, and cast thy mixture thereon, and serve forth. [Harleian MS. 279, xxviij, c. 1440]
49. Take egg whites, milk and flour, and a little yeast and beat it together ... then take a chauffeur [dish for heating] full of fresh boiling grease

and put thy hand in the batter and let thy batter run down by thy fingers into the chaffeur . . . [Harleian MS. 279, lj., c. 1440]
50. Take good porke and broil it, and grind it small with egg yolks; then take Pepper, Ginger, and grind it small, and mix it together, and a little honey, and garnish thy crust within and without, and cover them with thy lids, and let them bake, and serve forth. [Harleian MS. 279, iij., c. 1440]

A final new venue where the form and function of *your* are being exploited is advertising. Advertising copy is beginning to lend itself to the use of this formula with *your,* as in the following very recent examples.

51. The stars are out at your new K-Mart. [newspaper ad, 10/1/89]
52. Hi, I'm your basic frequent flyer. [TV ad for the TWA Frequent Flyer program]
53. The Sony Trinitron XBR. Your typical Over-Achiever. [print advertising, *Playboy,* November 1989]

One of the items in the corpus, the final token, sentence 54, is a monologic performance from a *Saturday Night Live* skit (30 Sept. 1989). It consists of 25 occurrences of *our,* 0 occurrences of *your,* and 3 occurrences of *my.* As exaggerated a pattern parody as it may be, it serves to reinforce the imitated naturalness of the social and linguistic usage.

54. Announcer: It's time for Home Improvement with the Anal Retentive Carpenter.
Gene: Hello, and welcome to the Anal Retentive Carpenter. I'm Gene. And today, we're going to be building a window box for *our* window. Now what do we need for this project? Well, we need *our* blueprint here. . . . Now, *our* blueprint calls for us to cut two boards but . . . but it doesn't call for a silly hazardous placement of pushpins. . . . And, of course, [demonstrating] *our* tool belt is loaded and ready for use. Now we've got *our* hammer, *our* pliers, *our* tape measure, *our* awl, clamp, extension cord, screwdriver, and marker. That's HPTACESM. I can remember it by repeating to myself "Howard plants tulips and chrysanthemums every Sunday morning." . . . Actually, I never use *my* awl but I need it to keep the syntax correct. . . . Now let's take a look at *our* lumber. We have a sturdy plank here and we have a matching 1x2. . . . It's not perfect by any means. It has this knot here, the grain is not exactly uniform as I'd like . . . there's a blemish. . . . So let's clamp *our* defective timber into *our* vise and get it ready to cut. . . . How do we cut *our* board? We remove *our* saw from *our* saw sheath. No corrosion on this little darling. . . . And let's uncover *our* little minivac . . . and, lining up *our* s-s-saw with *our* thumbnail . . . cut and clean, cut and clean, and cut and clean. . . . Now how do we discard *our* wooden refuse? Well, we get

> [pause] *our* little scrap basket here and we remove a scrap bag [pause] and place *our* scrap inside the bag and fold it over, keeping the corners square ... and we staple ... we ... and, of course, there is the problem of *our* staples punching through *our* plastic trash bag.... Now we staple again, but [pause] we do not fold over this time. [pause] Now I know what you're thinking: But, Gene, those staples could burst through that plastic trash bag as well.... And, this goes back under *our* workbench.... Let's replace [pause] you know, I'm replacing *our* minivac cozy. I call this *my* dustbuster duster.... All right, back to *our* project.... Now, we've premarked *our* 1x2 here, and, oh my, what a bold little mark we are.... I think we should take that down with an artgum eraser.... I'll just put *my* artgum eraser in there.... So let's get *our* toolbox. We put that on our table here.... We have everything arranged in alphabetical order, so we're going to have to bump things because awl starts with an A.... So that means *our* chalk is going to have to go where *our* chuck is.... ["The Anal Retentive Carpenter," *Saturday Night Live*, 30 Sept. 1989]

At this juncture in my research, I can only say that the setting for the forms is instructional and demonstrative, almost discoursally deictic. The triggers for the forms are social and syntactic, and, by frequency, mostly oral. Scripted forms, based on authentic language use, become performance forms. And, finally, the intent of the writer, speaker, or performer seems to be to engage the hearer by establishing some level of intimacy, informality, even to convey to the listener, by using such personal forms, information about roles, attitudes, and distance.

Among other things, what remains in this ongoing research is to discover other archival evidence for this particular usage earlier than 1430 and between 1430 and 1987. My research on this usage inevitably has to take me to other settings, including the hospital setting of doctor/patient and nurse/patient interactions (e.g., "How's our blood pressure today?"), the medicine, magic, or food recipes in older texts, certainly into other languages, and even into usages such as "I forgot to buy the wife an anniversary gift" which is a gender-specific form. At this stage, the sources look promising and support the claim that the forms are a function of the situation and of participant roles.

11. The Capitalization of Color Names and Other Terms for Ethnic Groups

ROBERT S. WACHAL
University of Iowa

The use of an initial capital letter to indicate that a term is somehow special, unique in reference, or a member of the category proper noun is a convention seldom explored, except in manuals of style, and they typically just list examples, categorized by the many semantic fields in which capitalization normally occurs. All too rarely they also list, for at least some categories, examples of exceptional forms that remain in lowercase. In an area of usage so often undescribed and presented only by lists, is the search for principles of capitalization likely to be fruitless? Or, the quest for internal logic aside, is there enough divided usage to merit extensive study? And, in any event, is it of any consequence that, for example, names of months are capitalized and names of seasons are not?

In a search for answers to such questions, this paper will explore capitalization patterns in names for ethnic groups. Through this examination, some principles of capitalization will emerge, some logical inconsistencies will be exposed, and divided usage will be documented. Because the use of uppercase in group names may be taken as conferring recognition or indicating respect, the use of lowercase may be perceived as belittling, disrespectful, or even bigoted. Thus, if the conventions of capitalization do not merit serious study in the socially sensitive area of ethnic identification, then they probably do not merit serious study at all.

Ethnic identification terms based on geographic names (*African, Caucasian*) or on political names (*Chinese, Sioux*) always begin with a capital letter; however, usage varies for terms derived from color words and other common nouns or adjectives. Thus, one may see Americans variously referred to as *Blacks, blacks, Negroes* (but no longer as *negroes*), *native Americans, Native Americans, Red Indians, red men, Whites,* or *whites*.

The fact that this inconsistency does not confine itself to racial terms is easily illustrated by the following examples from various dictionaries: *Black Mass* and *black mass,* Roman Catholic *red hats,* Tibetan *Red Hats* and *Yellow Hats, Black Friars, Black Monks,* and *black monks,* Russian *black clergy,* British *redcoats* and *Black and Tans,* nineteenth-century American *Blues* and *Grays, Red Army, Red Guard, Reds, reds, yellow rain, Yellow Pages, red poll* finches, *Red Poll* cattle, *Chester White* swine, *Black Death, Black Plague, black measles, black disease, Red Angus, Black Russian, Black Maria, black-eyed Susan, brown Betty,* and *brown betty.*

At one time, most English nouns were capitalized (Vallins 106), as they still are in German, and ethnic color names used as nouns or in nominal compounds remained capitalized up to 1660, judging from *OED* citations for *Negro, Black, Black Man, Black Boy, White, White Man,* and *Red Man.* Citations were variable from 1660 to the end of the eighteenth century, but in the nineteenth century there was a shift to the lowercase conventions of today. For at least half of the twentieth century, all color terms for races seemed almost invariably to begin with lowercase letters. *Negro,* a borrowed color word, came to be generally capitalized only after a fifty-year battle beginning in the late 1870s.[1] The use of *Native American* in the nineteenth century functioned to distinguish the established Anglo-Saxon Protestants from the Irish newcomers and other "Roman" immigrants.[2] The use of *Native American* or *native American* for American Indians (or more broadly for all indigenous Alaskans, Hawaiians, and U.S. Indians) is relatively recent.

For the present paper, over twenty dictionaries and manuals of style[3] were systematically surveyed to establish claimed patterns of usage and prescriptions of usage for ethnic names that use the color words *black, white,* and *red,* the common noun *native,* and the clipped terms *Gypsy* and *Chicano/Chicana.* The same list of words along with a few other color words (*brown, blue, yellow*) was checked to see if they appeared in other entries. Terms referring specifically to persons of mixed ethnicity, e.g., *mulatto, mestizo/mestiza,* and *half-breed,* which are usually lowercased, often derogatory, and mostly out of fashion, were not systematically investigated. Patently derogatory slang terms, regardless of their derivation, were not studied at all. A random selection of twenty college handbooks was also consulted, but they are not listed. A few general, but older or more derivative, books on punctuation and style also yielded interesting examples and comments. In spite of the modest (and occasionally generous) number of examples, specific pronouncements on the underlying nature of the regularities among cited forms are far from abundant, and the principles of capitalization often have to be derived by induction from lists of citations.

Six General Principles of Capitalization, which will be alluded to throughout this discussion, are summarized in table 11.1. The list is not intended to be exhaustive but to cite only those general principles which are relevant to the semantic field of ethnic names.

The notion of ceremonious capitalization is from Copperud (62–63). Carey (5) and a few others speak of consistency within a discourse, but the notion is broadened here to include consistency throughout a given semantic field, such as ethnic names. The other four principles are either readily induced from typical examples of usage or are commonplace distinctions, though not necessarily under the rubrics given in table 11.1.

Not all sources agree on the capitalization of the same examples. Besides the seemingly random variation that occurs, there is a tendency toward lowercase style in manuals of style, especially those based on newspaper practice, and a tendency toward uppercase style among dictionaries, but not always to the same degree.

TABLE 11.1
General Principles of Capitalization

Ceremonious Capitalization
   the Flag, the Queen Mother
Consistency
   ... said the Governor to the Bishop ...
   Negro, Black, White
Literalness
   Gypsy 'Romany' (but *gypsy* 'wanderer')
Name Preservation
   German measles (but *chickenpox*)
Semantic Distance (a downcasing principle)
   french fries, china plate
Specificity
   the President (but *a president*)
   the Age of Reason 'eighteenth-century England' (but *the age of reason* 'the age at which one can distinguish right from wrong')

No claim is intended that the principles are always conceptually independent of each other, and it is clearly true that, with respect to any given example, principles may support each other or conflict with each other. Literalness may be a subcategory of specificity (*Gypsy*); semantic distance may be one kind of non-specificity (*German measles*), or it may override name preservation (*china plate*); ceremonious capitalization might support other upcasing principles; and consistency could either support or override any of the other principles.

Current dictionaries, publication style books, usage manuals, and college composition handbooks mostly concur in either prescribing or preferring lowercase versions of those ethnic terms which are not derived from place names. However, the number of reference guides listing uppercase variants has clearly been increasing during the last decade or two, especially for *Black*. Sources using *Black* or recording its use as a variant include the second edition of the *OED*, the *Oxford American Dictionary*, the second edition of the *Random House Dictionary*, the second college edition of the *American Heritage Dictionary*, *Webster's II New Riverside University Dictionary*, the third college edition of *Webster's New World Dictionary*, (which also lists the spelling *White* as a variant for the noun but not for the adjective), the *Oxford Guide to the English Language*, and *International English Usage*. Unlike other sources consulted, *Webster's Third New International Dictionary* mentions the capitalized variant *White*[4] but no such variant for *black*; *Webster's Ninth New Collegiate Dictionary* gives only the lowercase versions of the racial color terms. Newspaper and university-press stylebooks invariably advise the use of lowercase for all racial color terms. A small (but growing) number of college composition handbooks note the variation and simply advise consistency of use, while others omit mention of minority group names altogether.

With respect to compounds, all dictionaries that list *Black English*, *Black Muslim*, and *Black Panther* capitalize them. Capitalization style varies for *Black African*, *Black American*, *Black Code*, *Black Nationalism/ist*, and *Black Power*. *Success With Words*, a usage dictionary, recommends using *black* for both noun and adjective, but states that "the capital is always used in such terms as *Black English* and *Black Studies*." However, the only dictionary listings found for *Black studies* all had lowercase *b* and *s*.[5]

As a term for North American Indians, the lowercase *red man* and uppercase *Red Indian* are the choices listed by most dictionaries consulted. Most sources give *Native American* but only a few downcase the *n*.[6] *RH2* lists both forms but with different glosses: *Native American* for 'Indian' and *native American* for 'a person born in the United States,' illustrating the principle of specificity (as opposed to generality) used for disambiguation. The principle of literalness (as opposed to figurativeness) also can be applied to avoid ambiguity. This principle is widely adhered to in the use of *Gypsy* for the Romany language and those who speak it and *gypsy* for those people supposedly resembling Gypsies in appearance or lifestyle. This distinction is observed by all American sources examined except for the *New York Times Manual of Style and Usage*, but ignored in favor of lowercase for both senses by all of the British sources consulted except the *Longman Guide to English Usage* and *IEU*. *WNW3Coll* and *W2* also noted variation in case style for the ethnic designation.

Several of the consulted dictionaries contain a section devoted to matters of style. Their pronouncements on capitalizing the initial letters of names of peoples are herein cited with the relevant entries from the body of the dictionary:

A capital letter ... usually begins the names of peoples, races, tribes, and languages. [*W3*, 26a; entries: *black, white/ White, native Indian, gypsy*]

Designations based on color or local usage are variously capitalized or lowercased by different writers; however, style manuals usually recommend lowercasing such words. [*WC9*, 1549; entries: *black, white, Native American, Gypsy*]

The following are ordinarily capitalized: ... The names of nationalities and languages, and the anthropological terms for races.... *Note*: In reference to races, *white* and *black* are not capitalized. [*WNW3Coll*, 1566; entries: *black* "sometimes B-", *white* "also W-," *Native American, Gypsy* "also g-"]

Capitalize the names of ... nationalities, races, etc. ... *Negroes, Caucasians*.... [*RH1*, 1900; entries: *black, white, Gypsy*; *RH2* (2465) omits the two racial terms, adds "sometimes cap." to the entry for *black*,[7] and adds an entry for *Native American*]

Capitalize the following: ... The names of nationalities, races, tribes, and languages.... [*WII*, 22; entries: *black* "often *Black*", *white, Native American, Gypsy*]

Unlike most style manuals, the *Oxford Guide* lists *Black, white, Red Indian*, and *gypsy*. More typically, the *Associated Press Style Book and Libel Manual* lists or uses *Afro-American, black, mulatto, American Caucasian, white*, and *red* (134), *American Indian* (102), and *Gypsy* (92). Except for the last item, *AP* usage is somewhat reminiscent of

Marshall Bigelow's *Punctuation*, published in 1885: "Words applied to certain races, or natives of certain regions, are also capitalized; as Creole, Hoosier, Yankee, Caucasian, etc.; but not *gypsy, negro, quadroon*, etc." (45).

One of the most widely used handbooks is *The Chicago Manual of Style*. The style books of many other university presses refer to it. Its brief presentation of capitalization conventions with respect to "Nationalities, Tribes, and Other Groups of People" has a list of uppercase "names" (including *Afro-American, Aryan, Chicano/Chicana*, and *Negro*) and a list of lowercase "designations based only [earlier editions said "merely"] on color, size or local usage (including *aborigine, black, colored, red man,* and *white*)." Two words appear on both lists: *bushman* and *pygmy*; although no explanation is given, ambiguity is avoided by observing the principles of specificity and literalness.[8] But the need to avoid ambiguity is overlooked when the manual lists only "native American (i.e., American Indian)" (194).

Are there any other principles such that most of the conventional uses can be subsumed under a set of general principles, leaving a relatively small set of exceptions? The principle of name preservation requires the capitalization of terms derived from place names[9] and other proper nouns, even when the derived form is clearly a common noun. The overriding of the principle of name preservation by the principle of semantic distance accounts for the downcasing of some terms derived from proper nouns: *brown betty, venetian blind, sandwich,* and *blackamoor* (from *black Moor*). But the principle of semantic distance is apparently not powerful enough to downcase the names of persons in *Black Maria* and *black-eyed Susan*. Also, most dictionaries list *French door,* and *RH1, RH2,* and the *American Heritage Dictionary* even list *French fries* (instead of the more usual *french fries*).[10]

Specificity of reference (a requirement of proper nouns) normally causes terms derived from common nouns like *united* and *states* to be capitalized (*United States*). Such a causative effect often takes place with color words that have no racial homonyms: thus, there is many a *blue Monday*, but there is only one *Black Friday*. The principle of name preservation works in harmony with the principle of specificity to maintain the capital on the day names in both compounds—one a common noun, the other a proper noun. However, the functioning of these two principles is not so straightforward in the case of racial terms. Inasmuch as the racial sense of *White* is denotationally coterminous with the racial sense of *Caucasian*, either both terms are proper nouns or both are common nouns. If *White* is a proper noun, can it be argued that the correct form is *white* on the grounds that it is derived from a common noun? Then what about *Boy Scout, Elk, Black Sea*? If *White* is a common noun, then so is *Caucasian*. But while it would make some sense to distinguish the members of the *caucasian* race from the *Caucasian* residents of the Soviet Union, such a violation of the principle of name preservation (apparently insufficiently mitigated by semantic distance) would totally fly in the face of convention.

The claims that ethnic terms like *White* and *Black* should not be capitalized because they are color words is a long-standing use of an etymological fallacy, occurring covertly, for example, in Spencer's *Practical English Punctuation* published in 1914:

> Nouns and adjectives of distinct nationality or locality are written with capital letters: as, *German, Yankee, Creole, Hoosier,* the *Old World,* etc. *Exception.*—The noun *negro* is not capitalized. This is not a discrimination against the colored race. It is due to the etymology of the word,—from the Latin *niger*, black. [17]

Does accuracy count for anything in the world of capitalization? And if it does, is *Black* just a color word? Not everyone would agree that it is:

> Black is conventionally (I am told) regarded as a color rather than a racial or national designation, hence is not usually capitalized. I do not regard Black as merely a color of skin pigmentation, but as a heritage, an experience, a cultural and personal identity, the meaning of which becomes specifically stigmatic and/or glorious and/or ordinary under specific social conditions. It is as much socially created as, and at least in the American context no less specifically meaningful or definitive than, any linguistic, tribal, or religious ethnicity, all of which are conventionally recognized by capitalization. [MacKinnon 516n]

> Unlike American blacks, a group with an inner coherence forged by the common experience of slavery and by many generations in this country, the label "Hispanic" conceals more than it clarifies. [Portes]

Furthermore, such collocations as *light-skinned Black person* and *dark-complexioned White person* clearly suggest that *Black* and *White*, in their ethnic senses, are not, in any literal sense, color words at all.

An appeal could also be made to social sensitivity or what Copperud calls "ceremonious capitalization . . . a personal matter of showing respect" (62–63).

An appeal to the desirability of avoiding ambiguity has apparently not yet been used in defense of capitalizing ethnic color designations, although such an appeal may underlie one of the principles given in Hart's *Rules*, the style book of the Oxford University Press:

The general rule is: capitalization makes a word more specific and limited in its reference: contrast a Christian scientist (man of science) and a Christian Scientist (member of the Church of Christ Scientist). [10–11]

Other examples come readily to mind: Locke, Berkeley, and Hume were *Empiricists*, but many of us are simply *empiricists*; or, if we are *rationalists*, we are not necessarily Cartesian *Rationalists*. The distinction is an especially clear one in instances of organized group names as opposed to their common-noun counterparts: *Democrats, Republicans, Odd Fellows, Elks, Lions,* and *Moose,* all involving the upcasing of common nouns. But as the *Longman Guide* and other sources have pointed out, the distinction may also lead to the downcasing of proper nouns:

Some words that were originally names are now used in a general sense and are no longer in capitals. . . . Contrast *Bohemian* (someone from Bohemia) and *bohemian* (someone living an unconventional life); *Bible* (the sacred scriptures) and *the lawyer's bible* (an authoritative work). [110]

Following principles of specificity and literalness, most authorities have avoided ambiguity by respectively distinguishing *Native Americans* from *native Americans* and *Gypsies* from *gypsies*. The fact that such a distinction has not yet been generally followed for the ethnic terms *Black* and *White* is, at best, a victory of arbitrary convention over common sense. As Carey pointed out, "the employment of capitals is a matter not of rules but of taste; but consistency is at least not a mark of bad taste" (5).

Bringing some semblance of logic to capitalization practice will not solve all ambiguity problems, however. In the nineteenth century, *black Republican* (like *black abolitionist*) referred primarily to White politicians who favored rights for Blacks, and it is possible that *Red Indian* could refer to a Communist from India. Perhaps, as

Vallins said regarding capitalization style, one "has to walk warily in a kind of no-man's land" (106).

But common sense would suggest reducing the extent of that "no-man's land" as much as possible. The ethnic terms not now consistently capitalized are few. Their origin notwithstanding, it would clearly be justifiable to capitalize them on all grounds of ceremony, consistency, literalness, semantic distance, and specificity. Perhaps the drift of usage will bring this about eventually. Be that as it may, editors and style manual authors have it in their power to hasten the change and establish a uniform and rational usage in this socially sensitive area.[11]

Notes

The assistance of Sharifa Daniels, John C. McGalliard, Michael Montgomery, and Arthur Peña in the research for this study is hereby gratefully acknowledged.

1. See Grant and Bricker, who trace the battle from its apparent beginning in 1878 to 1930, when most publications capitalized *Negro,* although the *Atlanta Constitution* was still using lowercase in the mid 1950s. The 1965 edition of H. W. Fowler's usage dictionary also has *negro* (391) in spite of his comment that "the use of Capitals [*sic*] is largely governed by personal taste, and my own, while not favouring seventeenth-century excess, happens to favour even less the niggardliness now sometimes apparent" (73).

2. See, for example, Billington, page 200.

3. See list of abbreviations, page 203.

4. In contrast, Sheridan Baker advocated lowercase "especially in phrases that contrast blacks and whites, since *white* is never capitalized" (454).

5. *W3* in the 1976 addendum, *RH2, AHD2Coll, WNW3Coll,* and *WC9.*

6. *AHD1, Chi,* and, as a variant only, *WDEU.*

7. There is a usage note at the end of the entry for *black*: "BLACK is usually not capitalized, except in proper names or titles (*Black Muslim, Black English*)."

8. *WC9* distinguishes between the "race of nomadic hunters of southern Africa" and the Australian rustic or pioneer for the former and between the race of dwarfs described by ancient Greek authors ("often cap") or short equatorial African ("cap") and "a short insignificant person" for the latter.

9. A rare exception among ethnic names is *chicano/chicana*, clipped forms of one pronunciation of *Mexicano/Mexicana*. *WDEU* comments that "contrary to the opinion of Copperud, *Chicano* is more frequently capitalized now than it used to be" (241). In fact, except in Copperud and *Longman Guide to English Usage*, it is difficult to find the lowercase variant advocated.

10. See the US Government Printing Office style manual for an extensive list of individual items (35–61), including downcased derivations of proper names (43–44).

11. For other aspects of capitalization, see Nunberg *The Linguistics* . . . ; for a general treatment of proper names, see Algeo *On Defining*. . . .

12. The Spread of Nonsexist Language: Planning for Usage That Includes Us All

KEITH WALTERS
University of Texas, Austin

> The *Old Mole* announces that it will no longer accept manuscripts or letters that use language such as emasculation, castration, balls to mean courage, letters addressed "Dear Sir" or "Gentlemen" or other examples of male supremacist language.
> Use of this language reflects values and patterns of thought that are oppressive to half the people of the world and harmful to all. . . .
> These words reflect a power structure (men having power over women) that we want to change. One way we can work to change this is to challenge the use, conscious or unconscious, of words and phrases that go along with this power structure. ["No 'Chicks'" 291–92]

Issues of usage are most often issues of lexical choice.[1] Traditionally, manuals of usage such as Follett's *Modern American Usage* resemble dictionaries in which readers find alphabetical listings of linguistic shibboleths and prescriptions about their status. Similarly, handbooks for students always contain one or more lists of words often confused because they are homophones or because their meanings in the most carefully edited writing and the most highly monitored speech of certain social groups differ from the meanings given them by the majority of the language's users. For example, as part of the entry for *impact* in the *St. Martin's Handbook*'s "Glossary of Usage," Lunsford and Connors in 1989 advised students to "avoid the colloquial use of *impact* as a weak and vague word meaning 'to affect'" (732). The editors of *The Old Mole* made a similar kind of pronouncement in 1969 when they proscribed the use of certain patterns of usage they deemed "oppressive" and "harmful." Although rarely, if ever, discussed by linguists, educators, or the public in terms of language planning,[2] such issues clearly fall within its domain and more specifically that of "cultivation planning." Following Fishman, Cooper offers a characterization of this type of language planning:

> When the problem is one of functional differentiation among registers and determining matters of "correctness" and "style," language planning refers to cultivation. Here, planners prepare style manuals and promote literary creativity

in a variety of genres for various purposes and audiences. [Cooper "Language Planning" 28]

Language planning and, more specifically, Cooper's efforts to understand the relationships between and among language planning, language spread, and language change offer an especially fruitful way to consider matters of usage, which largely represent conscious choices on the part of those who respect the canons of "good usage." Drawing heavily from the literature on the diffusion of innovations, especially the work of Katz, Levin, and Hamilton and of Rogers and Shoemaker, Cooper develops a heuristic for analyzing the diffusion of any sort of communicative innovation or new choice speakers or writers might make as users of the language. His heuristic suggests seven major rubrics for research: *who, adopts, what, when, where, why,* and *how.* Cooper's framework is particularly useful in helping describe the nature and spread of nonsexist usage[3] in American English and in analyzing how changes in usage and consequently in language use and language itself come about.

Who, for Cooper, includes both individual adopters and the "communications network" within which they are enmeshed (28). (See Cooper *Language Planning* for a slight revision of this paradigm.) With respect to recent interest in nonsexist usage, we might hypothesize that individual adopters were initially well educated, younger women and a small minority of men, all sympathetic to the goals of the feminist movement. These early adapters most likely used the written language in their professional lives, often to read or write about women and their experiences. As Bate points out, adopters among the academics she studied had been influenced by a "respected other"; for males, the encouragement of one or more females was especially important.

At the level of organizations or institutions, professional organizations and publishing houses led the way in encouraging the use of nonsexist language, as the list of guidelines in Frank and Treichler's *Language, Gender, and Professional Writing* (310–14) illustrates. Walters surveys the status of nonsexist usage in academic stylesheets, dividing them into three categories: those making no mention of the subject, those acknowledging it as an issue, and those encouraging or mandating its use. His 1981 research reveals, for example, that the Linguistic Society of America's 1979 stylesheet makes no mention of the subject (but see the 1992 "LSA Guidelines"), whereas the Modern Language Association's 1977 handbook contains a one-paragraph statement on the "social implications of language," which raises the issue. In contrast, guidelines of the National Council of Teachers of English (NCTE) (1975), the American Psychological Association (APA) (1977 "Guidelines"; cf. the 1975 APA Task Force "Guidelines"), the Council of Biology Editors (1978), and the Teachers of English to Speakers to Other Languages (TESOL) (1979) go beyond statement of the problem to offering suggestions for avoiding it. Since that time, academic stylesheets have undergone additional revision, and several book-length treatments of nonsexist usage have appeared, including those by Sorrels, Miller, and Swift, and Frank and Treichler. This last resource, published by MLA, is certainly the most exhaustive; it will no doubt serve in the coming years as a guide for writers in the humanities and other fields.

The appearance of such guidelines, especially those that require nonsexist usage, as do those of many publishers and professional organizations like the APA, is significant because they force changes in usage; publications that follow them not only insist on certain patterns of usage from writers published but also offer models of nonsexist usage to their many readers. The significance of these guidelines grows when one remembers that the APA stylesheet alone is used by well over a hundred journals, including many outside the field of psychology. If editors do their work and if researchers and textbook writers wish to be published, the language comes to be used in ways that it previously was not and ceases to be used in certain other ways. Consequently, the questions of *who* adopts nonsexist usage ranges from the level of individuals making choices to institutions mandating that particular choices be made.

Adopts, within Cooper's framework, "refers to the degree to which the communicative innovation has been accepted" (29), levels of adoption being distinguished along a four-point scale: *awareness* of the innovation, favorable or unfavorable *evaluation* of the innovation, *knowledge* about its appropriate use, and frequency of *usage* of the innovation. Awareness of nonsexist language has come to individuals in many forms: behavior of or comments from friends or colleagues, letters to the editor,[4] other reading, or the insistence of authority figures such as editors (cf. Henley and Dragun, cited in Henley "New Species"); institutions have no doubt been made aware of the issue because of the actions of individuals and small groups.

With respect to evaluation, nonsexist usage has given rise to a variety of responses, ranging from total acceptance (and indeed creed) to rejection, often through scorn and trivialization. Using evidence from the history of the language and from experimental studies, several writers, Blaubergs and Henley ("New Species") among them, have attempted to summarize and counter the arguments most frequently used by those who reject nonsexist usage. Like awareness, knowledge about appropriate and consistent usage comes in many forms, and frequency of usage depends on occasion for use and audience. Many of the students in my freshman composition class have been asked in the margins of their papers if only males attend their university much as authors of manuscripts I have read in draft form are occasionally asked if their findings should be generalized only to males. Certainly, when I fail to employ nonsexist usage consistently, friends, colleagues, and editors point out what I have done or failed to do.

The surprise of many of us who teach freshman composition when students arriving at college seem totally unaware of the practices or issues involved in nonsexist usage serves as evidence that teachers at the college level are at a different point in process of adoption than their colleagues who teach in secondary or primary education (cf. Nilsen "Guidelines Against"). Similarly, the behavior of university colleagues who continue to use sexist language is evaluated quite differently from that of students or those who taught them in high school.

For Cooper, the question of *what* is adopted includes questions of both form and function. Defining the exact nature and extent of sexist or nonsexist usage, whether in terms of form or function, is no simple task. Guidelines, stylesheets, and editors differ greatly on particular matters (cf., e.g., Nilsen "Guidelines Against"), but they share similar stated goals: to offer alternatives to linguistic practices that have traditionally ignored, overlooked, demeaned, or misrepresented women, their existence, their problems, their aspirations, and their achievements. Interestingly, such goals have extended to include fair and accurate representations of traditionally marginalized groups other than women such as ethnic minorities, people with disabilities, and lesbians and gay males (e.g., APA, 3rd ed. 44–45 and Treichler and Frank 203–06). These goals or functions are paralleled by a broadening of the forms included under the rubric "nonsexist usage" as well as an increasing awareness of their significance and ramifications. Early concern with the use of *he* and *man* as generic terms, issues that still comprise the bulk of discussions of the subject in student handbooks, has given way to lengthy discussions of such topics as questioning the canon, using sources from earlier historical periods, and balancing personal and academic freedom in scholarly publications, as found in Treichler and Frank's discussion of "special concerns in scholarly writing and professional activities" with respect to nonsexist language.

When, for Cooper, involves questions of the time of adoption of the innovation with particular interest in the characteristics of early and later adopters. As Cooper (35–36) notes, many diffusion studies report similar findings: the number of adopters grows slowly at first, mounts quickly, and then levels off until it reaches a ceiling, yielding an S-shaped curve when number of adopters is plotted against time of adoption. Whereas Walters charts the relative dates of adoption of policies on nonsexist usage by academic stylesheets, journalistic stylebooks, and the US government, Cooper ("Avoidance") and Tyler, for example, consider the actual practices of users, the former using samples from newspapers, popular magazines, and the *Congressional Record* and the latter investigating usage current among a sampling of the reports of Fortune 500 companies. Of course, concern with nonsexist usage in varieties of English did not begin in the decade of the 1970s or even the 1960s. Baron (*Grammar and Gender,* chapter 10) traces failed efforts to produce a novel, gender-neutral third-person-singular pronoun for English. The 1849 Seneca Falls "Declaration of Sentiments," based on the "Declaration of Independence," notes that "all men and women are created equal" (Hole and Levine 7). In 1895, Stanton produced *The Woman's Bible,* and in 1913, Parsons wrote about issues of women and language. Stanton and Parsons were certainly not the first women to question the linguistic practices of the society at large, but their work demonstrates that thinkers, especially female thinkers, have long been aware of the issue of sexist usage and have tried to combat it in a variety of ways. As many of us are reminded when reading texts from earlier periods, a growing number of readers have new kinds of expectations of writers and texts with regard to how women are included and represented.

Cooper's rubric *where* refers less to physical location than to "the socially defined location of the interactions through which the innovation spread" (37). Cooper's unit of analysis is the domain, which he, following Fishman, describes as "a constellation of social institutions, defined by the intersection of role-relationship, locale, and time, which are constrained by the same set of behavioral norms" (37). The domains associated with the initial spread of nonsexist usage in recent decades were surely domains in which women played the major role; they were most likely organizations created by women expressly for dealing with women's issues. From these groups, nonsexist usage and concern with related issues spread to places where women worked and organizations of which women were a part, ranging from underground newspapers to professional organizations. As nonsexist usage has become an issue for professional organizations and other societal institutions, it has become in many cases less an issue of choice than it was merely a decade ago. Many editors and teachers no longer abide sexist usage in written texts; they insist that it be revised. Furthermore, many readers are quick to write letters to editors about what they perceive as offensive usage. In like fashion, speakers in many professional and public settings risk criticism should their language offend proponents of nonsexist language.

Why, within Cooper's framework, attempts to understand the incentives adopters perceive to exist. In the case of nonsexist language, certain adopters have chosen to use it out of fear. They wish to avoid being labeled "sexist," or they desire to get something published; in these cases, not using sexist language appears a small price to pay. Indeed, some professional organizations or publishing houses may have adopted a policy of nonsexist usage for similar reasons. More positively, other adopters offer different arguments, ranging from individual affirmation to concerns with justice or the deleterious effects of sexist usage as demonstrated by research (Henley "Molehill").

Especially interesting in this regard is the difference in philosophy embodied in the statements of the NCTE and the APA with respect to motivation for encouraging nonsexist usage. Writers of the NCTE guidelines, as do most of the writers in the humanities who attempt to justify nonsexist usage, use the Sapir-Whorf hypothesis as basis for argument:

> Language plays a central role in socialization, for it helps teach children the roles that are expected of them. Through language, children conceptualize their ideas and feelings about themselves and their world. Thought and action are reflected in words, and words in turn condition how a person thinks and acts.

Eliminating sexist language will not eliminate sexist conduct, but as the language is liberated from sexist usages and assumptions, women and men will begin to share more equal, active, caring roles. [1]

Throughout the introduction, the focus is on NCTE members, their conduct in their various roles, and their influence on children and children's socialization. In contrast, writers of the APA statement characterize sexist language as a problem for the profession:

> APA as a publisher accepts journal authors' word choices unless those choices are inaccurate, unclear, or ungrammatical. Because APA as an organization is committed both to science and to the fair treatment of individuals and groups, however, authors of journal articles are required to avoid writing in a manner that reinforces questionable attitudes and assumptions about people. [*Publication Manual*, 3rd ed., 43]

Not surprisingly, the two sets of guidelines analyze the problems associated with sexist usage quite differently, NCTE's guidelines focusing largely on sentence-level problems of form (e.g., generic "man" and "he," and sex-role stereotyping) and APA's guidelines focusing on problems of function (e.g., problems of designation and evaluation, each with subsections on ambiguity of referent and stereotyping). In fact, in the most recent edition of the *Publication Manual of the American Psychological Association*, the guidelines, along with a section entitled "Avoiding Ethnic Bias," comprise a section labeled "Consideration of the Reader," part of Chapter 2, "Expression of Ideas." In contrast, the major concern of the NCTE guidelines appears to be the writer. Thus, these two professions, although agreeing in practice, have different sets of reasons for justifying that practice.

Cooper's final category, *how*, seeks to describe the process by which the innovation is diffused throughout a community. With respect to nonsexist language, the differences between NCTE's and APA's approach to the issue are again revealing. As Nilsen "Guidelines" documents, from the time they were initially proposed, the NCTE guidelines met with complaints of censorship. Potential authors were strongly encouraged, but not required, to conform to the guidelines; in fact, when the piece was accepted, they could insist that usage labeled "sexist" by the guidelines stand in the published version. In contrast, once adopted, the APA guidelines became part of the publication manual; consequently, potential authors have had to follow them or risk having their manuscripts returned unread by editors. By framing the problem as one of fairness and accuracy, values highly regarded among social scientists, the APA apparently managed to gain acceptance for its guidelines to a degree that NCTE has yet to achieve.[5] The difference in the justifications offered by these style sheets and in their reception by their respective communities demonstrates that how adoption takes place can differ from community to community; it likewise illustrates the complex nature of planning so as to increase the likelihood of gaining acceptance for a proposed change.

Cooper's framework for research offers a systematic way of analyzing how a communicative innovation such as nonsexist usage has spread during the last decade or so in this country. It helps document the birth of new standards by which certain patterns of usage are sanctioned and evaluated. Of course, a thorough analysis of the diffusion of this or any communicative innovation would require extensive empirical research of many kinds. The framework, however, is a useful one for thinking about language change, of which matters of usage are clearly a part. In linking the spread of a communicative innovation, whether a pattern of usage, a function of a language, or a language, itself, with language change, Cooper seeks to understand the specific mechanisms of change, a goal of many historical linguists and sociolinguists. Finally, by considering language spread and change in the content of language planning, Cooper moves into the dangerous buffer zone between linguistic description and prescription.

Students of usage who have received at least some training in linguistics usually desire to describe how the language is used by its many users, not to prescribe how it should be used. All of us who are interested in usage write, and in our writing, especially our professional writing, we either reinforce or call into question traditional pronouncements about usage. At the same time, most of us are academics who teach, and many of us teach writing, whether in courses so named or as part of other courses. In our classrooms, in our professional writing, and in our comments on student papers, we are constantly faced with the tension between the prescriptivism associated with the standard language, especially in its written form, and our descriptivist training, which would lead us to characterize fairly and accurately how the language—a part of which is the existence of the prescriptivist ideology accompanying the standard language—is used. Like language planners, we find ourselves trying to negotiate the mine field between descriptivism and prescriptivism.

Confronting the problem of sexist usage and finding creative solutions to it has challenged many students of language and usage to move beyond discussions of particular lexical items and possible alternatives to a re-examination and reconceptualization of our views of language as representation or creator of reality. It has also led us to move from issues of usage to questions of language use by males and females, whether individually or in groups, whether mixed or segregated. Consequently, thinking about our own linguistic choices and those of others as they are intended and perceived continues to help us plan responsibly as we seek patterns of usage that include us all.

Notes

1. Many of the issues discussed in this paper were raised in my 1981 thesis, where I also relied on Cooper's framework for analysis. At that time, resources about this topic were widely scattered and not readily available. Luckily, however, that situation has improved over the past decade as researchers in a variety of fields have investigated issues of language and gender. Consequently, citations in this article are, at best, representative.

2. Probably the most familiar and frequently used definition of language planning is "organized pursuit of solutions to language problems, typically at the national level" (Fishman 24), based on the work of Jernudd and Das Gupta, or one similar to it. From a slightly different perspective, Cooper ("Language Planning" 26) writes, "language planning can be viewed as an attempt to win or block acceptance for changes in language structure or use," a definition more clearly relevant to the discussion of issues in this article than that of Jernudd and Das Gupta.

3. Other terms commonly used to modify *language* or *usage* include *gender-neutral, sex-fair, gender-free,* or, more recently, *inclusive.* Other discussions of nonsexist language within the framework of language planning include, e.g., Nichols, Henley ("New Species"), and Frank.

4. Even though the American Anthropological Association's 1971 stylesheet did not mention the issue of nonsexist usage, nonsexist usage was the subject of a series of heated letters to the editor of the association's

newsletter beginning in 1972. After this time, at least some readers of the newsletter and the association's journals took the continued use of sexist language as a political statement (Walters 64n8).

5. My experience at NCTE and CCCC meetings has afforded me frequent exposure to criticism of the NCTE guidelines on grounds of censorship. On the other hand, in several years of experience working with a journal that follows the APA stylesheet and in dealings with researchers in psychology, I have never heard those guidelines criticized. Perhaps they are or were at one time criticized; if so, I predict the grounds for criticism have not been censorship.

13. Pan-Atlantic Usage Guidance

JOHN ALGEO
University of Georgia

Usage guides have been and continue to be produced on both sides of the Atlantic. Moreover, usage guides, whether produced in the United Kingdom or the United States, often take account of usage differences between the two countries, although not always the same differences or with the same judgments.

To illustrate the truth of the preceding generalizations, this essay compares four recent usage books—two British (*The Right Word at the Right Time*, henceforth *RWRT*, and *Longman Guide to English Usage*, henceforth *LGEU*) and two American (*Harper Dictionary of Contemporary Usage*, henceforth *HDCU*, and *Webster's Dictionary of English Usage*, henceforth *WDEU*). The books are similar in that they are recent, carefully prepared, and published by reputable houses.

The four books also, however, differ in noteworthy ways. *HDCU*, *LGEU*, and *RWRT* are generally similar to other examples of the genre in telling readers what they ought to say, although they differ in dependability, *HDCU*'s Panel of Consultants being inclined to deliver emotional jeremiads. *WDEU* is a different sort of usage dictionary because it presents evidence and encourages readers to make their own judgments—being thus the thinking person's guide to usage.

Of particular interest is what these four usage guides have to say about British-American differences. In the L's (chosen as a typical letter for comparison), *HDCU* has 121 entries, of which 30 (or 25 percent) include some information about usage differences in the UK and the US; *LGEU* has 198 entries, with 42 (21 percent) including British/American information; *RWRT* has 50 entries, with 10 (20 percent) including such information; and *WDEU* has 79 entries, with 19 (24 percent) including that information. The four dictionaries give information about usage differences on opposite sides of the Atlantic for a total of 80 different items. No items are treated in all four books; 7 are treated in three; 8, in two only; and 65, in a single book.

The wide variation among the four books concerning what items they comment upon is a function of the kinds of comments they make. *LGEU* frequently comments on matters of spelling and pronunciation, subjects rarely treated in the other three books. *HDCU* lists many gross vocabulary differences between British and American where no other usage question is involved; the other books rarely do so. *RWRT* and *WDEU* usually reserve their comments for grammatical and, to a lesser extent, semantic differences.

Spelling is commented upon for 13 items, all of which are in *LGEU*, the other three books each covering only 1 of those spelling items. In the following lists, the British variant is first, followed by the American: *l*-doubling in *labelled/labeled* and *labelling/labeling*, *levelled/leveled* and *levelling/leveling*, *libelled/libeled* and *libelling/libeling*; *labour/labor*; *leukaemia/leukemia*; the noun *licence/license*; *liquorice/licorice*; final *-re* versus *-er* in *litre/liter*, *louvre/louver*, *lustre/luster*, *liveable/livable*; *loth/loath*; *-logue/-log*.

Pronunciation differences are noted for 11 items (10 in *LGEU*, 3 in *HDCU*): stress placement in *laBORatory/LABoratory*, *LAMentable/laMENTable*; *lather* riming with *father* rather than with *gather*; *leisure(ly)* and *lever* with a first vowel like that of *fed* rather than *feed*; *lichen* beginning with the sound of *litch* rather than of *like*; *lieutenant* beginning with the sound of *left* (or sounding like "l'tenant" as a naval term) rather than beginning like *loot*; *lingerie* with stress on the first syllable and with the last syllable sounding like "ree" rather than with stress on the last syllable, sounding like "ray"; *liqueur* riming with *pure* rather than with *her*; *litchi* as "LIE-chee" or "lie-CHEE" rather than as "LEE-chee"; *loss* and *lost* with the vowel of *lot* rather than that of *law*.

LGEU also records variation for *launch* with a comment that is doubly misleading for Americans: *Launch* "is sometimes pronounced to rhyme with *branch*, but the pronunciation rhyming with *paunch* is now preferred for British English." In American, both *launch* and *paunch* have the vowel of *law* in some dialects and that of *father* in others; it is presumably the latter vowel that the comment about (British) *branch* is intended to refer to, and not the normal American vowel of the word. *LGEU* also misses a frequency difference between British and American when it comments that *launch* "is rather overused in the sense of 'start, initiate': *launch a programme / a subscription campaign*." The overuse of *launch* in that way is a British vogue that has not yet reached American shores.

Differences in morphophonemic shape account for usage comments on 5 items (all 5 in *LGEU* and 3 of them also in both *RWRT* and *WDEU*): adverbial *landwards/ landward, leftwards/ leftward*; preterit and past participle forms *leant/ leaned, leapt/ leaped, learnt/ learned.*

There is some disagreement about the verbs. *LGEU, RWRT,* and *WDEU* agree that American usually has *leaned* and *learned,* but either *leaped* or *leapt,* and that British has either *learned* or *learnt.* However, *LGEU* says that in British *leant/ leaned* and *leapt/ leaped* are equally common alternatives, whereas *RWRT* and *WDEU* say that *leant* and *leapt* are more usual in the UK. The frequency counts of the LOB corpus (Hofland and Johansson) indicate something different from either of those judgments. In the LOB Corpus, the regular forms *leaned, leaped, learned* are more frequent than the irregular ones *leant, leapt, learnt* in British use, just as they are in American. However, the irregular forms are more popular in British use than in American. For example, LOB has 65 percent *learned* to 35 percent *learnt,* but the corresponding Brown Corpus has 100 percent *learned.* Thus, the regular forms seem to be more common than the irregular ones in both countries; the irregular forms have some use in the UK but are quite rare in the US, at least in edited writing. Speech may be another matter.

Vocabulary and semantics are treated in 40 entries (25 in *HDCU,* 8 in *LGEU,* 3 in *RWRT,* and 7 in *WDEU,* with only three items commented upon in more than one book).

Specifically British words are the staple of British-American glossaries. Only *HDCU* notes many of them, but a good many: 23, which seem to have been chosen not because they are usage problems but because they have old-curiosity-shop interest for American readers. *RWRT* also notes 3, all under the entry for *lie, lay* as special instances of that usage problem. These Briticisms are *lacquer* 'hair spray'; *ladder* 'stocking run'; *ladybird* 'ladybug'; *lame duck* 'one with constant hard luck, one who defaults financially'; *larder* 'pantry'; *lashings* 'loads, scads'; *layabout* 'loafer'; *lay a duck's egg* 'lay an egg, make a zero score'; *lay-by* 'highway rest area'; *leader* 'editorial'; *legpull* 'gag, prank'; *lido* 'municipal pool'; *lie* 'rank in sports competitions'; *lie doggo* 'play possum'; *lift* 'elevator'; *lint* 'medical dressing'; *liverish* 'bad-tempered'; *local* 'neighborhood bar' (misdefined in *HDCU* as simply 'pub'); *long-sighted* 'far-sighted'; *loo* 'toilet'; *lorry* 'truck'; *loud hailer* 'bullhorn'; *lounge suit* 'business suit'; *love* or *luv*, an informal term of address; and *lumme!* 'for heaven's sake'.

Specifically American words become usage questions in Britain: *lawman* 'sheriff or police officer' (*WDEU* notes the anachronism of applying the word to sheriffs of the old West since the American sense was not invented until the early 1940s); *leery* or *leary* 'wary, chary'; *leeway* 'allowable margin of freedom or variation'; *lengthy* (*HDCU*—citing H. W. Fowler for British English—and *RWRT* prescribe its use only in the sense 'tediously long' although *WDEU* documents its standard use in the sense 'long' for about 300 years); *levee* 'embankment'; *liquor* 'distilled rather than fermented alcoholic drink'; *locate* 'settle oneself somewhere' (as in "The company decided to locate in Ohio"; *WDEU* points out that *locate* is historically an American form, whatever its sense, the *DA* dating it from 1652).

Trans-Atlantic polysemy is noted by *LGEU* in *lumber*, British 'surplus articles' and American 'dressed timber'. The discrimination of synonyms and subordinate terms leads *LGEU* under its entry for *lawyer* to distinguish American *attorney* from British *solicitor* and *barrister*. *HDCU*, after noting that in British *libel* and *slander* are synonyms, urges Americans to make a legal-jargonish distinction between them as written and spoken badmouthing respectively. *WDEU* discusses "an old controversy, limited to the United States"—the use of *love* in the sense 'like' and declares the issue dead. However, the discussion shows that the controversy was not quite limited to the US, since the *OED* pronounced the sense a US vulgarism. Under *lover*, *LGEU* puzzles over the problem of what to call a person to whom one is not married but with whom one lives as a sexual partner; an American candidate, *posslq* 'person of the opposite sex sharing living quarters' is noted unenthusiastically.

LGEU's comment on *legionary* and *legionnaire* is taken from the *Longman Dictionary of the English Language*. It is wrong in both places. *LGEU* gives the misimpression that both words mean 'ex-serviceman' in American use. Neither does. Either term can be used generically for a member of a legion. *Legionary* is specifically used for a member of the British Legion; the analogous American term for a member of the American Legion is *Legionnaire*. But an American Legionnaire is not equivalent to a veteran (the more usual American term for an ex-serviceman or ex-servicewoman), since there are many veterans who are not Legionnaires.

Words similar in both form and meaning are a ripe source for usage controversy. *Leave* and *let* are shibboleths of that kind. *Leave* in the sense 'let' ("Leave it be") has, however, been "held to be more reprehensible in American English than in British English. ... British attitudes seem more latitudinarian, or perhaps just indifferent" (*WDEU* 590). Despite *WDEU*'s opinion of British tolerance for "leave it be," the use is questioned in *RWRT* and interdicted in *LGEU*, without comment on national differences. *WDEU* also notes that *leave alone* as a variant of the conjunctive *let alone* is rather rare but standard in British use ("This argument... does not serve the author as a starting-point for prophecy, leave alone for any planning for Utopia" cited from the *Times Literary Supplement*), although it is called regional in *RWRT* and is foreign to standard American use.

Grammar is a less widely studied aspect of British-American differences than vocabulary, but it is dealt with in 11 different entries (1 in *HDCU*, 6 in *LGEU*, 5 in *RWRT*, and 8 in *WDEU*). As indicated by the total number of different entries in comparison with the number of entries in the individual books, some of the same grammatical items are treated in several books.

Conversion of one part of speech into another is exemplified by *lend* as a noun, which is found in neither American nor British mainstream use, but chiefly in the British fringes of northern dialect, Scots, and Irish-American, as well as in Australia and New Zealand, according to *WDEU*. The converse, the use of *loan* as a verb, is recognized by all four books as normal in American use, although *LGEU*, *RWRT*, and *WDEU* reject it, or report its rejection, in present-day British. *WDEU* points out, however, that the American use is a preservation of a pre-eighteenth-century English form that went out of fashion in the UK but was retained in the US. While acknowledging the historical fact, *RWRT* defensively urges that the use "should be regarded as an intrusive Americanism, and its invasion resisted." *LGEU* hypothesizes that in the US *loan* replaced *lend* because of an American reluctance to use *lent* out of a general uneasiness about participles in *-t*. That hypothesis is unconvincing in the light of the analogous *bend/bent* and *send/sent* and unnecessary in view of the evidence that what needs to be explained is British loss of the verb *loan*, not American preservation of it.

The back-formation *liaise* from *liaison* is another British innovation. The *OED* indicates it was originally British military slang from the early twentieth century. Today it is frequent in British English. *LGEU* comments on it, but only to observe that its use does not embrace the sexual sense of the noun: "People engaged in a sexual affair do not liaise." *WDEU* observes that the verb has not become normal in American English, where it is still regarded as a joke word, like *ush* from *usher*.

One of the most noticed function-word problems of usage is *like* as a conjunction. *HDCU* cites a snippy dismissal from W. H. Auden: "This seems to be standard American—but not English." *WDEU* shows that just as Britishers have thought it was American, Americans have thought it was British. It is in fact general English, attested since the fourteenth century. The complex subordinating conjunction *as long as* is used on both sides of the Atlantic in the sense 'while'; but *LGEU* says the sense 'because' (as in "As long as you're going, I'll go too") is American rather than British. *Let's* is a function word for introducing proposals that include the addressee. *WDEU* points out that American has an emphatic form, *let's us*; *LGEU*, *RWRT*, and *WDEU* mention the British negative *don't let's* beside the American *let's don't*.

Some grammatical collocations differ across the Atlantic, the verb *like* being involved in a number of differences. *LGEU* and *WDEU* note *like for* (somebody to do something) as an American regionalism, but *WDEU* suggests that it has now spread widely in the US. *LGEU* and *RWRT* also report the British preference for *should like* over against American *would like*; however, the preference is really a general one for *should* or *would*, quite apart from their collocation with *like*. *RWRT* notes the tendency of British to prefer a gerund and of American to prefer an infinitive after *like* ("I like leading / to lead when I dance"). *WDEU* notes two exclusively British patterns of complementation after *look*: *look like* plus a gerund ("looked like being a failure") and *look* plus a noun phrase ("looks a lucrative investment"), where American might have *look like* plus a noun phrase ("looked like a failure" and "looks like a lucrative investment").

Collocations like *second last* or *third last* are Briticisms that *RWRT* says are criticized by purists. *LGEU*, *RWRT*, and *WDEU* observe that unqualified adverbial *likely* ("He will likely be elected") is American; British requires a qualifier ("He will very likely be elected"). *WDEU* explains that the American use (which is also that of most of the rest of the English-speaking world) preserves the traditional English pattern, attested since the fourteenth century, and that the British use is a nineteenth-century innovation.

Finally, as a matter of text linguistics, *LGEU* points out that British correspondence draws on one set of complimentary closes (*yours sincerely, yours faithfully, yours truly, yours very truly, yours respectfully, yours ever, yours,* and *best wishes*) and American on another (*sincerely yours, very truly yours, respectfully yours, respectfully, cordially yours, cordially, as ever, best wishes,* and *best regards*). Both lists could be extended, but the patterned difference readily inferrable from *LGEU* is British *yours Xly* versus American *Xly yours*.

Four usage books are an inadequate basis for confident generalizations. However, it is at least suggestive (and is consonant with other evidence) that of the British-American differences noted in the books, more than 80 percent appear in only one of the four books. Usage guides, like other language books, do not agree on what British-American differences exist or deserve attention. What is needed is a more detailed and empirical study of how British and American differ than has yet been made.

Perhaps most noteworthy is the difference in aim of the usage guides. In aim, *WDEU* is uniquely distinguished. There have, to be sure, been earlier usage books that gave facts rather than unsupported advice. J. Lesslie Hall and Margaret M. Bryant (*Current American Usage*) wrote two of them and Albert H. Marckwardt and Fred Walcott wrote a third. However, the new *WDEU* is broader in its scope and more thorough in its treatment. It is a new monument in usage study, British or American, that will influence all serious usage books of the future.

14. Prescriptive Versus Descriptive: The Role of Reference Books

LYNN M. BERK
Florida International University

The debate over grammatical usage has been going on for centuries. Historically prescriptivism has dominated discourse about language, but it might seem that the rise of structuralism and subsequent Chomskyan revolution would have changed all that. During the last thirty years the visibility of linguistics in the academy has increased dramatically. Between 1961 and 1981 the number of bachelors degrees earned in linguistics increased by a factor of thirteen, the number of PhDs by a factor of five (Newmeyer 47). New linguistics departments sprang up and linguistics courses could be found in English, foreign language, anthropology, and even philosophy departments. Currently the ideas of linguists are well represented in the university and in the academic press.

But to what extent have linguists' views of language permeated the culture as a whole? Has the doctrine of usage that is normally taught or at least implicit in linguistics courses reached the average citizen or even the average college student? What kind of information is readily available to people who are interested in questions of language use?

One important source of information on grammar and usage is the reference section of the local bookstore. Most middle-class families own at least one usage guide or style book and students often own two or three. For many people these volumes provide the last word on language issues. But what sorts of language attitudes are promulgated in these volumes? In order to answer this question and those raised in the previous paragraph, I recently surveyed two bookstores, each serving a different clientele. First, I examined the reference holdings of a major national chain store, a Waldenbooks housed in a large shopping mall in Longmont, Colorado. The patrons of this bookstore are largely middle-class nonacademics. I also surveyed the Writing Aids section of the Colorado Bookstore, a typical college bookstore near the University of Colorado campus; this store serves the University community and some nonacademic citizens of Boulder, Colorado.

In order to apply a consistent standard of analysis to the books under scrutiny, I chose three well-known usage issues and evaluated each book's treatment of them. All three have generated well-known prescriptive rules, each based on Latin grammar and none valid in terms of modern or even historical English usage.

One of the most often cited prescriptive constraints on English is that proscribing the ending of a sentence with a preposition. Of course, in Old and Middle English speakers and writers often ended sentences in just this way, since, as Sweet notes in his *Anglo-Saxon Primer*, "Prepositions often follow instead of preceding the words they modify, sometimes with other words intervening" (57). However, John Dryden argued that such constructions were "non-Latin" and complained that Ben Jonson "writ not correctly" in part because of the "Preposition in the end of the sentence; a common fault with him, and which I have lately observed in my own writings" (167). Dryden was probably the first to proscribe ending a sentence in a preposition and his formulation has been touted by prescriptivists ever since.

A second commonly cited prescriptive rule is that which demands a subjective case pronoun after a copula verb. This, too, was based on an appeal to Latin grammar. In 1637 Ben Jonson discussed "the Verb, am, that requireth the like case after it, as before it" (541) and in the late nineteenth century Alexander Bain argued that this usage "follows from a principle adopted from the classical languages" (314). Of course, this rule too has little basis in fact for the history of English. In Old English, nouns in the accusative case were, in most declensions, identical to nouns in the nominative case; thus, a copula seldom had an effect on the form of the verb complement. Case distinctions did exist for pronouns, but constructions like *it is I/me* didn't exist; the complement pronoun in such a construction was always *hit* [it], which had the same form in both nominative and accusative cases—*ich hit eom* [I it am]. *It is I* constructions don't appear until the late fourteenth century and *it is me* appears in the sixteenth; both forms are well established by the time prescriptivists attempted to ban *it is me* in the seventeenth and eighteenth centuries.

Split infinitives were not actually proscribed in print until the nineteenth century, but they seem to have been tabooed as early as the sixteenth. This rule was undoubtedly inspired by the fact that the Latin infinitive, like its Old English counterpart, cannot be split (Visser 1036). But the English two-word infinitive emerged during Middle English, and from the outset the *to* was separated from its verb by a variety of elements including direct object pronouns, negative particles, and adverbs. Nevertheless, the split infinitive has now been successfully stigmatized for 350 years.

A grammar or style book's treatment of the rules noted above provides a measure of its sensitivity to usage questions. Some authors ignore such rules altogether or discuss them as archaic vestiges of historical interest. Others regard them as inviolable. The reference books surveyed here reflect the entire spectrum, but prescriptivism is the dominant theme. Table 14.1 summarizes each book's treatment of the rules discussed above.

The reference section at Waldenbooks was very disappointing. It boasted many dictionaries and only three grammar/usage books. Not surprisingly, Strunk and White's *Elements of Style* was prominently displayed. This best-selling volume supports the injunction against the split infinitive, arguing that "the construction should be avoided unless the writer wishes to place unusual emphasis on the adverb" (58). (Ironically, Strunk and White note elsewhere that modifiers should come near the words they modify.) *The Instant English Handbook* by Madeline Semmelmeyer and Donald O. Bolander proscribes the split infinitive and the ending of a sentence with a preposition, acknowledging that on rare occasions these rules may be justifiably violated. Semmelmeyer and Bolander also warn that "Mistakes are frequently made . . . when a pronoun is used as a predicate nominative" (99). The third book in the Waldenbooks collection, *A Pocket Guide to Correct English* by Michael Temple, ignores the prescriptive rules discussed above but invokes others.

Obviously, the information on grammar and usage available at Waldenbooks was meager and highly prescriptive. I had hoped that the books for sale in the reference area of a college bookstore might reflect a greater commitment to the doctrine of usage. The Writing Aids section at the Colorado Bookstore is large, occupying about forty feet of shelf space. I examined all writing/style/grammar books that contained discussions of grammar and usage, eliminating only those that focused exclusively on business or technical writing. Twenty-four books met these criteria. Only four

TABLE 14.1
Coverage of Rules by Reference Works Surveyed[a]

	PREP	INF	SUBJ
Anderson (1989)			
Baugh (1987)	+f		+
Bernstein (1965)	+r	+r	+f
Curme (1947)	–	–	+f
Ehrlich (1986)		+	+f
The English Handbook (1988)	–		+
Flesch and Lass (1947)			+
Fowler (1965)	–	+r	+
Gordon (1984)			+
Hopper, Gale, and Foote (1961)		+	+r
Karls and Szymanski (1990)			+f
Lewis (1948)	–	–	–
Longyear (1989)		–	
Luck (1972)	–		
Mallery (1944)	+	+	
Partridge (1947)	–	+r	
Reid (1989)			+
Roy and Roy (1989)	+		
Semmelmeyer and Bolander (1965)	+r	+r	+
Shertzer (1986)			+f
Strunk and White (1986)[b]		+r	
Temple (1982)			
Thomas (1954)	–	–	
Troyka (1990)		+r	+
Weiner and Hawkins (1985)	–	+r	+f
The Written Word II (1983)	–		+

a. + = rule invoked; – = rule rejected; +f = rule invoked for formal discourse only; +r = rule may be overridden by rhetorical concerns; blank = no discussion of rule.

b. Only Strunk and White (1986) appeared in both bookstores.

of these were free of prescriptivism. (While *Better English Made Easy* by Henry Thomas rejects the rules cited above, it accepts others.)

The most usage-oriented book in the collection was Norman Lewis's *Better English*, first published in 1948. In this delightful volume Lewis discusses traditional rules in terms of language change and modern usage. He coins the term "allowable error" and uses it to refer "to an expression which some old fashioned grammar texts and many handbooks of speech sweepingly, unrealistically and stubbornly condemn, despite the wide and general currency which such an expression may have in educated speech" (17). Lewis argues that "splitting an infinitive is no crime" and goes on to quote Robert Pooley's discussion of famous authors who do indeed split infinitives. Lewis also cites the NCTE's survey on the use of *it is me* and argues that this usage "is considered established acceptable English, even though a rule is being violated" (186).

Lewis's book is the only one in the collection to discuss the origins of prescriptive rules while consistently rejecting them. It does, however, acknowledge the role of prescriptivism in society and the academy and advises: "Should you be confronted with a choice between *I* and *me* as the complement of a copulative verb on, say, a civil service test or high school or college English examination, you would, of course, select the nominative form, for obviously you are being tested on your knowledge of grammatical rules" (186).

The other non-prescriptive books in the collection have very short grammar/usage sections. *Writing that Works* by Richard Anderson simply ignores traditional prescriptive rules. Marsha Longyear's *McGraw-Hill Style Manual* focuses primarily on misused words, although she does note that "good writers split the infinitive freely" (199). The *Instant Secretary's Handbook* by Martha Luck also ignores most traditional prescriptions, noting only that a preposition at the end of the sentence is perfectly acceptable.

With the exception of Thomas's volume, noted earlier, each of the remaining books in this collection supports at least one of the rules discussed above. A common pattern among them is to acknowledge that language does change but to justify prescriptivism in the service of a distinction between formal and casual use. Since there is little agreement over where this line should be drawn, the messages are mixed at best.

Some authors invoke prescription in all forms of writing, excusing violations only in the case of casual speech. *The Written Word II*, for example, maintains that "*I* not *me* is required in informal writing.... Informally in speech *me* is used acceptably after a form of *be*, as a concession to speech patterns" (256). Other authors demand adherence to prescriptive rules only in the case of formal discourse. *Essentials of English Grammar* recommends "In formal writing and business communication avoid putting the preposition at the end of the sentence" (Baugh 29) and *The Oxford Guide to the English Language* says that "Informal usage permits the objective case ... but this is not acceptable in formal style" (Weiner and Hawkins 157). The message is clear—it is acceptable to violate these rules in speech, but serious writers should not do so. *The Writer's Handbook* contains a particularly revealing statement in this regard. Karls and Szymanski describe formal standard English as a variety "used in special occasions—term papers, lectures, letters of application and academic discussions" (87). This definition at least hints that formal English is an artifact of the academy and little more.

Another common pattern in the Colorado Bookstore collection is to ban constructions for various rhetorical reasons, invoking vaguely articulated notions of logic, emphasis, and awkwardness. The *Simon & Schuster Handbook* (Troyka) and *Prentice-Hall Guide* (Reid) both maintain that ending a sentence with a preposition is awkward, while *Grammar, Rhetoric, and Composition* argues that "Prepositions are emphatic words. As a rule, therefore, it is well to avoid placing them at the end of the sentence" (Mallery 109). *The Bantam Concise Handbook* (Ehrlich) bans *it is me* because it is "illogical."

Conversely, some authors argue that a rule may sometimes be violated for rhetorical reasons. Bernstein, Troyka, and Weiner and Hawkins all note that a split infinitive is occasionally necessary to avoid clumsiness and ambiguity, while Eric Partridge delivers this gloriously ambiguous message: "Avoid the split infinitive wherever possible, but if it is the clearest and the most natural construction, use it boldly. The Angels are on our side" (*Usage and Abusage* 296).

Despite these concessions to register and rhetoric, the message in the Colorado Bookstore reference section is decidedly prescriptive. Only Norman Lewis discusses usage in terms a contemporary linguist might use. (Ironically, this is one of the oldest books on the shelves, as is Thomas's volume.) Over sixty percent of the reference books in this collection support the nominative case after the copula (despite the fact that this construction rarely occurs in essay writing). Thirty-eight percent of these books object to the split infinitive and seventeen percent object to the preposition at the end of the sentence.

Why have the views of linguists had so little influence on grammar and usage books? Is it because the publishing industry is more interested in prescription than description? Or is it simply a vicious cycle in which readers have come to expect prescription and this is what they demand?

In any case, it is clear that linguists have a job to do. If we believe that the doctrine of usage is important, we must see that linguistically responsible grammar and style books are written, published, and appropriately marketed. The chasm between linguists and writers of reference works must be bridged. If we don't take this challenge seriously, seventeenth-century prescriptivism may last another three hundred years.

15. "Broad Reference" in Pronouns: Handbooks Versus Professional Writers

CHARLOTTE C. CRITTENDEN
Georgia Southern College

Language scholars realize that the most effective way to decide when standard English has changed is by noting, recording, and counting the usages that defy long-established but sometimes no longer realistic rules. Paul Roberts, for one, states in an article in *American Speech* that counting is the reliable method of determining standard English usage (178). John Algeo, for another, has stated that usage is a primary consideration and can be determined only by accurate data, but he makes the following observations about popular usage guides:

> The popular usage book is doubtless like the poor in that we will have it with us always—though it certainly has made some of its producers rich enough. The popular usage book fills a need, and popularity is no fault. But if it is to fill that need well rather than shoddily, it must rest upon the kind of serious studies that have recently been all too rare. ["Grammatical Shibboleths" 70-71]

Composition teachers are often aware of the lack of data on which English handbooks are based, as shown by the striking discrepancies between textbook rules and those followed by contemporary professional writers. As an attempt to begin addressing the situation, this present study, one component of a more comprehensive survey of pronoun reference (Crittenden "A Study of"), examines "broad reference," specifically in relation to the pronouns *which, that,* and *this* (examples will be provided below). In order to determine the actual use of these three words, one must read, record, and count. The conclusions of this study are therefore based on a reading of approximately one million words published in 1983: 400,000 words from twenty nonfiction best sellers, some published a year or two earlier, but best sellers during 1983; 400,000 from ten periodicals representing a range of readerships, from the popular home-oriented magazine, like *Better Homes and Gardens,* to the professional and scholarly journals such as *College English*; and 200,000 from editorials in five newspapers representing different geographical areas.[1] Additionally, rules from six frequently used college handbooks were a part of the study. The method used was to identify, record, and count usages that differ from those prescribed in these traditional handbooks.

A survey of the history of the three pronouns reveals that what we refer to as "broad reference" has long been accepted as useful. The *OED* states that *which* has repeatedly been used to refer to a "fact, circumstance, or statement" (s.v. 7c) and cites Gower, Shakespeare, and Dickens among others. The pronoun *this* is described as "referring to a fact, act, or occurrence, or a statement in question mentioned or implied in the preceding context" (s.v. B. Ic). *That* is described in a similar way.

Some of the best known twentieth-century usage studies are consistent with the historical background. Bergen and Cornelia Evans, for example, in *A Dictionary of Contemporary American English* state that broad reference is a function of *this* and *that*, particularly of the former: "The word *this* is preferred when the reference is less specific. It is often used as a summarizing word and means 'all that has just been said'" (510).

Margaret M. Bryant's *Current American Usage* also reports on the status of *this, that,* and *which*. Her conclusions are very much like the ones of this current study:

In standard English, *this* occurs more often without a summarizing noun that refers to a preceding clause or sentence than it does with a definite antecedent or reference; *that* . . . [and] *which* are used in the same manner, but less frequently. [172]

On the other hand, there are studies like that of the journalist Wilson Follett, whose *Modern American Usage* was published in 1966.[2] Quick to suggest a return to what he believes to be the traditional, Follett comments disapprovingly on broad-reference *this* and *that*:

The unanchored *that* is often found but is so far outnumbered by *this* that it may be ignored. In some kinds of modern writing—e.g. editorial pages in the best dailies and weeklies—it is almost impossible to get through a column without stumbling on at least one *this* used in summary of unspecified elements that precede. . . . One can hardly overstate the dependence of modern writers on the unfocused *this*. [70–71]

Follett's attitude is obviously an accepted one, especially in handbooks of grammar, many used as reference texts for college composition courses. Most such handbooks advocate using pronouns only with specific antecedents or rephrasing a statement to eliminate a pronoun having broad reference and thereby any possible ambiguity. Selected handbooks from the 1970s and 1980s illustrate this approach.

The Concise English Handbook by Guth, published by Wadsworth in 1977; *Handbook* by Good and Minnick, published in 1979 by Macmillan; *The Little, Brown Handbook* by Fowler, published in 1980—all advise against broad use of the pronouns. For example, the Wadsworth handbook recommends avoiding "ambiguity caused by idea reference" and explains that "vague idea reference results when a *this* or *which* refers to the overall idea expressed in the preceding statement" (42). Noteworthy in that assertion is the word *statement* in the singular; this handbook does not even consider the possibility of *this* or *which* referring to more than one. The other two handbooks contain similar advice.

The strongest advocate of restricted usage is the 1986 edition of Houghton Mifflin's *Practical English Handbook* by Watkins and Dillingham: "Pronouns should not refer vaguely to an entire sentence or a clause or to unidentified people" (63). An example is given and the analysis that follows deals with the possibility of complex problems of interpretation: "'Some people worry about wakefulness but actually need little sleep. *This* is one reason they have so much trouble sleeping.' *This* could refer to the worry, to the need for little sleep, or to psychological problems or other traits which have not even been mentioned" (63). This last option would indeed make interpretation rather complex if not impossible.

In spite of the obvious trend to reiterate traditional rules (that is, rules that form part of the handbook tradition), two recent handbooks at least recognize current usage although at the same time, in an almost contradictory manner, they warn against pronoun usage that is not specific.

Scott Foresman's *Handbook of Current English*, contains the following observation: "*This, that, which,* and *it* are often used to refer to ideas or situations expressed in preceding statements. . . . In such constructions *the idea* to which the pronoun refers should be obvious" (Corder and Ruszkiewicz 150, emphasis added). Similar to this treatment is that of the *Harbrace College Handbook* (Hodges and Whitten): "Pronouns such as *it, this, that, which,* and *such* may refer to a specific word or phrase or to the sense of a whole clause, sentence, or paragraph" (280). However, the handbook then warns against reference to an expressed idea unless the meaning is quite clear. Additionally, there are examples of "vague" and "clear" references that are like those of other handbooks, the implication being that the student writer should avoid any chance of referring to more than one or two concepts or to any combination or summarizing of ideas.

Present-Day Usage

Actual usage of *which*, *that*, and *this*, exemplified by the nonfiction best sellers, articles in periodicals, and newspaper editorials, reveals an acceptance of the three pronouns, especially *this*, used with broad reference. In fact, broad-reference *this*, *that*, and sometimes *which* serve as strong summing-up and transitional words, often being preceded by the qualifier *all*. In this capacity, the pronoun becomes a collective word, grouping and unifying many concepts into a useful transitional phrase, i.e. *all this, all that*, and *all of which*. Perhaps we need to add the term "collective pronoun" to the descriptive grammar texts. For the purpose of this study, all uses of broad reference for the three pronouns were not recorded, only those which traditional grammar and most modern-day handbooks would consider vague or ambiguous.

As selective as the process was, many examples surfaced to illustrate the broad-reference usage of all three pronouns. *Which*, for example, was noted 35 times in the nonfiction, 30 in the periodicals, and 20 in the editorials. For *that*, the nonfiction sources provided 45 examples; the periodicals, 25; and the editorials, 40. This evidence is impressive, but the use of *this* in such capacity is striking.

Broad-reference *this* was noted 347 times: 114 in nonfiction, 136 in periodicals, and 97 in editorials. Such common use suggests that a necessary function of the pronoun is to serve in a collective capacity, to tie together many ideas. This function of the pronoun seems especially useful for beginning paragraphs and, like *which* and *that*, *this* is often combined with *all*. A few examples of broad-reference *this* demonstrate the tendency of modern-day writers to use a pronoun (whether *which, that,* or *this*) that refers to more than one word or concise statement and does so effectively.

Representative of the nonfiction examples are the following (emphasis mine):

[¶] *This* is not intended to diminish the value of full-time motherhood. [Friedman 1983, 13]

[¶] *This* brings us to the next step. [Kiley 1983, 12]

[¶] Paul was puzzled . . . when Gallagher reported all *this.* [Follett 1983, 14]

[¶] *This* should not be surprising. [Naisbitt 1982, 240]

Through all *this* she lay in bed. [Baker 1982, 1; sums up a descriptive passage]

[¶] I think that *this* is reflected in the success of my first book. [Allen 1983, 25; sums up the previous nine-sentence paragraph]

I thought: It is for *this* I have come. [Moon 1982, 33; refers to several sentences]

[¶] But *this* assumes there was something magnificent to spoil. [Manchester 1983, 10]

How could *this* be happening to my family? [Kushner 1981, 2; refers to several paragraphs]

Articles from the periodicals also indicate a need for broad-reference *this.* The 136 collected examples include the following:

[¶] A visionary brought all *this* about. [Robert P. Jordan, "High-Flying Tulsa," *National Geographic,* Sept. 1983, 385).

National Geographic has 20 examples, most of them *all this* constructions or *this* at the beginning of a paragraph.

[¶] The reason for *this* is the way that flounder capture their prey. [Louis D. Rubin, Jr., "Tales of an Elusive Flounder," *Southern Living,* Mar. 1983, 164; refers to last several sentences of previous paragraph]

This is why physicians will often ignore a low serum calcium level. [Ellen McFadden et al., "Hypocalcemia: A Medical Emergency," *American Journal of Nursing,* Feb. 1983, 228; refers to a long statistical description]

From a total of 25 examples in *Society*:

This translates into approximately 14,850 caesareans. [Nancy Cohen and Louis Estner, "Silent Knife: Cesarean Section in the United States," *Society*, Nov.–Dec. 1983, 96; summarizes many statistics]

This is near-biography set in an autobiographical frame. [Linda Wagner, "Lillian Hellman: Autobiography and Truth," *Southern Review*, Spring 1983, 278; refers to 2 sentences]

We should take *this* rather as one of those touches of humor which she enjoys revealing in others. [Daniele Pitavy-Sougues, "Watchers and Watching: Point of View in Eudora Welty's 'June Recital,'" *Southern Review*, Summer 1983, 483; refers to several sentences]

All *this* the bored voice subliminally conveyed to him. [Timothy Foote, "In New York: Be Kind to Your Mugger," *Time*, 21 Feb. 1983, 11; refers to 3 or 4 sentences]

All *this* and more his biographers have put down. [Hugh Sidney, "Above All, the Man Had Character," *Time*, 21 Feb. 1983, 25; refers to many sentences]

Because these data are preliminary. . . . I do not want to make too much of *this*. [Mike Rose, "Remedial Writing Courses: A Critique and a Proposal," *College English*, Feb. 1983, 115; has an antecedent of many sentences]

The newspaper editorials contribute their share of uses of the broad *this*. Note: *New York Times* has 8 while *Wall Street Journal* has 40.

Since only the most carelessly fabricated data are easy to detect, *this* may be the tip of the iceberg. ["The Scandal in Chemical Testing," *New York Times*, 16 May 1983, A18; refers to a previously outlined situation]

[¶] *This* may be the most severe test yet. ["Dealing Race Out of Politics," *Atlanta Constitution*, 15 Apr. 1983, 12B]

[¶] All of *this* has led to a certain amount of paranoia. ["Education Task Force Overdue," *Atlanta Constitution*, 15 Apr. 1983, 18A]

[¶] Is *this* discrimination? And does the television industry have a right to 'discriminate' if audiences prefer female glamour and if the industry stands to lose profits if it does not oblige? *This* is a whole area of case law. ["The Craft Case," *Christian Science Monitor*, 12 Aug. 1983, 24]

[¶] At the center of all *this* is something yearned for. ["Bringing in the Savings: A Goad to Better TV News," *Wall Street Journal*, 1 Mar. 1983, 34]

Conclusion

As Dennis Baron states in his *Grammar and Good Taste*, language change "is not normally a rational and deliberate process" and "any attempt to make it so must be supported by a mechanism to implement planned changes" (6). Defining or creating such a mechanism is difficult, to say the least. Certainly, Americans do not want to promote legal means to "fix" or change usage. The necessary mechanism is simply factual information, the kind provided by carefully documented observation.

The problem of determining acceptability is not a new one. As long ago as 1917, Lesslie Hall in his *Studies in the History and Uses of English Words and Phrases*, describes his own frustration:

> The idea has frequently occurred to me while teaching usage with certain popular textbooks in hand that I was criticizing and correcting sentences that might have been taken from the most distinguished authors. Words mercilessly condemned by these textbooks would fall from the lips of some distinguished speaker that addressed the students on the very day on which the words had been treated as barbarous in the lecture room. [5]

All this is indeed perplexing. Modern-day usage handbooks seem to be a fulfillment of the old hankering for some sort of "academy" to prescribe what usage should be, not describe what it actually is. One must consider, however, that these handbooks do have the task of guiding the fledgling writer and therefore must include guidelines that are supportive of usage that has been labeled "correct" by some authority. Unfortunately, the foremost authority for these handbooks seems to be previously published handbooks. Even though usages are established by appearing in top-level publications, as evidenced in this study, handbooks continue to promote and reinforce traditional usages prescribed by handbooks themselves, a cycle of stifling entrapment.

Writers and composition teachers, therefore, must determine what actual usage is and challenge the handbooks when there is an obvious contradiction between "rule" and usage. Many professional writers obviously approve of using *which*, *that*, or *this* to refer to several sentences or several paragraphs, a construction most often labeled "broad reference" in college-approved handbooks. The one sure way to verify this conclusion is to continue counting, recording, and analyzing.

Notes

1. Nonfiction best sellers: Robert G. Allen, *Creating Wealth*; Russell Baker, *Growing Up*; Helen G. Brown, *Having It All*; William F. Buckley, *Atlantic High*; George Burns, *How To Live To Be 100—or More: The Ultimate Diet, Sex, and Exercise Book*; Leo Buscaglia, *Fall of Freddie the Leaf*; Robert A. Caro, *The Years of Lyndon Johnson, the Path to Power*; Jimmy Carter, *Keeping Faith*; Ken Follett, *On Wings of Eagles*; Jane Fonda, *Jane Fonda's Workout Book*; Sonya Friedman, *Men Are Just Desserts;* Seymour Hersh, *The Price of Power, Kissinger in the Nixon White House*; Dan Kiley, *The Peter Pan Syndrome*; Harold Kushner, *When Bad Things Happen to Good People*; Shirley MacLaine, *Out on a Limb*; William Manchester, *The Last Lion*; William Least Heat Moon, *A Journey into America, Blue Highways*; John Naisbitt, *Megatrends*; Thomas J. Peters and Robert H. Waterman, Jr., *In Search of Excellence*; Andrew Rooney, *And More by Andy Rooney*.

Periodicals: *American Journal of Nursing; Better Homes and Gardens; College English; National Geographic; Smithsonian; Society; Southern Living; Southern Review; Time.*

Newspaper editorials: *Atlanta Constitution; Christian Science Monitor; New York Times; Wall Street Journal; Waycross Journal-Herald.*

2. Actually Follett had already died. The book was completed and published after Follett's death by, among others, Jacques Barzun.

16. A Comparison of Usage Panel Judgments in the *American Heritage Dictionary 2* and Usage Conclusions and Recommendations in *Webster's Dictionary of English Usage*

VIRGINIA G. McDAVID
Chicago State University, emerita

Until the twentieth century, books containing information about usage—about which of a number of optional ways of expressing a given meaning are part of the standard language and which are not—have largely been authoritarian and prescriptive in nature. In Samuel Johnson's *Dictionary* (1755) for example, more than a thousand words or uses of words are accompanied by restrictive labels or comments expressing Johnson's opinion, often forcefully stated, as to the suitability or correctness of a locution. Subsequent dictionaries have continued Johnson's practice, and they have been joined by scores of grammars, handbooks, and guides to "good usage."

With only a few exceptions, for example Joseph Priestley's *The Rudiments of English Grammar* (1761), not until this century have there been usage books which, instead of expressing the judgment of the author about the appropriateness or correctness of a usage, have attempted to determine and describe standard spoken and written English. Two recent works are representative of the two ways of treating usage. The older tradition is represented in a special way by *The American Heritage Dictionary* (Boston: Houghton Mifflin; ed. William Morris; hereafter *AHD1*). It first appeared in 1969 and was advertised as the answer and antidote to a claimed abrogation of responsibility in matters of correct usage by the editor of *Webster's Third New International Dictionary* (1961). A second edition of the *American Heritage,* published in 1982, carried on the tradition, claiming to contain "hundreds of usage notes [reflecting] the opinions of the distinguished Usage Panel." The source of guidance in both editions is a Usage Panel (105 persons in the first edition) of "those professional speakers and writers who have demonstrated their sensitiveness to the language and their power to wield it effectively and beautifully" (*AHD1*, p. xxiii). Their judgments were reported in percentage form, for example, "89% reject" or "42% approve," and sometimes the usage notes included quotations of Panel members who expressed opinions on the usage items, for example "abominable," "loathsome," "O, God no," and the like.

There are some differences between the two editions of the dictionary in the constitution of the Panel and in their findings. In *AHD2* the number of Panel members was increased from 105 to 165. Actual quotations by Panel members were eliminated, as was the reporting of the actual percentages of those approving or disapproving a given usage; instead phrases like "a large majority accepts" were used.

In *AHD2* the number of notes reporting votes by the Panel is slightly less than half that in *AHD1*, and the number of separate votes reported in *AHD2* is about two-fifths of that in *AHD1*. Of the 112 Usage Notes containing Panel votes in *AHD2*, only 15 are entirely new; that is, there was no usage note at that entry word in *AHD1*. Five more of the 112 are new notes in the sense that, although there was a usage note in the same entry in *AHD1*, there is some difference in the problem treated in the *AHD2* note. This leaves 92 usage notes containing a Usage Panel vote which deal with the same matter as did the notes in *AHD1*. Because some notes consider more than one problem, for example the difference in status between noun and adjective use of a word, a total of 94 usage questions are considered here. The reports on 23 of these, or 24%, indicate the acceptability of the item in a specific medium—speech or writing; the others do not make this distinction. The usage notes in *AHD2* consist of brief paragraphs attached to the entry being considered; the reports of the Panel votes usually comprise only a sentence or two of the entire usage note.

The second recently published work is, instead of a collection of judgments or opinions, a report of the status of items based on observation of actual usage—usually in published edited writing: *Webster's Dictionary of English Usage* (ed. E. Ward Gilman; hereafter *WDEU*). As its title indicates, *WDEU* is not a general dictionary containing only occasional notes about usage but one dealing only with words or expressions about which questions of appropriateness or correctness have at some time been raised. Each item receives the space the editors have felt it merits, and the discussion of some items runs to five or six columns. (Of the items considered here, the discussions of *anticipate, burgeon, comprise, deprecate, dilemma, discomfit, disinterested, fortuitous, infer,* and *nauseous* are particularly detailed and interesting.) Each entry presents much more than a conclusion and recommendation on the item. It begins with a history of the usage, illustrated by quotations; continues with a history of the criticism of the usage, also with quotations; continues further with an analysis of contemporary usage with examples; and finally draws a conclusion and often but not always makes a recommendation. Occasionally, as with *above, comprise, fortuitous, head up,* and *unique* for example, there is a warning that although the disputed usage is standard, the user may attract some adverse attention. The conclusions and recommendations for the approximately 2,000 items (the number of problems considered is far greater) in *WDEU* are thus based upon extensive evidence, not upon the tastes of an individual writer on usage like Theodore M. Bernstein, or the votes of a usage panel. The summaries of the conclusions and recommendations given in the following tables fail to do justice to the complexity of the entries of the *WDEU*.

The recommendations in *AHD2* are quite simple and straightforward—either a majority of the Panel accepts a disputed usage, or it does not. The conclusions and recommendations in *WDEU* are more complex, and take into account the medium, and not only whether speech or writing, but the kind of writing—fiction, reportage, literary use. Even with these differences, however, it is instructive and interesting to compare the conclusions on 94 items considered by the *AHD2* Usage Panel and those in *WDEU*.

The two dictionaries agree on the status of 48 of the items. Of these, they agree that 30, or 62.5%, are acceptable for unrestricted use; and 18, or 37.5%, are not. The dictionaries disagree, then, on whether 46, or 49%, of the 94 items are acceptable. For these, *WDEU* says that 45 are acceptable; a majority of the *AHD2* Panel rejects them. Only one ("look badly") is accepted by the *AHD2* Panel but receives something less than full acceptance by *WDEU*, which says "most writers use bad."

If the total judgments for acceptability or the lack of it are compared in the two dictionaries, the AHD Panel accepts 31%, or 29, of the items, thus rejecting 69%, or 65; *WDEU* accepts 79%, or 74, thus rejecting 21%, or 20. Clearly opinions about usage questions are more conservative and more likely to be adverse than are evaluations (e.g. *WDEU* s.v. *burgeon*) that let the evidence make the point. Further, as *WDEU* points out repeatedly, if a usage is both new and common, it inevitably attracts criticism.

In tables 16.1 and 16.2, the opinions of the *AHD2* Usage Panel members accurately reflect actual usage as described by *WDEU*. Table 16.3, however, reveals that so-called authoritative judgments about usage are often not borne out when usage is studied and described. In forty-six, about half the items reported on here, the judges condemned what actual practice reveals as established and standard.

TABLE 16.1
Items approved by the *AHD2* Usage Panel and described as standard or established by *WDEU*
(Abbreviations: sp = speech; wr = writing)

	AHD2	WDEU
above (adj)	wr	"standard"
advise 'inform'	wr	standard
agenda (sg. cst.)		"standard"
aren't I	sp	"winning respectability"
anticipate 'expect'		standard
cannot but		"an old, established idiom"
celebrant 'celebrator'		"both in reputable use"
(fairly) certain		"dead issue"; standard
(more) complete		standard
data (is)	sp	standard
deprecate 'belittle'		"impeccably standard"
discomfit 'distress'		standard
done 'finished'	wr	standard
doubt whether		*if, that, whether*: writer's choice
dove (pret.)	wr	either standard; *dived* more common
each other 'one another'		"interchangeable from beginning"
farther (or *further*) from the truth	either	"further has eclipsed farther in adj. use; farther chiefly distance"
fault (vt)		"no fad; standard use"
idle (vt)		standard; chiefly journalistic
(more) importantly	(tie)	either adj. or adv. is standard
intrigue (vt) 'interest'		standard since 1919
leave alone		standard in both senses
like (conj.)		widely used in standard prose
materialize 'take shape'		standard
one of every ten is		standard
predicate (vt)		standard
presently 'now'	(tie)	in standard use since 1485
responsible (impersonal subj)		standard; "entirely reputable"
will 'shall'	wr	*will, would* more common than *shall, should*

TABLE 16.2
Items Both Rejected by the *AHD2* Usage Panel and Restricted by *WDEU*

	AHD2	WDEU
(not) about to	wr	"speech & edit. wr.; little lit. use"
(not) all that	wr	"fiction, reportage, occas. serious writing"
better 'more'	wr	"not in more formal writing"
contact (v.)	wr	"standard"
debut (vi, vt)		standard in gen. prose; no lit. use
drunk (adj.)		chiefly before driver, driving
either of them are	wr	rare in writing
hung 'executed'		*hanged* more common in writing
infer 'imply'		chiefly oral use with personal subject; disappearing in writing
likely (no qualifier)		little literary use
quote (n.)		standard; mainly casual writing
raise (vi)		"dialectal & some general use"
rarely ever		*rarely* alone most common
try and		more typical of speech
type (no of)		not common in edited prose
unique 'unusual'		well-established but disapproved of; best to avoid
various (of)		regarded as a mistake
-wise		used for formation of nonce words

TABLE 16.3

Items Disapproved or Rejected by the *AHD2* Usage Panel but Described as Standard or Established by *WDEU*

	AHD2	WDEU
above (n.)	wr	"standard"
alibi (n.)	wr	"established"
alibi (v.)	wr	"established"
of any 'all'		"old, well-established, & standard"
anyone 'everyone'	wr	"old, well-established, & standard"
(look) badly[a]		"most writers use *bad*"
in (or *on*) *behalf of*		"used interchangeably in Am. Eng."
burgeon 'grow'		"firmly established by 1950s"
cohort 'companion'	wr	"firmly established in standard use" commentate, vt [implied approval]
(is) comprised (of)		"established and standard"
data (is) (tie)	wr	standard
dilemma 'problem'		"fully standard"
disinterested 'uninterested'		"confusion doesn't exist"
doubt if		if, that, whether all established
due to		"impeccable grammatically"
finalize		"well established as standard"
fortuitous 'lucky'		"established"
gift (vt)		"standard, but uncommon & unpopular"
headquarter (vi, vt)	wr	"clear, concise verb that is guilty of no offense other than newness"
head (up)		"nothing wrong; may be criticized"
help but	wr	cannot but, cannot help but, cannot help are all standard
individual 'person'		standard personal subj. disappearing in wr.
lack (for)		for in neg. const.; standard
loan (v.)		entirely standard; always literal
materialize 'happen'		standard
most 'almost'		standard; estab. Am. idiom
-oneself (subj., obj.)		standard; not limited to inf. wr.
nauseous 'queasy'		standard in general prose
only (conj.)	wr	standard
personality 'celebrity'		not overused
practically 'nearly'		"entirely standard"
premiere (v.)		established by 1940s
proven (ppl)		proven, proved both standard as ppl and attrib. adj.
providing		provided, providing both standard; provided more common
regarding, as regards		in regards to not in edit. prose; all others standard
(a) savings		"clearly estab. as idiomatic"
so (*that* omitted)		"little difference in level of formality"; both standard
sometime 'occasional'		standard
stomp	wr	"standard syn of stamp in some senses"
tend 'attend'		standard
thusly		standard; distinct from thus
(not) too 'not very'	wr	"impeccably standard"
transpire 'happen'		standard; somewhat formal
(from) whence		standard; "use it where it sounds right"
reason why		standard

[a] *(Look) badly* is accepted by the *AHD2* Usage Panel but is qualified by *WDEU*.

17. Usage Items in Current Handbooks of Composition

WALTER E. MEYERS
North Carolina State University

Apart from the occasional newspaper column or alarmed editorial, the vast majority of Americans encounter comments about usage only in the glossary of a handbook of composition, where one should look first to find out what kind of information the public is being given and what kind of attitude is being promoted. Lynn Quitman Troyka, for example, has a statement at the head of the glossary in the *Simon & Schuster Handbook for Writers*[1] that might make one optimistic: "little demonstrates as dramatically as does a usage glossary that standards for language use change. Some words slip away from usage: for example, *thee* and *thou* are no longer used in everyday life. Some constructions considered nonstandard a decade ago are accepted as standard today: for example, *shall* used to be required for the first-person future (*I shall finish the work tomorrow*), but today most dictionaries and usage surveys report that *shall* and *will* can be used interchangeably in such constructions" (797). On second look though we might question that optimism. First, the description of the rule for *shall* and *will* is oversimplified: no one ever said that *shall* was required for the first-person future in every case. Second, one wonders why she chose this example, implying that in 1977, a decade before the book's first edition, "I will finish the work tomorrow" was considered nonstandard. Third, dictionaries and surveys of usage, one would think, reveal what *is* used, not what "can be used." And finally, the phrase "today most dictionaries and surveys of usage" raises the question of which dictionary or survey of usage done since 1977 states that "I will finish the work tomorrow" is nonstandard.

At least, Troyka asserts that glossaries are good indicators of the change in standards of usage. Specialists in usage like Edward Finegan are not so sure: "Today's condemnations of the double negative, of the objective case in *it is me*, or the use of *lay* for *lie*, and of the 'confusion' of *shall* and *will* were invented in the eighteenth century by men like Robert Lowth and promulgated by his imitators, especially the American-born Lindley Murray. Many such prohibitions have continued without significant alteration into the middle of the twentieth century" (16).

Do glossaries reflect a change in usage or not? To answer the question, I have spent the last several years in a point-by-point examination of the usage glossaries of 59 handbooks of freshman composition published from 1980 to 1993 and 12 works offering advice on usage—most in the familiar handbook form—published between 1867 and 1941.[2]

Some statistics from the survey are startling: the glossaries of the 59 works offer advice on 1584 separate items. *Item* here means a writer's comment about an individual question of usage.[3] A separately headed entry may therefore contain more than one item: a work's entry for *so*, for instance, may include any or all of the following items: its use in negative clauses, as an adverb of extent, as an intensifying adverb, or as a coordinating conjunction. Questions of classifying the survey material also arise: should *myself* for *me*, *yourself* for *you*, *himself* for *him*, and so on, be counted each as a separate item, or should they be grouped as the single item, reflexives? (Here, because handbooks listed a variety of combinations of reflexives, I counted them as the single entry "*-self* for personal pronoun.") Someone else surveying the same material might have divided the entries differently, so the total should be considered only a close and reasonable estimate.

Of these fifteen hundred and some items, 763—almost half—appear just once in 59 usage sections; 976 items, 62%, appear in only one or two texts. Despite claims by many of the authors that the usage items in their glossaries represent the most common problems, the chances are almost nil that a given student will see any one of these 976 items. If we ask how many items appear in the majority of the glossaries—how many appear in from 30 to 49 works—the answer is 83. To put it another way, the majority of handbook authors collectively agree that an item is a usage problem only 83 times. And if we ask how many items appear in each one of the 59 books—on how many there is unanimous agreement—the answer is: one.

The usage items therefore divide sharply into two groups: the first—the great majority of items—clearly does not include the most common problems of usage if consensus counts for anything at all. Take the 763 items that occur once: for every text that presents each of these as a usage problem worth including, there are 58 other texts that do not. But this centennial publication of the American Dialect Society provides a particularly timely occasion to consider the second group—the 83 items to be found in the majority of today's handbooks—and to test the claims often made about the currency and importance of these items.

For those who believe that English is threatened with imminent collapse (Edwin Newman, say), there is good news indeed: the rate of deterioration of the language has been brought almost to a standstill. According to the survey, of the 83 most troublesome usage problems, only 12 have appeared in all the years since the beginning of World War II (the number of texts listing each item appears in brackets): *hopefully* as a sentence adverbial [53]; *amount* and *number* [52]; *irregardless* [52]; *alot* [50]; *center around* [40]; *awhile, a while* [35]; *who's, whose* [35]; *criteria* [34]; *anyone, any one* [33]; *suppose to* [31]; *and/or* [30]; and *media* [30]. None of these was found in the 1941 edition of *Harbrace Handbook* or in any of the earlier works consulted.

How long in the tooth are the remaining 71 items? Two of them are over 50 years old, having appeared in handbooks since 1941 at least: *being that* [39] and *maybe, may be* [33].[4] Two more have passed retirement age, having appeared in handbooks at least since 1925: *all ready, already* [48]; and *might of* [36].

Ten have been in handbooks for 77 years, at least since 1917: *advice, advise* [42]; *all, altogether* [43]; *allusion, illusion* [47]; *anyways* [33]; *anywheres* [30]; *beside, besides* [49]; *censor, censure* [33]; *imply, infer* [56]; *ok, o.k., okay* [34]; *sure* adverb [33]. The difference between *farther* and *further* [54] is a year older: it has been a handbook item at least since 1916. And *try and* [46] was objected to in a glossary of usage printed in 1914. Ten have been in handbooks for 87 years, at least since 1907: *all right, alright* [56]; *and etc.* [34]; *disinterested, uninterested* [54]; *due to* adverb [42]; *good, well* [47]; *principal, principle* [52]; *should of* [51]; *than, then* [35]; *to, too, two* [40]; *use to* [40]. One has been appearing in texts at least since 1902: *so* 'very' [30]; nineteen more, having been included since 1893, are 101 years old: *a, an* [45]; *accept, except* [52]; *aggravate* 'irritate' [39]; *apt, likely, liable* [40]; *as* 'because' [34]; *bad, badly* [48]; *data* number [46]; *enthuse* [43]; *its, it's* [51]; *leave, let* [34]; *most* 'almost' [34]; *off of* [41]; *raise, rise* [40]; *real* 'very' [45]; *-self* for personal pronoun [38]; *that, which* [38]; *there, their, they're* [44];

thusly [31]; *unique* [40]. Two—110 years old—have been appearing at least since 1884: *ain't* [35] and *but that/what* [30]. Twelve are 127 years old: you can find them in composition texts in an unbroken string at least since 1867: *affect, effect* [54]; *awfully* 'very' [32]; *being as* [39]; *comple-, compliment* [41]; *continual, continuous* [47]; *could of* [52]; *fewer, less* [54]; *kind of, sort of* [42]; *like* conjunction [54]; *loose, loosen, lose* [46]; *theirself, -selves* [30]; *would of* [48].

The 11 majority items that remain are superannuated indeed: as the bracketed numbers show, they occur and have occurred in many handbooks of composition over the past century. But more interestingly, the age of these items shows the birth of the "usage" attitude: besides appearing in handbooks, they appear in the works that fathered the handbooks. One dates from 1779: *kind, sort* (number of) [31]; and six from 1770: *among, between* [59]; *different from/than* [53]; *is when, is where* [32]; *lay, lie* [52]; *reason is because* [52]; *set, sit* [48].

The four most bewhiskered items are *hanged, hung* from 1769 [39]; *shall, will* from 1763 [40]; *who, which, that* from 1762 [39]; and *can, may*, going right back to Johnson's *Dictionary* in 1755 [51].

Space allows just one extended example of the handbook treatment of an item: when to use *among* and *between*—an item appearing in all 59 surveyed handbooks. Johnson said in 1755 that "*Between* is properly used of two and *among* of more; but perhaps this accuracy is not always preserved,"[5] and his stricture was amplified into the familiar handbook form by Robert Baker (1770), who added, "Some very incorrect speakers would say 'a statue between every pillar.' . . . To be quite clear we must say 'between every two *proximate* pillars'" (Leonard, 113). Two hundred and twenty years of advice, and native speakers of English have still not learned to say either "He has athlete's foot among his toes" or (to be quite clear) "He has athlete's foot between every two proximate toes."

The Johnsonian rule of *between* for two, *among* for more than two is by no means dead: 27 of the current handbooks (Beale, Crews, Dietrich, Dunbar, Fergenson, Gefvert, Hairston, Hodges, Hunt, Jacobus, Kennedy, Kirkland, Lindberg, Lunsford, Neeld, Neman, O'Hare, O'Hare-Memering, Packer, Perrin, Reinking, Rosen, Schiffhorst, Skwire, Troyka, Watkins, White) essentially repeat it; one more (Kirszner) limits the rule to formal writing. Howell says that *between* "suggests" two; Hacker, that *between* is used for two "ordinarily"; and Gere, Heffernan, and McKernan, that it is used for two in general.

Most of the remaining 26 have qualifications of some kind, but not all of these qualifications are either helpful or bring the rule in line with usage. Willson, for example, says that *between* is used with more than two "sometimes," and provides example sentences; Corder says much the same thing without providing examples, and labels this use "informal English." Kirszner says that the use of *between* with more than two is becoming "increasingly acceptable" (a glacial change indeed, if proceeding since 1755), especially when *among* would be "awkward" or unclear. Also in this group belongs Trimmer, who provides example sentences, then summarizes: "The general distinction...should be modified when insistence on it would be unidiomatic" (574). Such entries presume that the students already know what they are supposed to be consulting the glossary to learn.

Nor should it be assumed that individual handbooks have marched steadily toward a closer description of established usage. In the first edition of Crews we read: "*Between* can be used for any plural number of items, though some writers reserve it for two items" (344). "Some writers" changes in the second edition, becoming: "Many careful writers also reserve *between* for sentences in which only two items are involved" (542). In the first edition, students were told that *between* "can be used for more than two items . . . but it does require at least two" (346). The second edition deletes that permission, and the revised sentence reads only that *between* "Requires at least two items" (544). The reason for the revisions is not explained, but I doubt that usage changed significantly between 1985 and 1989.

Barnet's statement is probably the closest to reality: "Only English teachers who have had a course in Middle English are likely to know that it comes from *by twain*, and only English teachers and editors are likely to object to its use (and to call for *among*) when more than two are concerned . . ." (395). But Barnet is a voice crying in the wilderness on this item. If handbooks had existed in the twelfth century, they would no doubt have insisted on the similar distinction between the dual and plural numbers in the personal pronouns.

We began with Troyka's statement about handbook glossaries, but the fact is that the situation is almost exactly the reverse of her assertion. We could say with much more evidence that "little demonstrates less than does a usage glossary that standards for language use change."

How then do items get into the glossary? Why do 40 texts find it necessary to have any entry at all on *shall* and *will* when to my knowledge no one has ever refuted the argument made by Charles Carpenter Fries 65 years ago that there is no *shall/will* error ("Periphrastic Future")?[6] Asking why a glossary includes certain items and excludes others is a reasonable question, and one might think a handbook would invariably answer it, as justfication for the list that follows if for no other reason. Not so. Many handbooks (among them, Baker, Crews, Heffernan, Howell, Irmscher, Jacobus, Kirkland, Kolln, Lindberg, O'Hare, Watkins, and Willson) are silent about why their lists of usage items are composed as they are.

A few handbooks have statements of inclusion that describe the glossary as everything from an encyclopedia—"alphabetically arranged, brief entries to answer any question a student is likely to raise about syntax, usage, capitalization, punctuation, spelling, and rhetorical figures" (Neman x)—to an attic—"an assortment of specific problems that do not fit neatly under more general headings" (Hacker, first and second editions; her third edition gets more specific). But most handbooks that defend their selections fall into two groups. Members of the first ring various if limited changes on the assertion that their glossaries identify pests in the garden of prose: they claim to include words and phrase that "often cause problems for writers" (Fowler 748); "frequently cause problems for writers" (Reid 509); "frequently cause problems for inexperienced writers" (Dornan 402).

Texts in the second group imply how useful the glossaries will be by asserting that their items address questions that constantly arise: "the common errors" (Packer 539); "the most common usage problems" (Hodges 212); "the most common problems of usage in student writing" (Millward 422); "the most common of these troublemakers" (Reinking 569); "most of the common problems in formal writing" (O'Hare and Memering 542); "some commonly confused words and phrases" (Lunsford 745); "commonly confused words and phrases" (Carter 644).

These two kinds of statements are closely related: although one emphasizes the gravity of the problem and the other stresses its frequency, words like *common, frequently,* and *error* turn up in both. The statements ask us to accept that the major problems of usage found in student compositions today include: spelling *maybe* as *may be* or vice versa (found in 33 texts); a "confusion" among the meanings of *apt, likely, liable,* and *prone* (found in 40); using *hanged* and *hung* "incorrectly" (found in 39); using *enthuse* as a verb or participle (in 43 texts); using *continual* for *continuous* or vice versa (in 47 texts); a "misuse" of *beside* and *besides* (in 49 texts); "misusing" the word *disinterested* (in 54 texts); and a "misuse" of *can* and *may* (found in 51 of 59 texts). If inclusion is a vote for the importance of an item, then all of the many authors of the surveyed texts collectively conclude that the most important usage questions facing students in 1994 are the difference between *imply* and *infer*, found in 56 glossaries, and the use of *between* and *among*, found in all 59.

A few handbook authors know and admit that the glossaries have no connection direct or indirect with the most common problems in student writing: Beale says that his list includes "the most commonly *cited* problems of written usage" (328, my emphasis). Shaw's note is similar: "some of the more often *raised* points of word usage" (292, my emphasis), as is Guth's: "words, word forms, and constructions that are frequently criticized" (525). Or, as Barnet says, "expressions that set many teeth on edge" (717).

Do the lists of items in usage glossaries depend on a tooth count? To answer that question, let me first supply some anecdotal evidence. Some decades ago I wrote a handbook myself. Today I would repeat many of the same steps, but one step can be most charitably described as youthful folly: when it came to compiling a usage glossary, I gathered a number of the popular handbooks and combined their lists to see which items were most often discussed. Like a handbook Frankenstein, I was robbing the textbook graveyard for parts to stitch together into my very own monster. When I was done, it lay before me on the desk, dead but conventional.

The melancholy conclusion is that handbooks throughout the 1980s and early 1990s cannibalized their predecessors, duplicating items without concern for whether they presented real problems now or ever. When the authors departed from the items they found in older texts, the result was an explosion of individual quirks and crotchets. The average handbook gives no hint whatsoever that such a thing as research on usage exists.[7] One would think that the very beginning of the usage glossary is the most appropriate place to list the sources of the judgements recorded therein, and indeed some handbooks do. But only Watkins' and Bell's headings are models, citing the specific works from which they draw their judgements: only Bell lists the *Oxford English Dictionary*; only Bell and Watkins name current unabridged and abridged dictionaries. But the forthrightness and relative currency of their two texts are not typical: most of the texts name no sources whatsoever. The most frequently cited source, found in 12 texts, is H. W. Fowler's *Dictionary of Modern English Usage*, and only one of those 12, Lunsford's, notes that the work was first published in 1926. The next most frequently cited source, in ten texts, is Wilson Follett's *Modern American Usage*. If one makes an exhaustive and exhausting search of all the places where advice on usage sources is likely to be found—the acknowledgements, the section on dictionaries, the section on the research paper—the works mentioned are by and large the same ones found in the glossary headings. And if the question is asked, what about within the glossaries themselves? Are there any footnotes citing sources? The answer is no: in 59 glossaries there is precisely one footnote citing a source for a judgement.

In the glossary headings, one finds Edwin Newman recommended once, and Theodore Bernstein recommended a couple of times, but among the authorities not cited, not even mentioned in all these usage glossaries are: Leonard Bloomfield, Dwight Bolinger, Thomas Creswell, Edward Finegan, Charles C. Fries, J. Lesslie Hall, G. P. Krapp, Sterling A. Leonard, Albert H. Markwardt, Raven McDavid, H. L. Mencken, Holger Pedersen, Robert C. Pooley, Thomas Pyles, Allen Walker Read, I. Willis Russell, Fred Newton Scott, James Sledd, and Fred G. Walcott.

Notes

1. Unless otherwise stated, all references in this chapter are to the most recent editions of works in the list of references.

2. The early handbooks and usage guides were: J. M. Bonnell, 1867, *A Manual of the Art of Prose Composition* (Louisville, Kentucky); Henry Alford, 1884, *A Plea for the Queen's English: Stray Notes on Speaking and Spelling*, 2nd ed. (New York); Adams Sherman Hill, 1893, *The Foundations of Rhetoric* (New York); Robert Herrick and Lindsay Todd Damon, 1902, *Composition and Rhetoric for Schools*, rev. ed. (Chicago); Edwin C. Woolley, 1907, *Handbook of Composition* (Boston); Gerhard R. Lomer and Margaret Ashmun, 1914, *The Study and Practice of Writing English* (Boston); James C. Fernald, 1916, *English Grammar Simplified: Its Study Made Easy*, rev. ed. 1946 (New York); H. N. McCracken and Helen E. Sandison, 1917, *Manual*

of Good English (New York); Roy Ivan Johnson, 1921, *Mechanics of English* (Boston); Garland Greever and Easley S. Jones, 1925, *The Century Collegiate Handbook* (New York); Paul Sidwell and Russell Grant Siegfried, 1928, *Handbook of Grammar* (New York); John C. Hodges, 1941, *Harbrace Handbook of English* (New York).

3. *Usage* very loosely defined, as handbooks typically do: 20 or so of the 83 "usage" items are simply spelling errors by anyone's definition—*advice* and *advise*, for example.

4. The reason for the cautious "at least" is that a given item may well be older than the dates supplied here—the next old handbook examined may turn up an earlier proscription than those cited here.

5. Johnson's second clause shows with crystalline clarity a near universal failing of popular commentators on usage: when examining how a term is used, they first formulate a simple rule. Then, if the facts of usage are more complex than the rule states, the commentators do not amend the rule; instead they condemn speakers and writers for not following it.

6. The key word here is *refute*, not *ignore*, which many writers uncomfortable with the idea of varieties in language have done. But even Wilson Follett, whose *Modern American Usage* devotes 23 pages to telling us why his use of *shall* and *will* is better than ours, says, "No one who is well read in English literature or who reviews attentively the great mass of examples collected by Jespersen can continue to believe that there is a canonical usage which by a large consensus writers regularly apply throughout the domain bounded by *shall* and *will* and *should* and *would*" (371).

7. Gefvert is a happy exception to this generalization: as the basis for her usage statements, she conducted a survey of her own of professional people who use writing in their work, a survey she describes in her preface.

18. *Drug* Usage among High-School Students in Silsbee, Texas: A Study of the Preterite

CYNTHIA BERNSTEIN
Auburn University

Purpose

As part of A Phonological Survey of Texas, interviews were conducted with more than 500 high-school and college students representing the major cultural areas of the state.[1] One portion of the interviews is a sentence-completion task, in which students read sentences, at the same time selecting the word in parentheses that most closely fits what they would ordinarily say. The idea is that when their attention is directed toward making grammatical or lexical choices, their pronunciation is less guarded.

An unexpected benefit of the task has been the information the sentences have provided about grammatical preferences among young people in Texas. Although the sentences are designed to elicit phonological information, listening to the taped responses indicates that there are also systematic differences in the students' grammatical choices. In two of the sentences, students are asked to select between a strong form of the preterite (that is, a preterite involving a vowel change) and the weak form (in this case, a preterite formed in the regular manner with the addition of *-ed* or *-d*). This study focuses on possible reasons for the choice of one form of the preterite over another among high-school students from one small community in East Texas.

The Sample

Silsbee, one of the sites for the Phonological Survey of Texas, is a rural community, located north of Beaumont in East Texas, with a population of under 8,000. With one exception, all of the respondents were high-school students, aged 14 to 19. (The exception was a teacher, a forty-year-old white female, whose grammar in speaking very much resembled that of her students.) As indicated in table 18.1, this study includes interviews with 48 respondents: 22 males and 26 females; 30 whites, 18 blacks.

TABLE 18.1
The Sample (N=48)

	Males	*Females*	*Total*
White	14	16	30
Black	8	10	18
Total	22	26	48

Methods

During the sentence-completion portion of the interviews, conducted mostly by graduate students at Texas A&M University, students were asked to pick the word they would most naturally say—without pausing to figure out the "right" answer. They were assured that this is not a test. Although the entire task consists of 25 sentences, some involving more than one choice, just two of those sentences involve a choice between a regular *-ed* (or *-d*) pretcrite and an alternative strong form. Those sentences, listed below, require a choice between *drug* and *dragged* for the past tense of *drag* and between *dived* and *dove* for the past tense of *dive*:

1. Mary let out a whimper and a whine when Mother (drug, dragged) her to the sink to wash out her mouth with soap.
2. Father has a tin plate and a steel pin in his right leg from a wound he got when he (dived, dove) into a pool that had been drained.

A data set was compiled that includes the choices for each sentence (coded, for example, 1 for *drug*, 2 for *dragged*), along with the student's sex and ethnicity. Then, using an SAS statistical package, the grammatical variables were cross-tabulated with the demographic ones.

Results

The cross-tabulations show the extent to which the preterite varied with the sex or ethnicity of the informant. As shown in tables 18.2 and 18.3, neither verb tested varied significantly according to

TABLE 18.2
Preterites for *Drag* by Sex

	Males	Females	Total
Drug	45% (10/22)	35% (9/26)	39% (19/48)
Dragged	55% (12/22)	65% (17/26)	61% (29/48)

TABLE 18.3
Preterites for *Dive* by Sex

	Males	Females	Total
Dove	73% (16/22)	73% (19/26)	73% (35/48)
Dived	27% (6/22)	27% (7/26)	27% (13/48)

the sex of the speaker. Males were slightly more likely than females, though not significantly so, to use *drug* instead of *dragged* (45% of the males, as opposed to 35% of the females, preferred *drug*). Whereas less than half of both sexes chose the strong preterite *drug*, far more than half—73%—preferred the strong past tense *dove*. The only thing surprising about the high acceptance of *drug* and *dove* is that the percentages are not even higher than they are. Although earlier surveys have identified *dove* as a Northern feature, preliminary analysis among students at Texas A&M University had shown almost universal preference for *dove* over *dived*.[2] The same university students also showed a strong preference for *drug* over *dragged*. One might have assumed that younger, less-educated, rural students would be even less likely to use what might be considered the "educated" forms: *dragged* and *dived*.

The literature on the subject reinforces the expectation of *drug* especially among less educated speakers. E. Bagby Atwood writes in *The Regional Vocabulary of Texas*, "The past tense of *drag* is preponderantly *drug*, which is favored in all areas and in all age and education groups."[3] *Dragged*, he says, "is clearly an educated form" (74). In the 273 Texas interviews in Atwood's survey, *drug* occurs 66 times, to 19 for *dragged*. The 1934 Webster's (as Harold Wentworth's *American Dialect Dictionary* indicates) identifies *drug* as a dialectical, illiterate form. In fact, *dragged* is so clearly the "educated" choice that *The American Heritage Dictionary* (Second College Edition) completely excludes the preterite *drug*.

The status of *dove* versus *dived* is less clear. *American Heritage* does include *dove* as a variant of *dived* but calls *dived* "historically correct"; *dove* is acceptable in writing to only half of their Usage Panel. Although Atwood does not make the same claim for *dived* being an educated form that he did for *dragged*, stating, in fact, that *dove* is used "at all levels" of education (75), the *OED* indicates that *dove* is a dialectical variant of *dived*.

One expects, then, to find *drug* and *dove* among some rural Southern speakers. In Silsbee, males and females alike use these strong forms with some frequency. The frequency differs, however, according to the ethnicity of the speaker. As table 18.4 shows, whereas 53% of the white students use the "dialectal" *drug*, only 17% of the blacks do so. An astounding 83% of blacks use the standard *dragged*. The same trend is observed in the *dove/dived* distinction, shown in table 18.5. The "historically correct" *dived* is selected much more frequently by blacks than by whites. Just 13% of the whites in the sample selected *dived*, compared to 50% of the blacks.

Looking at these forms alone, one might conclude that blacks speak more "grammatically" than whites. But the pattern does not hold for two other preterites in the sentence-completion task. In the context of those sentences in the exercise, *swam* and *saw* are the "grammatical" choices, as opposed to *swum* and *seen*:

> 3. Although the horse was slower than the car, it (swam, swum) the eight foot deep stream, which the car couldn't do.
> 4. As the sun came up in the east, she wiped the dew off the glass, looked out the window, and (seen, saw) the mule eating the crop.

Although once again there is no significant difference between boys and girls, whites do prefer the "grammatical" forms of these verbs significantly more often than blacks (see tables 18.6 and 18.7).

The survey would at first seem to admit conflicting observations: for some verbs, blacks use the standard form more often than whites; for others, they use the standard form less often. If, however, we look more closely at the verbs themselves, there seems to be a pattern in the choices being made. Blacks, more often than whites, choose as the preterite the form not requiring a vowel change. What seems to be happening, other things being equal, is a regularization of the past tense, whether it leads to the more

TABLE 18.4
Preterites for *Drag* by Ethnicity

	Whites	Blacks	Total
Drug	53% (16/30)	17% (3/18)	39% (19/48)
Dragged	47% (14/30)	83% (15/18)	61% (29/48)

TABLE 18.5
Preterites for *Dive* by Ethnicity

	Whites	Blacks	Total
Dove	87% (26/30)	50% (9/18)	73% (35/48)
Dived	13% (4/30)	50% (9/18)	27% (13/48)

TABLE 18.6
Preterites for *Swim* by Ethnicity

	Whites	Blacks	Total
Swum	13% (4/30)	39% (7/18)	23% (11/48)
Swam	87% (26/30)	61% (11/18)	77% (37/48)

TABLE 18.7
Preterites for *See* by Ethnicity

	Whites	Blacks	Total
Seen	13% (4/30)	39% (7/18)	23% (11/48)
Saw	87% (26/30)	61% (11/18)	77% (37/48)

correct or the less correct form by dictionary standards. This "rule" explains *dragged* and *dived,* and it helps to explain the occurrence of *seen.*[4]

Conlcusion

The regularization of the past tense in BEV was noted over a century ago by James A. Harrison. The feature is exploited by Langston Hughes in the utterances of BEV speakers in his poems (italics added):[5]

After all them dollars I *gived* her these last two years. ["Broke," *The Negro Mother*, 1932]

I *seed* the river Jerden. ["Sylvester's Dying Bed," *Selected Poems*, 1959]

I *knowed* we was through! ["Madam and Her Might-Have-Been," *Selected Poems*, 1959]

I never *knowed* how. ["Wide River," *The Dream Keeper*, 1932]

In spite of this general awareness of the feature, studies of BEV pay it little attention. To the contrary, Fasold and Wolfram note, "Verbs which form their past tenses in an irregular way distinguish present and past forms in the overwhelming majority of cases in Negro dialect" (68). If the present study is any indication, however, the completed Phonological Survey of Texas will reveal a systematic distinction in the preterite formation by black and white speakers.

Notes

1. A Phonological Survey of Texas was undertaken with Guy Bailey as part of a National Science Foundation study on Urbanization and Language Change, grant number BNS-8812552.

2. Raven I. McDavid, Jr. (515) identifies *dove* as a Northern feature.

3. Note, though, that Atwood's sample includes no one under the age of 20.

4. Unfortunately, *seed* was not an option for the preterite of *see*. *Swam* and *swum*, of course, both involve vowel changes, and *swimmed* was not an option.

5. Mandelik and Schatt have a helpful concordance of Hughes's poetry. They list no instance of *dragged*, but two instances of the preterite *drug*, both of which are in "Angel Wings," *Selected Poems*.

19. Dictionary Recognition of Developing Forms: The Case of *snuck*

THOMAS J. CRESWELL
Chicago State University, emeritus

How the form *snuck* as preterit and past participle of *sneak* came into being, whether by analogy or by retention from some earlier but unrecorded dialectal use, is not known. But it was first recorded in US use and is generally regarded as an Americanism.[1]

The earliest recorded appearance of *snuck* as the preterit of the verb *sneak* was reported by R. M. Lumiansky. He cited a passage from *The Lantern*, a weekly published in New Orleans: "SNUCK. Sneaked. Dec. 17, 1887, 3/3: 'an' den snuck home'." The complete sentence from which Lumiansky drew his citation is included s.v. *sneak* in the *Oxford English Dictionary*, Second Edition: "He grubbed ten dollars from de bums an' den snuck home." Assuming that *grubbed* is intended to represent a nonstandard pronunciation of the preterit of *grab*, the context makes clear that *snuck*, in its earliest recorded appearance, is intended to represent a dialectal or nonstandard form.

As will be shown in what follows, in the slightly more than 100 years since its first appearance, *snuck* has become a standard variant for *sneaked*, both as preterit and past participle. But for a long time its rise in status escaped the notice of lexicographers.

What Triggered the Research on *snuck*

Late in 1975, this exchange occurred in Ann Landers' daily newspaper column:

> Dear Ann: Will you kindly consult your experts and settle an argument: is "snuck" a proper word? I say no, it is slang. My husband says it must be a proper word because Dick Cavett used it. As you know, Dick is a graduate of Yale, and they don't turn out dummies there. Please answer in the paper. I need to shove the column under my husband's nose.—(Signed) Love to Win This One

Dear Love to Win: While Yale doesn't turn out dummies it is possible to graduate from there and use a word that is not grammatically correct. "Snuck" does appear in some dictionaries but it is labeled "colloquialism" (or slang) for "sneaked." So I'd say you win. (November 23, 1975)

This selection from popular literature is appropriate here for several reasons (aside from its demonstration of conjugal tenderness and connubial non-competitiveness): First, it is responsible for triggering this exercise in intensive, perhaps obsessive, microlexicology. Second, since Ann Landers can safely be regarded as the quintessential exemplar of the mind-set and values of the general public, it may serve to call to mind the credence and trust placed in dictionaries by the general public—their tendency to accept without question anything they find in any dictionary, to say nothing of their tendency to misinterpret or overinterpret stylistic labels.

The shock of Ann Landers's casual condemnation of what had been, as far as I could remember, my own lifetime preterit and past participle form for *sneak* led me to wonder whether, by any chance, Ann had misread the dictionaries or dictionary she consulted. So I began looking up *snuck* in dictionaries. In my first search, only those published up to 1975 were included. I have since checked the treatment of *snuck* in newly published dictionaries as they have come to hand. Table 19.1 reports the results of the search. (See page 203 for an explanation of the abbreviations.)

Snuck in Dictionaries

No dictionary that I have been able to discover even acknowledged the existence of *snuck* prior to the publication of the second edition of *Webster's New International Dictionary* (W2) in 1934. In W2, *snuck* appeared below the line at the bottom of page 2383 among words described in the "Introduction" to the dictionary as "vocabulary entries which are no more than cross references to other entries. . . ." The complete entry reads thus: "snuck [pron.] past tense and past part. of sneak. Dial. U.S."

As table 19.1 makes clear, the maiden appearance of *snuck* in W2 did not set off a rush by other dictionaries to include it; not even

TABLE 19.1
Dictionary Treatment of *snuck*

OED1 (1933)	Not Entered
W2 (1934)	Below the line; Dialectal
ACD (1937)	Not Entered
WNW1Coll (1953)	Not Entered
W3 (1961)	Chiefly Dialectal
WC7 (1963)	Not Entered
SCD (1963)	Not Entered
RH1 (1966)	Chiefly Dialectal
RH1Coll (1968)	Chiefly Dialectal
AHD1 (1969)	Nonstandard
WNW2Coll (1972)	Colloquial
WC8 (1973)	No label
DD (1975)	Not Entered
S-B (1977)	Dialectal
RH2Coll (1979)	Chiefly Dialectal
OAD (1980)	"Use only to portray regional dialect"
AHD2Coll (1982)	Nonstandard
NYT (1982)	Regional or Informal
WC9 (1983)	No label
WII (1984)	Nonstandard
RH2 (1987)	No label. Usage note: "standard"
OEDSupp2 (1987)	Orig. & chiefly U.S.
WNW3Coll (1988)	S.v. sneak: No label. S.v. snuck: Colloq.
OED2 (1989)	Orig. & chiefly U.S.
RHWColl (1991)	No label. Usage note: "standard"
AHD3 (1992)	"Usage Problem." Usage note: "67 percent of Usage Panel disapproves"
WC10 (1993)	No label. Usage note: "standard"
AHD3Coll (1993)	Same as *AHD3*

the ensuing editions of *Webster's Collegiate Dictionary* did so. In fact, with the sole exception of *Webster's Third New International Dictionary* (*W3*) (1961), which elevated *snuck*, labeled "Chiefly dial.," to a position in the entry for *sneak*, more than thirty years passed before a dictionary by another publisher, *The Random House Dictionary of the English Language* (*RH1*) (1966), even acknowledged the existence of *snuck*. After that, lexicographical chaos ensued.

In all the dictionaries I have surveyed, what is claimed to be authoritative, up-to-date information leaves users with the following choices:

1. There is no such word: *ACD* (1937), *WNW1Coll* (1953), *WC7* (1963), *DD* (1975). It should also be noted here that no Oxford dictionary, with the sole exception of an American edition *The Oxford American Dictionary* (*OAD*) (1980), included *snuck* until the publication of *OEDSupp2* in 1987.
2. It is dialectal or regional, or chiefly or especially so: *W2* (1934), *W3* (1961), *RH1* (1966), *RH1Coll* (1968), *S-B* (1977), *OAD* (1980), *NYT* (1982).
3. It is colloquial or informal: *WNW2Coll* (1972), *NYT* (1982). *Webster's New World Dictionary. Third College Edition* (*WNW3Coll*) (1988) enters *snuck* s.v *sneak* as an alternative preterit and past participle, with no restrictive label. But in a separate entry s.v. *snuck*, it labels the form "Colloquial."
4. It is nonstandard: *AHD1* (1969), *AHD2Coll* (1982), *WII* (1984).
5. It is a standard alternative form to *sneaked* with no restrictions on its use or occurrence: *WC8* (1973), *WC9* (1983), *RH2* (1987), *OEDSupp2* (1987), *OED2* (1989), *RHWColl* (1991), *WC10* (1993). The *OEDSupp2* and *OED2* entries are not entirely without restriction: *Snuck* is labeled "Originally and chiefly U.S." The "originally" is probably accurate, but, as we shall show, the range of *snuck* is now wider than "chiefly U.S."
6. It is a "Usage Problem" and, although widely used in all varieties of writing, is disapproved of by 67% of a Usage Panel and is therefore to be avoided: *AHD3* (1992), *AHDColl* (1993).

Obviously, not all these dictionaries can be right. The research reported in the following pages shows relatively incontrovertibly that *snuck*, whatever its status in the past, is now well established, fully standard, and in widespread general use in both the U.S. and Canada, and in growing use in Britain and Australia.

The data to support this contention come from seven major sources:

1. Forty-one citations collected by my students, friends, colleagues, and me.
2. Seventy-two citations from the Merriam-Webster citation file for *snuck* through 1986, provided through the kind cooperation of Fred Mish, editor in chief, and E. Ward Gilman, managing editor of the Merriam-Webster dictionaries.
3. Twenty-three citations collected for *OEDSupp2* up to 1977, secured for me by my friend, teacher, and mentor Raven I. McDavid, Jr. through the kindness of Robert Burchfield, *OEDSupp* editor in chief, plus a few more citations not then available but included in *OED2*.
4. Maps and tabular analyses derived from the data bank of the *Dictionary of American Regional English* (*DARE*) (1985–) provided through the kindness of *DARE* Chief Editor Frederic G. Cassidy. These data are not yet generally available as only Volumes I (A–C) and II (D–H) have so far been published.

5. The results of a survey of Canadian usage reported by M. H. Scargill (1974).
6. More recent information on Canadian usage from an article by Gaelan Dodds DeWolf of the University of Victoria, B.C. (1990).
7. Data from NEXIS citing journalistic uses of *snuck* for the years 1977–1987. KWIC [Key Word in Context] printouts from the NEXIS files were made available for study through the kind cooperation of David A. Jost, Editor, *The American Heritage Dictionary.*

The Citation Evidence

The citations from my own, the Merriam-Webster, and the *OEDSupp2* files include 136 instances of the use of *snuck* dating from 1887 to the present, including both transitive and intransitive and both preterit and past participle uses. Eighty-seven (64%) of the 136 are from 1977 to the present. Of these 87, 18 (21%) are from works of fiction, 69 (79%) from other varieties of published writing. Twenty of the 87 instances are clearly intended to represent dialectal or nonstandard speech. The other 67 occur in mostly serious contexts—passages dealing with topics such as love-making, murder, body-snatching, recording of classical music, antique hunting, marine navigation, taxes, political elections, and the like. These instances can in no way be characterized as dialectal or nonstandard uses, nor can the great majority of the 67 instances reasonably be classified as informal.

Among the literary authors who have used *snuck*—sometimes, but by no means always, to represent dialectal, nonstandard, or informal speech—are Ring Lardner, Raymond Chandler, James T. Farrell, Jack Kerouac, Conrad Richter, Leon Uris, Wilfrid Sheed, Simon Brett, John MacDonald, John Irving, and John Updike.

Publications from which the citations come include *The New Yorker, New York Times Magazine, Readers Digest, Saturday Evening Post, Saturday Review, Esquire, Harper's, Atlantic Monthly, Sports Illustrated, Newsweek, Time, Car and Driver, Boating, Rolling Stone, Downbeat, The National Observer, The Black Panther, Vassar Quarterly, The American Scholar, Fanfare* and *Globe Magazine* (both Canadian); *Oz* and *The Listener* (both British).

Finally, a substantial number of the citations are from news or feature stories in daily newspapers. The citation evidence on *snuck* deals with occurrences of *snuck* in edited printed sources. To learn about its use in speech, we must turn to other sources.

Evidence from *DARE*

The *DARE* data bank provides information on the spoken use of *snuck* by a selected sample of Americans. In the late 1960's a questionnaire for the *DARE* study was completed by 1002 respondents from all 50 states in the United States. The questionnaire contained the following item: *To walk very quietly: The children filled their pockets and ——— out the back way.* Responses to this item included 365 *sneaked* from 47 states, and 171 *snuck* from 40 states; other respondents supplied words such as *slid, escaped,* and the like. The *DARE* population was heavily skewed, as is well known, toward older speakers: 66% of *DARE* respondents, or 660, were 60 years old or older; they supplied 42% or 72 of the *snuck* responses. Twenty-four percent, or 240 of the speakers, were from 40 to 59 years of age, and they supplied 33% or 56 *snuck*s. Only 10%, or 100, of the *DARE* respondents were below age 40; they supplied 25% or 43 of the *snuck* responses. To put these figures in another way, approximately 1 in 9 of the over-60 speakers supplied *snuck*, 1 in 4 of those aged 40 to 59 did so, and almost 1 of every 2 of the under-40 respondents. Quite clearly, the younger the speaker, the more likely it is that *snuck* is the habitual form.

Computer analysis of the *DARE* figures makes clear that *snuck* is not regional or dialectal; it occurs in 40 of the 50 states. Further, use of *snuck* in no way correlates with level of education of the respondents. This lack of correlation shows that *snuck* is not nonstandard or substandard: it is used more or less equally by well educated, moderately educated, and poorly educated speakers. The only social variable with which use of *snuck* has a high positive correlation is the age of speaker: The younger the speaker, the more likely that *snuck* is the preferred form.

The Canadian Usage Survey

A 1974 usage survey of Canadian speakers reported by M. H. Scargill reveals even more forcefully the strong relationship between age of speaker and use of *snuck*. Respondents in this survey were 8,500 ninth-grade students and 6,000 of the parents of those students, representing, more or less equally, every province in Canada. Here is the *snuck* question:

Which do you say?
A. He snuck by when my back was turned.
B. He sneaked by when my back was turned.
C. Either one.

Nationwide, 30% of the parents and 64% of the students indicated *snuck* to be their usual form. This survey was conducted in and through the schools of Canada, and the results reveal without question that *snuck* is the preferred form among younger speakers. It is highly unlikely that in the school atmosphere and under school auspices students would choose a form felt to be nonstandard or in any other way objectionable.

More Recent Canadian Studies

A more recent Canadian study, by Gaelan Dodds DeWolf (1990), compared data from two studies conducted in the late 1970's: one with 100 informants in Ottawa, the capital city of Canada, located at the eastern edge of the province of Ontario, approximately due north of Syracuse, N.Y.; and one with 240 informants living in Vancouver, B.C., about as far west as you can get in Canada. Sixty-five percent of the Ottawans used *snuck,* 32% *sneaked.* In Vancouver 50% used *snuck,* 45% *sneaked*; others either did not respond or substituted a verb like *stole.* The truly astounding figure in DeWolf's study is that 88% of the respondents under age 40 in the two cities chose *snuck*; only 25% of those over 40 did so. These results indicate that not only is *snuck* the majority form in the two cities studied, but among speakers below age 40 it is the overwhelmingly more common. These data corroborate the correlation found in the *DARE* study and the earlier Canadian usage study between age and use of *snuck. Snuck* is the preponderant choice of younger speakers.

The NEXIS Files

A search of the NEXIS files from 1 January 1977 to 15 July 1987 reveals that *snuck* appeared in 1,168 separate "stories" (newspaper stories, editorials, magazine articles, book reviews, etc.). Table 19.2 shows the number of occurrences each year and reveals that the

TABLE 19.2
Occurrences of *snuck* in NEXIS Files

1977	16	1982	108
1978	12	1983	107
1979	21	1984	157
1980	58	1985	230
1981	96	1986	226

1987 (1 Jan.–15 Jul. only)   138
1987 Full year (Extrapolated)   250

use of *snuck* has increased considerably during the years reported—from 16 occurrences in 1977 to 226 in 1986, the last full year for which I have data available. For 1987, only the period January 1 to July 15 is covered in the table, showing 138 appearances. Extrapolation projects a likely total of approximately 250 occurrences in 1987. The years are not truly comparable, however, due to the fact that not all of the sources in which occurrences are found in 1987 were included in the NEXIS corpus in the years 1977–82. By 1983, however, all sources covered in 1987 were included in NEXIS files, so the years 1983–87 are directly comparable, and in that period the increase was from 107 occurrences in 1983 to an extrapolated 250 in 1987, an increase of 136% over five years. Table 19.3 presents data on use of *snuck* in those two years.

In the two years analyzed, 1983 and 1987, slightly more than half of the uses of *snuck* occur in sports stories, mostly from Associated Press and United Press International wire services. Other contexts for *snuck* are highly varied and include newspaper crime reporting, book reviews, editorials, articles on computers, medicine, business, the arts, music, international news, politics, and law. Perhaps the

TABLE 19.3
Occurrences of *snuck* in NEXIS: 1983 and 1987

	1983	*1987 (1 Jan.–15 Jul.)*
Total Occurrences	107	138
In Sports Stories	57	61
In Other Contexts	50	77
Quoted Speech	43	65

most formal context in which *snuck* appears is in an article in *Legal Times* of 27 June 1983:

> Deeming that amicus curiae status would have to do for Justice—which snuck into the case at the 11th hour, arguing that the case was important to the government's Title VII enforcement interests. . . . (3)

A high proportion of the occurrences of *snuck* in the NEXIS corpus occur in direct or indirect quotations of reported speech: 43 of the 107 occurrences in 1983 and 65 of the 138 in 1987 are quoted from someone's speech. In other words, close to 50% of the NEXIS occurrences in the two years analyzed represent reports of use of *snuck* in spoken language.

It should be noted that most of the quoted speech instances occur in sports stories, quoting players or coaches. From the NEXIS data we can conclude that in the 1980's the use of *snuck* became firmly established and standard in sports reporting, it was occurring with increasing frequency in newspaper and magazine writing on all sorts of subjects, and it was well established in speech.

Snuck Today

Taken together, the data presented here demonstrate unequivocally that *snuck* is not dialectal, not nonstandard, not informal, but well-established, fully standard, and widely used in speech and writing in the U.S. in all but the most pompously formal or frozen contexts. And the evidence shows that it is well established and standard in speech in Canada. Because I have not had access to a large number of Canadian publications, I cannot provide substantial evidence of its use in print there, but I do have five citations from Canadian publications, and, based on its wide occurrence in Canadian speech, I think it most likely that a search of Canadian published material would yield ample evidence of use of *snuck* in all kinds of contexts. *Snuck* is also spreading to other parts of the English-speaking world: *OED2* has three recent citations from British publications, and I have two instances of Australian use in my files.

Despite the extensive evidence of the standard status of *snuck*, some—perhaps remembering with pleasure the elitist foofaraw over the scaling down of the use of restrictive labels in *W3*—persist in disputing its status. On the basis of the information reported in these pages, my colleague Virginia McDavid and I composed the following usage note, which was included s.v. *sneak* in *The Random House Dictionary of the English Language*, second edition:

First recorded in writing toward the end of the 19th century in the United States, SNUCK has become in recent decades a standard variant past tense and past participle of the verb SNEAK: *Bored by the lecture, he snuck out the side door.* . . . It is not so common in highly formal or belletristic writing, where SNEAKED is more likely to occur. SNUCK is the only spoken past tense and past participle for many younger and middle-aged persons of all educational levels in the United States and Canada. SNUCK has occasionally been considered nonstandard, but it is so widely used by professional writers and educated speakers that it can no longer be so considered.

Perhaps nostalgic for the *W3* donnybrook, Christopher Porterfield, a senior editor at *Time*, in a mixed review of *RHD2* included a superciliously hostile evaluation of the dictionary's general treatment of usage (*Time*, 2 Nov. 1987, 86). Among other pontifications, he wrote, "And because many people wrongly consider the past tense of sneak to be snuck (instead of sneaked), the word has been promoted from 'chiefly dialect' in RHD-I to full respectability in RHD-II." I wrote to Porterfield at *Time* enclosing an earlier version of this paper and pointing out to him that in a co-authored biography of his friend Dick Cavett (Dick Cavett and Christopher Porterfield, *Cavett* [New York, 1974], Cavett is quoted once using *snuck* (41), and Porterfield, writing in what I presume to be his own "voice" also uses *snuck* (116). Porterfield did not reply to my letter.

Webster's Dictionary of English Usage (1989) includes a long, well-informed note on *snuck*, concluding: "in about a century *snuck* has gone from an obscure and probably dialectal variant of the past and past participle to a standard and widely used variant." The judgment is followed by citations from *The Wall Street Journal*, the English publication *The Listener*, a formal address by Robert MacNeil, the PBS newscaster, and *The New York Times Magazine*. This judgment is repeated in the recently published *Merriam-Webster's Collegiate Dictionary*, tenth edition (1993).

One American dictionary, however, still prefers to dismiss the evidence of wide use in favor of the opinions of its usage panel. The *American Heritage Dictionary*, third edition (1992) and its college edition (1993) both label *snuck* "Usage Problem," and report in a usage note that it is disapproved of by 67% of the AHD Usage Panel. Predictably, and consistent with evidence reported earlier here, more than half of the usage panel members are over 60 years of age, and some are in their 90s. Older persons are still squeamish about *snuck*.

The Future of *snuck*

The extensive and apparently increasing use of *snuck* by the young suggests that it may be in the process of replacing *sneaked* as the standard preterit/past participle of *sneak*. E. Ward Gilman, Managing Editor, has sent me copies of two letters about *snuck* recently received in the Merriam-Webster offices. The first is signed by 24 pupils from an English class at Yelm Middle School in the state of Washington. Here is the entire message: "Our class has decided that 'SNUCK' should be an accepted word. Snuck sounds better as the past tense of sneak. The word 'SNEAKED' sounds awkward and clumsy. Thank you for your consideration." The second is from a junior high school student from Grenada Hills, California. Here is an excerpt:

> ... I ran into a horrible sounding sentence. I checked it over and found that the cause of the ill-sounding sentence was the word "sneaked." That word does not sound in the slightest bit correct to me. Therefore I am writing to petition that you make "snuck" a word.

The future models for standard English have spoken. We may yet see the day when a carefully edited, newly published, database dictionary will say, in its entry for *sneak*, "pret. and p. part *snuck*; also, esp. in older use, *sneaked*."

Note

1. The first version of this report was presented at the MMLA/ADS meeting in Minneapolis on 2 Nov. 1978. A more fully developed, updated report was made to the joint DSNA/ADS meeting in Philadelphia, 6 June 1987. This paper is an updated and expanded version of the latter.

20. The Suffix -ee

MICHAEL R. DRESSMAN
University of Houston — Downtown

Most English borrowings have been of root-source (or lexical) morphemes, falling into the traditional form classes of nouns, verbs, and adjectives. We know that historically the English lexicon is most indebted to French and the typical pattern in the Anglicization of these French terms is that, though the root remains recognizably French, the usual productive English system morphemes are affixed to form plural and possessive forms for nouns, tense markers for verbs, and comparative and superlative markers for adjectives.

The impact of French on English has been so great, however, that a number of French derivational suffixes also have passed into English, and it would be difficult to imagine English as we know it without such suffixes as *-able* (as in *unthinkable*), *-ous* (as in *thunderous*), or *-age* (as in *shrinkage*). One such French suffix, *-ee*, seems to have been well established in Late Middle and Early Modern English, occurring in a host of legal terms, e.g., *appellee*, 1531; *assignee*, 1419; *lessee*, 1495; and *mortgagee*, 1584.[1] Considering the fact that the law courts were among the last English institutions to surrender the use of Anglo-Norman French, this is no particular surprise. The common pattern was that these *-ee* words were paired with agent nouns ending in *-or*, *-er*, or *-our*, and the word bearing the *-ee* suffix expressed a passive sense. Thus an appellee was one against whom an appeal was made, and a mortgagee was one to whom a mortgager granted a mortgage. Rather early, however, this *-ee* suffix was affixed in English to words which ordinarily would not bear it in French, e.g., *vendee*, 1547; *legatee*, 1688. Still, it seems that *-ee* enjoyed only limited productivity, namely with certain English words in legal contexts; it was not freely added to just any transitive English verb root in order to designate the direct or indirect recipient of an action. Today, however, *-ee* is more widely distributed; constraints limiting the use of the form to legal contexts are progressively weakening. Especially for purposes of humor, nonce forms with *-ee* seem unlimited, bound only by the conventional meaning of the morpheme—not any set stock of words or any particular context.

Serious, quasi-legal words with *-ee* entered the language early. *Nominee* dates from at least 1664, *trustee* from 1647, *referee* from 1621, *grantee* and *committee* (in the singular sense of an individual to whom something is committed) from the late fifteenth century. Newer words with *-ee* endings also have received wide acceptance since the eighteenth and nineteenth centuries. Many of these are found in the jargon of government, education, the military, and other professions—especially the social sciences. *Examinee* is first attested in 1788, *trainee* in 1850, *draftee* during the American Civil War (Flexner *I Hear*), and *interviewee* in 1884.

Initial acceptance into the language does not guarantee full utilization. Some terms seem to have existed for a time and then to have slipped out of general use. For a while in the nineteenth century, it was accepted to call a photograph's model or human subject a *photographee*. Walt Whitman used several *-ee* words in *Leaves of Grass*, and the possibilites of the suffix clearly interested him. In his private notes on language he welcomed the new term *employee*, calling it "a good innovation"; and he records other possible parallel terms such as *offendee, lovee, hatee, suspectee, servee*, and *receivee* (Dressman "Walt Whitman's Study"), many of which have subsequently disappeared.

Other terms have emerged during and since the nineteenth century which are hardly legal at all. The subject of a biographer's work has been called a *biographee* since 1941. The recipient of an honor is called an *honoree* in twentieth-century newspapers (Mencken *The American Language*), and this usage appears to have been transferred to *awardees* and *enshrinees*, such as those mentioned in a recent radio ad for the Pro Football Hall of Fame. American educationists and British university lecturers refer to pupils of tutors as *tutees*; the term *tutoree* is also found. Someone under investigation is an *investigatee*. Branches of the government of the State of South Carolina unabashedly refer to *recommendees, ratees*, and *evaluatees*. The Federal Bureau of Indian Affairs labels some of its charges *relocatees*. The military has its *selectees, inductees*, and *enlistees*. Adopted children are *adoptees*. Merrill Lynch, in one of its investment brochures, refers to *optionees*. Omicron Delta Kappa, an honor society, holds a tapping ceremony for its *tappees*. The Houston Grand Opera occasionally sends out calls for *auditionees* for the chorus. *The College Board Review* refers to college students as *enrollees*. The *New York Review of Books* talks about a person contacted as a *contactee*. Richard Connell's famous short story "The Most Dangerous Game" contains a reference to the hunter and the *huntee*.

More striking than the examples of *-ee* as an English derivational suffix is the use of *-ee* to create an essentially humorous effect. If a speaker says, "The inquisitor was the torturer and the heretic was the torturee," or "During the sermon, the minister is the preacher and the congregation are the preachees," the hearer understands the relationship being described but also knows that the tone is jocular. This use of *-ee* as a signal of humor is often associated with traditional African-American comedians such as Flip Wilson and Redd Foxx or the pseudo-Black comedy in the old *Amos 'n' Andy* radio and televison shows. Yet, it seems that this humorous usage of *-ee* dates back to the eighteenth century. Richardson wrote, "The Lover and Lovee generally make the happiest couple" in 1754; and Sterne wrote of "the jester and jestee" (Jespersen *Growth and Structure*). The humorous use of *-ee* continued into the nineteenth century. Carlyle appears to have been particularly enamored of it, having given us both *cursee* and *laughee* (Jespersen). L. Harcourt wrote in 1860, "You are the beater, I am only the beatee."

Some of these humorous forms may have been questionable at first, but they moved into accepted use. In 1853 Thomas DeQuincey used *gazee*, perhaps with humorous intent, perhaps not. But DeQuincey also used *addressee* in 1858, a term now in general use. Also found during the nineteenth century is the borrowing from French, *employe*, which was soon anglicized to *employee*. Apparently the usage gained popularity first in the United States. The *OED*'s first citation for employee is from Thoreau's *Walden* (1854), but it also appears in Melville's "Bartleby" (1853). Richard Grant White, writing over a century ago, advised Americans to eschew a French spelling and pronunciation of the term and recognize it as an English word (White, 1880).

The humor found in the nonce application of *-ee* is difficult to account for unless it may derive from the pseudo-intellectual, pedantic sound of it, since the majority of terms ending in *-ee* are legal jargon. However, the phenomenon of a language feature moving from humorous use toward greater acceptance is not unique to *-ee*. D. E. Houghton ("Humor as a Factor in Language

Change") shows that words or affixes (e. g., the suffix *-wise*) may become fashionably jocular for a time and then shift into the lexical mainstream.

Journalists, long ago and to this day, have contributed to the humorous possibilities of *-ee*. The *British Monthly Magazine* in a 1798 issue referred to a person who had been snubbed, or socially "cut," as a *cuttee*. The term *kickee* appeared in a London newspaper in 1832 and cropped up again in another London journal in 1864. Mencken's *The American Language* contains several joking instances of *-ee* words, including *holdupee* and *tryoutee*. Modern news commentator Paul Harvey has made *-ee* a part of his stock of oral humor, referring to a person answering a telephone as the *callee*; advocating that we let "the punishment fit the punishee"; and speaking of giver and the *givee* at Christmas. Eric Sevareid referred to the "planners [in government] and the plannees, the people." William F. Buckley, Jr., writing of President Jimmy Carter's pledge to whip Ted Kennedy's butt in any future election, referred to Kennedy as the *whippee*. The *New York Review of Books*, in a review of a book by swindler Bobby Baker, spoke of Baker's list of "senatorial bilkees." Howard Rosenberg of the Los Angeles Times News Service, in a review of TV's *Dallas*, wrote of the victims of the evil J. R. Ewing as *shaftees*. Jack Kroll of *Newsweek* labeled Woody Allen's schlemiel character as a *conqueree*.

Sports reporters, too, have employed the nonce *-ee*; Howard Cosell called people dunked in water *dunkees*. Glenn Rollins in the *Charlotte Observer* said that Cedric "Cornbread" Maxwell was frequently the object of other players' jokes, that is, the *jokee* rather than the joker. Tom Higgins, also of the *Observer*, wrote a piece about stock car driver Buddy Baker, who was the guest of honor at a dinner "roast," as the *roastee*. And every spring there are several non-roster *invitees* that show up in major league baseball training camps, according to the *Houston Chronicle*.

The *-ee* continues to thrive in the world of comedy. Note such examples as *dumpee*, *stinkee*, and *sublettee* in Neil Simon's movie *The Goodbye Girl*; the complaint of the Muppet Grover on *Sesame Street* to his horse: "I am the rider. You are the ridee"; Fonzie's use of *rentee* and *pinnees* on *Happy Days*; Bob Newhart's psychologist character's reference to the chair for the helper and the couch for the *helpee*; Jeff MacNelly's cartoon that speaks of the editor and the *editee*; and the caption on a *Dunagin's People* cartoon: "Our guest today is a Congressman who was stung by a recent FBI sting operation, but maintains he meant to be the stinger instead of the *stingee.*" (Emphasis in this last case is not added.)

Outside of explicitly comedic contexts, other media examples of *-ee* used in quasi-humorous ways include a reference on TV's *Knots Landing* to a *seducee*; Norman Corwin's statement on National Public Radio that he was one of the early *enticees* of radio; August Eberle's use of phoner and *phonee* in the *Chronicle of Higher Education* in reference to the participants in a telephone conversation; and on the TV show *To Tell the Truth* the reference to a woman tattooed over 75 percent of her body as a *tattooee.*

In general, the examples of *-ee* words maintain the passive quality of the original uses of the form. (See Elna Bengtsson's *Studies on Passive Nouns*, as cited in Jespersen *Morphology.*) Certain words with *-ee* are, however, less clearly passive, for example, *absentee, escapee, debauchee, refugee, resignee,* and *retiree.* In each instance one might experience an active sense in these words. Nevertheless, for each of these terms there exists a French reflexive verb such as *se retirer*, which suggests a remarkably close association still to the source language for the *-ee* morpheme and that, as these words moved into English, they maintained their passive sense in a reflexive mode. Thus an *absentee* is one who absents himself or a *retiree* is one who retires himself or has been retired. A similar sense might explain the popular sports term *signee,* for a college athlete who signs a grant-in-aid. This athlete might be considered one who signs himself to a contract or one who has been signed up by a coach.

It is more difficult to explain certain other attested forms such as *dilutee*, a British term for an unskilled worker who assumes a skilled worker's place (as in wartime); also note *standee* and *attendee.* Why not simply say stander or attender? *Webster's New World Dictionary* handles the reflexive *-ee* terms and such forms as those cited here as designating a person in a specified condition. In other words, one who is standing is in the condition of standing himself. This may be a useful categorization synchronically, as an extension in Modern English of the French reflexive.

Except in the instances of the reflexive and like forms, *-ee* words seem always to have a possible agent noun counterpart—usually bearing an *-er* or *-or* suffix. In some cases, though, the agent word ends in *-ator,* as in *evaluator* and *nominator.* Morley Safer, on *60*

Minutes, referred to seductresses and *seductees*. We may also note that certain reflexive forms have parallel *-er* forms which have a sense that differs from the *-ee* form. For example, a *debaucher* is one who causes another to become debauched, that is, a *debauchee*. However, there are attested forms such as *signer* and *retirer*, which seem to carry much the same sense as *signee* and *retiree*.

Another feature of *-ee* words is that they all tend to be animate. For example, a *rider*, like Grover, may consider his horse the *ridee*; but an *eater* does not consider an apple an *eatee*, unless he regards it in an unusually personal manner. Similarly, a *dancer* who dances a samba could in no way consider the particular variety of dance the *dancee*.

The *-ee* suffix is a living and often playful element in English. Its growth as an accepted non-humorous form in certain governmental, educational, and social science circles may be noted and dismissed by some as further evidence of bureaucratese or gobbledygook. The acceptance (with neither shudder nor chuckle) of many new *-ee* words, however, may point to the more general acceptability of the morpheme—or it may just go to show the profound lack of a sense of humor and lack of awareness of self-parody in certain quarters in our society.

Note

This essay is a revised and updated version of "The Suffix -ee: Laughing All the Way to Acceptance," *SECOL Bulletin* 5 (Fall 1981): 101–07.

1. All dates, unless otherwise referenced, are from the *Oxford English Dictionary*.

Additional *-ee* Examples

allocatee	*Chronicle of Higher Education*
arrestee	CBS Radio News
baptizee	*Chronicle of Higher Education*
bitee	*Newsweek*
bouncee 'ejected by a bouncer'	*Houston Post*
firee	*Parade* (magazine)

investee	*Fortune* (magazine)
pickee 'victim of pickpocket'	CBS Radio News
rear-endee	*Houston Chronicle*
shelteree 'disaster victim housed by Red Cross'	KKBQ Radio News, Houston
shootee	KTRH Radio News, Houston
kidnappee	"Sylvester and Tweety" (cartoon)
surprisee	*Good Times* (TV show)
auctionee	*Full House* (TV show)
rentee	*Hooperman* (TV show)
hustlee	Betty White on *The Tonight Show*
boomee 'one on whom the boom is to be lowered'	*Silver Spoons* (TV show)
weanee 'one who is to be weaned'	*Night Court* (TV show)

21. More on Proximity Concord

W. N. FRANCIS
Brown University

In 1986 I published an article dealing with 'proximity concord.' I pointed out that 'proximity concord,' also called 'attraction,' denotes the situation where a finite verb in the present tense agrees in number with a nearby, usually preceding, noun rather than with the head of the noun phrase which is the true grammatical subject. It is to be distinguished from 'notional concord,' in which the verb agrees with an underlying meaning of the subject rather than with its surface form, as in the case of collective nouns like *team, faculty, jury,* and semantically closely bound coordinates of the *ham and eggs* sort. It is also distinct from cases where nouns of quantity followed by *of*-phrases actually have become plural quantifiers, as in "a lot of people" and "a number of reasons," both of which take a plural-marked verb. It further differs from cases of agreement of a copular verb with a predicate nominal rather than the grammatical subject (e.g. "The weather to keep an eye on are these clouds" from a TV weather broadcast). I pointed out that proximity concord proper is purely grammatical, with a nearby noun overriding the true subject and taking over the verb concord (e.g. "The full impact of the cuts haven't hit hard yet").

I cited numerous examples, chiefly drawn from educated speech and writing, and ventured the hypothesis that the noticeable increase of this phenomenon in current English is a symptom of the ultimate loss of the third person *-s* inflection, as the last vestige (except in the verb *to be*) of the full subject-verb concord in Old English, a system still surviving in modern German but completely gone in the Scandinavian languages.

Here I would like to pursue the subject further by observing the types of constructions which display this phenomenon. The most frequent and characteristic type of expression exhibiting proximity concord is one having a singular noun as subject followed by some type of postmodifier (usually a prepositional phrase) ending in or at least containing a plural form. Some typical examples:

1. The *thrust* of these allegations *are* baseless. [witness on TV, 28 Feb. 1985]
2. The sheer *weight* of all these figures *make* them harder to understand. [Ronald Reagan on TV, 13 Oct. 1982]
3. The *variety* of these *allow* many possibilities of change. [W.P. Lehmann, *Historical Linguistics*. 2nd ed. 1973, 142]

It is possible that *variety* in (3) is a quasi-quantifier as it would be, for example, in "a variety of solutions were proposed." But in this example it seems to be closer to its basic nominal meaning. Although the great majority of the intervening elements evoking plural concord are prepositional phrases (101 of 140 in my collection), other constructions may appear. For example, relative clause:

4. The second *thing* that local meetings have in common *are* observers from the Barrington League of Women Voters. [Barrington RI *Times*, 16 Jan. 1985; the plural predicate may be of influence here]

Gerund clause:

5. *Violating* the rules of personal reference probably *have* no special consequences that *violating* other social rules *do* not share. [MS paper by colleague, Feb. 1987]

Although most of the examples I have collected have a singular subject and plural verb (117 of 140), the reverse is also possible:

6. *Portions* of tonight's broadcast *is* made available by ———. [TV announcement]
7. . . . we will have in this country the tax equivalent of the Boston Tea Party, except that it will be the *politicians* instead of the tea that *gets* thrown overboard. [Rep. Wm. Roth, quoted in *Time*, 20 May 1985]

It is of interest also to note the heavy preponderance of *of* in the intervening phrases and of forms of *be* in the verbs.[1]

The question arises whether instances of this phenomenon are to be considered evidence of grammatical change in process or mere careless mistakes. Linguists incline to the former explanation; "pop grammarians" and other schoolmarmish folk to the latter. But there are some major differences between this phenomenon and favorites of the latter group, like *between you and I, I don't have no money, I seen him yesterday* and the rest of the tiresomely repeated list cited by pop grammarians and linguistic martinets who write letters to the newspaper. The first is that this solecism (if indeed it is one) is largely confined to the speech and writing of the educated. My rather desultory collection contains spoken examples from the President, a couple of cabinet secretaries, some professors (including three linguists, myself being one), and various TV newscasters, and written examples from newspaper stories, columns, and letters to the editor (this may, of course, be because these are the spoken and written materials most ready to hand and encountered at times when it is possible to make notes). The second difference is that none of the deplorers of the state of the language have hit upon it as something to wring their hands over. It is as though they don't notice it at all. Which seems to me to be a strong bit of evidence that it has become sufficiently embedded in the language to be accepted or at least overlooked. And isn't that how change in language comes about?

Note

1. The late Dwight Bolinger was kind enough to send me a copy of his collection of 62 examples of proximity concord. This raises my corpus to over 200 cases. The numbers in the Bolinger corpus agree closely with my own, as shown in table 21.1.

TABLE 21.1
Incidence of Negative Concord as Found by Francis and Bolinger

	Francis (N = 140)		*Bolinger* (N = 62)	
Intervening elements				
Prepositional phrases	101	(72%)	45	(72%)
With *of*	69	(68% of PPs)	32	(71% of PPs)
Relative clauses	11		2	
Gerund clauses	8		1	
Infinite clauses	1		3	
Other	19		11	
Verbs				
are	64		23	
were	10		14	
have	10		1	
has	6		5	
Other	50		19	

22. The Lawyer's *imply*

BRYAN A. GARNER
LawProse, Inc.

The phrase *by implication* signifies "by what is implied, though not formally expressed, by natural inference" (*OED2*). Anglo-American judges, who continually evaluate facts, often use the phrase, along with its various cognates. Judges (by implication) draw "natural inferences" and thereby decide that something or other was, in the circumstances, "implied." Through the process of hypallage—a semantic shift by which the attributes of the true subject are transferred to another subject—the word *imply* has come to be used in reference to what the judges do, as opposed to the circumstances. This specialized use of *imply* runs counter to popular lay use and is not adequately treated in English-language dictionaries. The usage is unrecorded in all dictionaries of which I am aware, apart from my own *Dictionary of Modern Legal Usage.*

Specifically, the word *imply* often means "(of a court) to impute or impose on equitable or legal grounds." An *implied* contract is not just one implied from the facts of the case, but implied by the court, i.e., imposed by the judge or judges as a result of their inferences.

In using *imply* in this way, courts are said to find a doctrinally posited fact (a condition, restriction, remedy, right of action, or the like) that controls a judicial decision. Thus:

[I]t would be more literally accurate to acknowledge that . . . the *court* implies the conditions from reasons of equity. [*Susswein v. Pennsylvania Steel Co.*, 184 F. 102, 106 (C.C.S.D.N.Y. 1910)]

This court cannot, upon some supposed hardship, defeat an estate by *implying* a condition which the grantor has not expressed, nor in the least intimated by the language of his conveyance. [*Brown v. State,* 5 Colo. 496, 504 (1881)]

The difficulty with the arguments seeking to *imply* Mary Silva's survival of Joseph as a condition is that they would result in holding that because it is expressed that Joseph must survive until the period of distribution to take an inheritable interest, a similar contingency should be *implied* as to Mary. [*In re Estate of Ferry,* 361 P.2d 900, 904 (Cal. 1961) (in bank)]

165

Judicial willingness to *imply* new remedies in areas governed by federal law has been expressed in a number of ways. [*SEC v. Texas Gulf Sulphur Co.*, 312 F. Supp. 77, 91 (S.D.N.Y. 1970)]

[I]n my view, the Members of Congress merely assumed that the federal courts would follow the ancient maxim "ubi jus, ibi remedium" and *imply* a private right of action. [*California v. Sierra Club,* 451 U.S. 287, 300 (1981) (Stevens, J., concurring)]

When put in the passive voice, this use of *imply* may be especially confusing, because the person who does the implying is left unclear. The user of any unabridged English-language dictionary either would find it hard to divine precisely what *imply* means or would deduce an incorrect meaning:

[T]he remaining provisions of the Insurance Law would lack substance if no private right of action were *implied.* [*Corcoran v. Frank B. Hall & Co.,* 545 N.Y.S.2d 278, 284 (N.Y. App. Div. 1989)]

Here the passive voice masks the subject. The writer apparently means to say that a court would allow such a cause of action: Thus the court would *imply* a right of action, i.e., impose it on equitable or legal grounds.

This special legal sense is most keenly demonstrated when *imply* is coupled with *impute,* as here:

When deciding the shares, we look to their [the husband's and the wife's] respective contributions and we see what trust is to be *implied* or *imputed* to them. [*Cracknell v. Cracknell,* [1971] 3 All E.R. 552, 554]

Often one could actually read *impute* in place of *imply* and have the same sense (read *impute to* for *imply on*):

Under special circumstances the Court may *imply* knowledge *on* the speaker, such as the inventor of a machine, "who must be fully informed as to [the machine's] good and bad qualities." [*Brickell v. Collins,* 262 S.E.2d 387, 390 (N.C. App. 1980)]

In some contexts, *imply* seems to take on a slightly different sense, "to read into (a document)," as here:

[O]ne has merely to look at what is clearly said. There is no room for any intendment.... Nothing is to be read in, nothing is to be *implied.* One can only look fairly at the language used. [*Cape Brandy Syndicate v. I.R.C.,* [1921] 1 K.B. 64, 71]

But such uses comport with the general sense here outlined, since "reading in" provisions has the same effect as "imputing" them.

The lawyer's *imply* has directly encroached on the word *infer*. Whereas nonlawyers frequently use *infer* for *imply*, lawyers and judges conflate the two in the opposite direction, by using *imply* for *infer*. In analyzing the facts of a case, judges will *imply* one fact from certain others. (*From* is a telling preposition.) Nonlawyers believe they must be *inferring* an additional fact from those already known; if contractual terms are *implied*, they must surely be implied by the words or circumstances of the contract and not by the judges.

Perhaps using this reasoning, some legal writers have recoiled from *imply* and have resorted instead to *infer*:

Apart from the difficulty of *inferring* a contract where none has been made, no agreement between husband and wife for future separation can be recognised. [*Pettitt v. Pettitt*, [1970] A.C. 777, 811 (H.L.)]

When a party voluntarily accepts a valuable service or benefit, having option to accept or reject it, the Court may *infer* a promise to pay. [*Lewis v. Holy Spirit Association*, 589 F. Supp. 10, 13 (D. Mass. 1983)]

In the following sentence, in which the court writes *imply or infer from*, the word *imply* adds nothing, unless *by the circumstances* (i.e., *implicit in the circumstances*) is to be understood, and *or* is to be read as *and*:

Rather, the crucial question is when can a waiver of rights be *implied or inferred from* the actions and words of the person interrogated. [*McDonald v. Lucas*, 677 F.2d 518, 520 (5th Cir. 1982)]

In the following sentences, *infer* might have served better than *imply*. One would be tempted to call these misuses, were not some specimens so ancient:

[T]here is nothing averred from which the court can *imply* that those conditions were performed. [*Cutting v. Myers*, 6 F. Cas. 1081, 1082 (C.C.D. Pa. 1818) (No. 3520)]

The requirements of the rule are met if such an intention may be clearly *implied* from the language, the purposes of the agreement, and all the surrounding facts and circumstances. [*Salamy v. New York Central Systems*, 146 N.Y.S.2d 814, 817 (N.Y. App. Div. 1955)]

Note that the facts here posited (performance of a condition, intention) are of a lower level of abstraction than those in the examples given at the outset of this paper. Using *imply* with low-level abstractions, as opposed to doctrinally posited facts, is comparatively uncommon in modern legal usage.

Adding still more color to this chameleon-hued word in legal contexts is the ordinary nonlegal sense:

> We do not mean to *imply* that where joint ownership is set up in conformity with the statutory provisions, a court of equity is thereby foreclosed from looking behind the form of the transaction and determining questions of real and beneficial interest as between the parties. [*Frey v. Wubbena*, 185 N.E.2d 850, 855 (Ill. 1962)]

> There is nothing in the former decision that would *imply* that the "sole discretion" vested in and exercised by the trustees in this case is beyond court review. [*In re Ferrall's Estate*, 258 P.2d 1009, 1013 (Cal. 1953) (in bank)]

Similarly, the nonlegal confusion between the words inhabits the legal realm:

> Exclusion from venires focuses on the inherent attributes of the excluded group and *infers* [read *implies*] its inferiority.... [*United States v. Leslie*, 759 F2d 381, 392 (5th Cir. 1985) (en banc) (Garwood, J., dissenting)]

It is not wholly surprising that the legal uses of *imply* have not found a place in English-language dictionaries. Common in American and British law alike, the uses here outlined have not yet spread from legal to nonlegal contexts—and may never do so. Moreover, because lexicographic reading programs seldom glean citations from legal texts, lexicographers often overlook linguistic innovation in law (see Garner "Missing Words"). Any attempt to marshal such a voluminous specialized vocabulary, whatever the scale of the effort, will fail to uncover every new item. But we certainly ought to direct more lexicographic energy into a field as important as law, which affects myriad aspects of everyone's life.

23. *Vice president* and *president*: Syntax and Semantics

JAMES B. McMILLAN
University of Alabama, emeritus

In recent years the lexeme *vice president*, as a result of changes in organizational structures in American business and educational institutions, has undergone syntactic and semantic changes that are (perhaps properly) ignored by dictionaries. The kindred lexeme *president* has also undergone a subtle semantic change that may not call for dictionary notice.

Syntax of *Vice President*

The term *vice president*, old in English, had only one meaning for several centuries, defined in *Webster's Third New International Dictionary* (1961) as "an officer next in rank below a president and acting as president in case of that officer's absence or disability." In the 1930s corporations began appointing more than one vice president and assigning to such officers limited duties, so that *Webster's Third* had to add a second meaning: "one of several officers serving as a president's deputies in charge of particular locations or functions." Since World War II universities have followed the practice of corporations, with vice presidents for finance, development, student affairs, and other functions.

The style of the title varied from, for example, *vice president for finance* or *vice president for the midwest region* to styles with a dash, a hyphen, a comma, or a space between *vice president* and the limiting phrase in the title. In recent years the preposition *of* instead of *for* has become common, as in *vice president of finance* (administration, sales, public relations, etc.) Although there is never a president of finance or public relations, or sales, the anomaly of a vice president of something that has no president has not inhibited spread of the usage.

The *of*-form as recorded originated in newspapers and magazines and is not found on corporate letterheads. The first occurrence that I saw was in a student newspaper, and I assumed it was an undergraduate *lapsus calami* caused by hearing weak articulation of unstressed *for*, but I soon began noticing it in newspapers, including the conservatively edited *Wall Street Journal.* The *American Heritage Dictionary* Second College Edition, generally considered conservative, lists the newer, second meaning of *vice president* and illustrates it with the phrase *vice president of sales*, with no comment on the unorthodox syntax.

The older form with a dash, hyphen, comma, or space between *vice president* and the limiting phrase shows that the preposition is redundant, and redundancy provides the occasion for much syntactic change. The analogical model for the *of*-form is titles like *director of, manager of, dean of, superintendent of, chairman of,* and, of course, *vice president of X Institution.* The following citations, arranged chronologically, illustrate the variety of contexts in which the *of*-form occurs:

1970 Mar. 17 *Wall Street Jour.* 16/4 "Alex B. Owen . . . vice president of the components group [of Litton Industries]."

1973 Feb. 3 *Birmingham* [AL] *Post-Herald* 16/1 "Walter F. Johnsey, the company's vice president of administration and finance."

1974 Aug. 21 *University of Alabama Crimson-White* 3/4 "Dr. Joab Thomas has been appointed vice president of Student Affairs." Ib 3/5 " Dean Neal R. Berte was named vice president of Educational Development."

1975 Arthur Haley *The Moneychangers* 166 "As vice president of public relations, French . . . ran his department knowledgeably." Ib. 325 "The stern, black, handsome vice president of security."

1976 Nov. 9 *Tuscaloosa* [AL] *News* 7/1 "Sutton is the University's vice president of planning and operations."

1977 Apr. 4 *Wall Street Jour.* 20/1 "David L. Litten . . . was elected vice president of the Great Lakes region."

1977 July–Aug. *NRTA News Bulletin* 1/1 "Joan Patota, vice president of public affairs" [at Rhode Island School of Design].

1977 July 6 *New York Times* 45/6 "John M. Farley, vice president of the raw materials division" [of Jones and Laughlin Steel Corporation].

1978 Jan. 13 *Wall Street Jour.* 27/4 "Richard F. Schulte, senior vice president of marketing" [of the Deltona Corp.].

1979 Jan. 1 *Wall Street Jour.* 1/1 "According to Mike Wineblatt, NBC's recently appointed vice president of entertainment."

1983 Nov. 14 *Business Week* 58/1 "Robert M. Scott, 45, who had been vice-president of Porter's automotive parts and industrial hose division."

1989 Oct. 14 *New York Times* 13/2 "The assignment of Ebersol as senior vice president of news, in charge of the 'Today' show."

1993 Sept. 3 *Wall Street Jour.* B2/6 "James R. Collins, 52 years old, was appointed vice president of strategic planning and development of" [E-Systems Inc.]. (The "Who's News" column in the *Wall Street Journal* provides abundant evidence of the continuing occurrence of the variant.)

The *of*-form remains an unofficial style. Leafing through 100 recent corporate annual reports randomly selected, I found not one corporation that used the *of*-form. I have not yet seen it in a catalog of an educational institution, but I have seen it in a letter from a faculty committee addressed to a "Vice President of Academic Affairs" whose letterhead titles him Vice President for Academic Affairs.

Semantics of *Vice President*

The semantic change in the title *vice president* has been in both its denotation and its connotation. In its denotation the phrase *vice president for (of)* does not mean 'deputy' or 'substitute,' so that the term *vice* loses its connection with the *vice* in *vice chancellor, vice consul, vice regent*, and the like. In connotation the title has been devalued. A "vice president for . . ." is not next in rank below a president who acts as a substitute for the president but is the head of a specific division or region. In many universities the treasurer or bursar is now the vice president for finance; the dean of students is now the vice president for student affairs; the assistant to the president for fund raising is now the vice president for development. Banks now have a vice president for legal affairs, for trust operations, for marketing (formerly director of public relations or advertising), and for various other functions.

Aljean Harmetz, a writer in the *New York Times* (1981, May 18, C13/1), reported that in Hollywood "The vice president of [n. b.] production is likely to be the third-, fourth-, or even fifth-ranking executive at a studio." An executive quoted by Harmetz said that "title inflation in the entertainment industry started at the television networks 'where even the guy who pushes the coffee cart is called a vice president. The advertising agencies then made their account executives vice presidents so they'd be on the same level.'"

A standard directory of corporations, *The Corporate 1000* (New York: Monitor Publishing Co., Spring, 1989, V, No. 2) lists for W. R. Grace & Company five executive vice presidents, 12 senior vice presidents, and 31 limited vice presidents, a total of 48; the International Business Machines Corporation has eight senior vice presidents and 42 limited vice presidents, a total of 50; the Proctor & Gamble Company has 14 group vice presidents and 40 limited vice presidents, a total of 54; and Motorola, Inc. has seven executive vice presidents, 21 senior vice presidents, and 45 limited vice presidents, a total of 74. Page after page of the directory shows the proliferation of the title in many kinds of businesses. It is a truism that as a title increases in incidence it declines in prestige (the connotative change).

Semantics and Syntax of *President*

A similar decline in prestige of the title *president* was caused by the rise of the conglomerate in the 1960s. An umbrella corporation may have several presidents of component businesses, who "report to" (in PR euphemistic jargon meaning 'is subordinate to') a *chief executive officer* (*CEO*), or a *chief operating officer* (*COO*), who outranks the presidents. Some companies call the highest-ranking officer *chairman* or *chairman and chief executive officer*, titles which may also outrank *president*.

In the academic world the nearest thing to a conglomerate is a state university system, in which an executive, usually called *chancellor*, outranks the presidents of the component universities. But a state system is not an educational institution; it is a legal entity that doesn't have a campus, a faculty, students, or alumni; the title *president of a state university* retains its prestige.

No syntactic change in the word *president* has occurred except a difference in collocation. Where formerly *president of* was usually followed by the name of a corporation, now it is frequently followed by a noun phrase referring to some component of a corporate conglomerate.

The following citations illustrate the newer use of *president*:

1970 Mar 2 *Wall Street Jour.* 10/3 "Donald N. Johnson, president, insurance operations" [of Aetna Life and Casualty Co.].

1973 Mar. 6 *Wall Street Jour.* 36/4 "Three division presidents and chief executives of this diversified concern were elected vice presidents of the parent" [Walter Kidde & Co.].

1977 July 25 *Wall Street Jour.* 17/3 "James McDermott, president of Levi's womenswear division."

1977 Sept. 4 *Tuscaloosa* [Ala.] *News* A-1/2 "John F. Tynan, manager of the Gayfers Store here since it opened in 1969, has been named president of the six stores in the Montgomery Gayfers group."

1984 Sept. 14 *Wall Street Jour.* 24/2 "Four new vice presidents have been elected by this conglomerate [Litton Industries]. They are Alton J. Brann, president of the guidance and control systems division; Neal P. Cramer, president of the western geophysical division; Richard D. Fleck, president of the data systems division, and Randolph E. Lang, Jr., vice president of the advanced electronic systems group."

1993 Sept. 3 *Wall Street Jour.* B2/5 "Richard A. Pisce III, 44 years old, was named . . . president of the staffing services division of" [Olsten Corp.].

Prospect

Only time can tell whether the *vice president of* style will become official. It is quite possible that if people who write to and about vice presidents continue to use *of*, the form may be adopted by organizations as formal style. Purists may cite logic and tradition in opposition to it, but historical dictionaries and grammars are littered with logical and traditional forms that usage has discarded. The frequency of the construction and its durability (in use for at least 25 years) argue for its survival, even if only as unofficial style.

24. Current Generic Pronoun Usage: Evidence from the Writing of Two Generations

MIRIAM MEYERS
Metropolitan State University, Minneapolis

Interest in "the generic pronoun problem" in English has long been evident in the scholarly literature.[1] Over the last two decades, however, concern for inclusive language has brought generic pronoun usage under unusual scrutiny. During this time, grammarians have reviewed the options available to English speakers and writers historically (Bodine; Baron *Grammar and Gender*), as well as problems inherent in those options (Nunberg "The Decline"). Efforts to suppress forms such as singular *they* and *he or she* have continued, mostly unsuccessfully; linguists such as Lawson, Quirk et al. (*A Comprehensive Grammar*), Cooper ("The Avoidance"), and Meyers ("Forms of") have documented British and American speakers' and writers' continued use of these sex-neutral options. As Sklar writes of singular *they*, "given the choice between agreement in gender and agreement in number, we evidently choose gender over number—in this case, gender indefiniteness" (419).

But to exactly what extent we do so is not known. Some work has been done to document actual generic pronoun choices of writers and speakers. Green, Martyna ("What Does"), Wheeless et al., and Boyd examined college students' writing to discover their usage, and Langendoen did the same with English teachers. Cooper traced changes in usage over the decade of the 1970s in the mass media, in both the U.S.A. and Great Britain. Richmond et al. studied the usage of third- through twelfth-grade student writers and Martyna ("The Psychology") looked at that of kindergarten through college students.

Whitley solicited generic pronouns from American speakers and found them to prefer singular *they* over masculine or feminine pronouns in certain contexts. He acknowledged, however, that singular *they* is probably more common in colloquial English and suggested that written usage "would probably prove more *he*-ful" (37). Whitley further suggested that future researchers consider age as a variable in studies of generic pronoun usage.

Method of the Present Study

This paper reports results of a study of the recent (mid-1980s) generic pronoun usage of Minnesota school-age and adult writers. The adult writing samples came from degree plans filed by upper-division university students of an average age of 34 years. The samples are considered serious pieces of writing because students must produce an acceptable degree plan, reviewed by both faculty and community-based professionals, to achieve B.A. degree candidacy. Each plan includes an introductory statement detailing the writer's views on the subject "What Is the Educated Person?" Besides lending themselves well to investigation of generic pronoun usage, these statements have the advantage of being written in a natural, non-experimental setting.

The youngsters' writing samples also reflect these advantages. They are essays submitted to the *Star Tribune*, a Minneapolis-based Twin Cities newspaper. Monthly, during the school year, the *Star Tribune* invites Minnesota youngsters to submit essays on a particular topic. The paper then publishes selected essays in a special youth feature called "Mindworks." The two sets of essays sampled for this study addressed the topics "What Is the Ideal Teacher?" and "When Is a Person Grownup?" (henceforth to be called the ideal teacher and ordinary grownup groups).

A brief description is in order of the adults and youngsters whose writing was studied. Roughly half the writers in all three samples were female and half male. The adults were mostly residents of the seven-county metropolitan area of Minneapolis/St. Paul. All held at least college junior standing upon admission to the university. Most were employed full-time outside the home, and many had children the age of the youngsters in this study, who ranged in age from seven to sixteen years but were mostly fifth, sixth, and seventh graders between 11 and 12 years of age. About three-quarters of the youngsters attended school in the seven-county metropolitan area and one-quarter in greater Minnesota.

All writing samples were marked and coded for usage characteristics of interest. These data, along with available demographic data, were then analyzed to obtain statistical descriptions of the writers and their usage, as well as tests of significance on particular points of usage.[2]

Results and Discussion

In all three groups, about one-third of the writers used approaches to writing about a hypothetical person that did not require a third singular generic pronoun. Some of these approaches involved repeating the noun, pluralizing the noun, choosing a particular sex openly for the hypothetical person, or projecting the writer or the reader as the hypothetical person. After elimination of those writing samples with other than third singular approaches, the adult sample contained 269 essays and the school-age samples 100 each.

The next area of investigation concerned consistency of approach—whether or not the writer chose and held to one pronoun, or mixed different approaches, making it impossible to categorize the approach precisely. The comparison in the present study indicated that school-age writers were generally no more inconsistent in their pronoun use than were adults. In the most comparable adult/youngster samples—the adults' educated person writing and the youngsters' ideal teacher writing—25% of the adults and 27% of the youngsters were inconsistent. Some writers in both age groups used only one instance of a third singular generic pronoun, so that consistency was not a relevant criterion.

Table 1 details choices of writers in the three groups who did choose and maintain a third singular generic pronoun approach. One can see in this table a real difference in the way the youngsters dealt with the ideal teacher and ordinary grownup topics. The very large proportion of writers in the ordinary grownup group choosing and maintaining singular *they* and ignoring the other options available to them—in particular, masculine, feminine, and *he or she* type pronouns—raises questions. The concept 'grownup' is a more abstract, less immediate, concept than 'teacher' for school-age children; singular *they* may be these youngsters' choice for this more abstract creature and may therefore be a more truly generic pronoun for them than other available options.

Nilsen ("Sexism in") has commented on the tendency of children, when writing about a person of unspecified sex, to use masculine pronouns when they have a male model in mind and feminine pronouns when they have a female model in mind. This tendency may be what's operating in the ideal teacher essays. One twelve-year-old male illustrates in his essay the shift from an overtly male or female model teacher to an unidentified sex-neutral model teacher, with attendant shifts in pronoun use:

An ideal teacher is a person who doesn't allow home-work but will give you enough work to keep you busy during the day. The teacher would be fair to all students.... [I]f the teacher was a woman, she'd have to be fair to the boys as much as the girls. If the teacher was a man he'd have to be fair to the girls. A teacher would never assign you something they didn't understand, and they would always give you study[hall] after they assigned something.

He or she type combinations were perhaps chosen more, too, by youngsters writing on the ideal teacher topic because of direct experience with teachers of both sexes and because teacher preference is of more concern to children than is what it means to be grownup.

One final remark on table 24.1. The two most comparable sets of results are those of adults writing on the educated person and youngsters writing on the ideal teacher. The major differences between the two are that youngsters tended to use more feminine pronouns and adults to use the pronoun *one* more—not surprising differences at all. It is interesting that the youngsters used masculine pronouns over twice as much to describe the ideal teacher as they used feminine pronouns, even though teaching is a female-linked profession.

Table 24.2 shows all the writers' generic pronouns of choice—used consistently or one time only. The same general pattern of usage obtains here as in table 24.1, except that in the ideal teacher group, singular *they* and *he or she* type forms tie for the lead,

TABLE 24.1
Third Singular Generic Pronouns Applied Consistently[a] by Adults and School-Age Writers

Third Singular Generic Pronoun Approach	Adults Educated Person (n = 138)	School-age children Ideal Teacher (n = 49)	School-age children Ordinary Grownup (n = 56)
Singular *they*	32%	27%	87%
Gen. masculine	34	33	7
He/she type forms	22	22	4
Gen. feminine	4	16	2
One	8	2	—
It	—	—	—

a. Writers who used only one instance of a singular generic pronoun throughout their essays were not included in the consistency count.

overtaking the generic masculine. Adults did use more masculine generic pronouns than either of the school-age groups. Furthermore, adult writers used a wider variety of approaches than did either group of youngsters.

Just as adults used more different approaches than did youngsters, so did female adults use more different approaches than did male adults. This finding, detailed in table 24.3, is consistent with other research on generic pronoun usage. Martyna ("What Does"), for example, found that Stanford University female students were more likely than their male counterparts to choose alternatives to the generic masculine, as well as a wider variety of approaches overall. The tendency of the adult female writers in the study reported here to avoid the generic masculine accounts for the probability value of .01 on the chi square test of approach by sex (χ^2 [11, N = 267] = 23.17).

Within the ordinary grownup group of youngsters, a striking difference is girls' use of singular *they*, consistently or one-time-only, at the rate of 86.5%, compared to the boys' rate of only 50%. In addition, boys in this group were more inconsistent and used masculine generic and *he or she* type pronouns more than did girls. Though the ideal teacher group demonstrated some of these same differences by sex, none are of the magnitude of the differences in the ordinary grownup group.

A difference worth pointing out in that group is the extent to which males used masculine pronouns and females feminine pro-

TABLE 24.2
Third Singular Generic Pronouns Applied Consistently or One Time Only by Adults and School-age Writers

Third Singular Generic Pronoun Approach	*Adults Educated Person* (n = 202)	*School-age children*	
		Ideal Teacher (n = 73)	*Ordinary Grownup* (n = 87)
Singular *they*	29.7%	30.1%	79.3%
Gen. masculine	34.6	21.9	8.8
He/she type forms	23.2	30.1	1.5
Gen. feminine	4.4	16.4	1.1
one	7.4	1.3	—
it	.5	—	—

TABLE 24.3
Approach by Sex to Generic Pronoun Choices of Adult and School-age Writers

Third Singular Generic Pronoun Approach	Adults Educated Person (n = 267)		School-age children Ideal Teacher (n = 85)		Ordinary Grownup (n = 100)	
	female	male	female	male	female	male
Singular *they*	15.6	17.5	21.1	8.5	61.5	35.4
Sing. *they* once	7.1	4.8	7.9	6.4	25.0	14.6
Inconsistent	26.2	23.8	21.1	34.0	7.7	18.8
Gen. masculine	14.2	21.4	10.5	25.5	1.9	6.3
Gen. masc. once	4.3	13.5	—	—	—	6.3
He/she type forms	12.1	8.7	10.5	8.5	1.9	2.1
He/she once	7.1	5.6	10.5	8.5	—	16.7
Gen. feminine	4.3	—	13.2	4.3	1.9	—
Gen. fem. once	2.1	—	5.3	4.3	—	—
it	—	—	—	—	—	—
it once	.7	—	—	—	—	—

nouns in describing their ideal teacher. This pattern by sex provides some support for the idea that young writers choose generic pronouns consistent with their own sex.

Table 24.4 shows the percentage of writers in each sample using singular *they* or any feminine pronoun at least once—whether freestanding or in *he or she* type combinations, consistently or inconsistently. The table shows in effect the extent to which these traditionally proscribed forms appear in the writing of two generations. Again, it is in the ordinary grownup group that singular *they* prevailed most dramatically, with 81% of the youngsters using the pronoun at least once. Yet 45% of the ideal teacher group did this as well. As for the higher feminine pronoun use in the ideal teacher group, it cannot be attributed to females alone, since 8.6% of the male youngsters in that group used feminine pronouns exclusively, reflecting perhaps their experience with female teacher models. While no males in the ordinary grownup group used feminine pronouns exclusively, males accounted for 78% of all feminine pronoun users in that sample when *he or she* type combinations are considered. This, probably more than any other

TABLE 24.4
Percentage of Writers in Each Group Using Singular *they* or a Feminine Pronoun at Least Once

	Singular they	*Feminine pronoun*
Adults ("Educated Person")	39%	35%
Youngsters ("Ideal Teacher")	45%	58%
Youngsters (Ordinary Grownup)	81%	23%

factor, was responsible for the statistically significant difference (χ^2 [1, N = 100] = 9.44, p < .002) in feminine pronoun use by males and females in the ordinary grownup data.

The results reported in this table and others contrast with those of Richmond et al. in which both female and male youngsters depended heavily on masculine pronouns in writing about a gender-neutral person. Whether the differences in their group and the Minnesota group are due to region, nature of materials examined, or other variables is not clear but is worthy of further investigation.

This study indicates that topic makes a difference in generic pronoun use—at least for the youngsters studied here. The indefinite nominal *grownup* elicits singular *they*, while *ideal teacher* elicits more of a variety of options, including many more masculine, feminine, and *he or she* type forms, similar to the distribution of options chosen by adults writing on "the educated person." This may suggest that some sex-indefinite nominals are more sex-indefinite than others. Or, to put it another way, singular *they* may be more truly generic than other third singular generic pronoun options. The study further indicates that while singular *they* use declines with age and education, it still competes strongly with generic masculine forms in the written usage of adult writers with two or three years of college. Finally, a comparison of these findings with those of other researchers suggests that usage of *he or she* type forms is increasing.

Notes

1. An earlier version of this paper was read at the American Dialect Society annual meeting 30 December 1989, Washington, DC. A more

detailed report of the adult usage may be found in Meyers "Adult Writers'" and "Current Generic."

2. I am indebted to the Center of Youth Development and Research at the University of Minnesota for access to the Mindworks essay archives and in particular to Rebecca Satio for her hospitality. Leah Harvey, academic dean at Metropolitan State University, gave generously of her time to consult on statistical analysis and to provide moral support during all stages of the study.

25. The Unmarked Plural Noun Following Compound Adjective Phrases

AVIS KUWAHARA PAYNE
New Mexico State University

In the English language a regular, countable noun, such as *mushroom* or *computer*, is made plural when it refers to two or more of its kind, as in *mushrooms* or *computers*. In fact, it is sometimes difficult to persuade a newcomer to the language that we have exceptions to this rule, as in *fish* or *information*.

However, there is an instance in which native speakers do not—actually, refuse to—pluralize a regular, countable noun that is indisputably plural in meaning and is clearly followed by a plural verb. This is the case in which a noun is not marked as plural after adjective phrases joined by *and* as in "A diseased and a healthy branch were knocked off the tree"; a native speaker would never say "A diseased and a healthy branches were knocked off the tree."

In *Syntax*, the second volume of *A Modern English Grammar on Historical Principles*, Jespersen notes what we readily accept as a basic rule of modern-day English:

> 1. A substantive with two or more adjectives (or other adjuncts) joined by *and* and indicating each a separate thing or individual is fairly regularly put in the plural: the eighteenth and nineteenth centuries (= the 18th century and the 19th century).... (73)

However, on occasion in English, too, the noun may remain uninflected, though countable in type and plural in reference, as Jespersen shows us (75, 491):

> 2. the canonicall bookes of the old and new *testament* [Francis Bacon, *The New Atlantic*, 1900]
> 3. no better lyrics than he could find in the Old and New *Version* [George Eliot, *Adam Bede*, 1900 (1859)]
> 4. His grandfathers on the maternal and paternal *side* [Horace A. Vachell, *The Hill*, 1905]
> 5. In the sixteenth and to a great extent in the seventeenth *century* [Henry Bradley, *The Making of English*, 1904]
> 6. we see in the seventeenth and still more in the eighteenth *century* a period [John R. Seeley, *The Expansion of England*, 1883]

7. The eldest and the youngest *child* of the family sat at the piano in the act of performing a duet. [Arnold Bennett, *Clayhanger*, 1912]

In the cases of (5–6), Jespersen says "the reason of the [singular] is the qualifying addition to the second adjective" (75). He maintains that "obscurity can be avoided by the use of the [singular] in such collocations" (75), as we see especially in (7) where we particularly appreciate how the use of the singular noun avoids obscuring the number of eldest and youngest children. Note that the noun phrases in question here all begin with a definite article, in some cases repeated before the second modifying phrase. Note also that with the exceptions of (5–6) we would today probably pluralize all the nouns in question in (2–7) above. Jespersen's explanation regarding (5–6) seems to hold for present-day speakers.

In his *Syntax*, George O. Curme sees the definite article and the plural marking of the noun as significantly affecting meaning:

8. *the* red and white rose (one rose with two colors)
9. *the* red and *the* white rose (two roses, each with only one color)
10. *the* red and white roses (a number of roses, each of which is red and white)
11. *the* red and *the* white roses (a number of roses, some of which are all red and others of which are all white)

Jespersen and Curme were writing sixty years ago. Today, even at the cost of ambiguity as in the cases of (9) and (11), we would usually pluralize all the nouns in (2–7) and (9–11), with (8) alone being singular in reference, although we would probably consider Jespersen's and Curme's examples well formed. (Jespersen's [5–6] are possible exceptions, as discussed above.)

Confirming the plural meaning of the nouns in question, both Jespersen and Curme show us instances of an unmarked plural subject followed by a distinctly plural verb:

12. The elder and the younger son of the house of Crawley were never at home together. [William M. Thackeray, *Vanity Fair*, 1890 (1847)] (Jespersen 75)
13. *The* red and *the* white *rose* are both beautiful. (Curme 59)

Today, (12–13) would usually have plural subjects and would consequently not merit notice for lack of agreement between subject and verb, though these sentences are well formed for us. In other words, while we might not generate Jespersen's and Curme's sentences ourselves, we might not notice someone else producing them in conversation.

While the definite article does not mark number, the indefinite article does, and current English usage attests to the seemingly anomalous occurrence of a singular noun as the subject of a plural verb.

> 14. A coniferous and deciduous tree grow nearby.
> 15. *A coniferous and deciduous trees grow nearby.

This usage did not escape Jespersen. He notes the plural verb in (12) and elsewhere comments, "The singular [noun] is regularly found when the indefinite article is repeated with each adjunct" (74), with examples:

> 16. two styles essentially distinct . . . a speaking and a writing style [W. G. Collingwood, *Life of John Ruskin*, 1905]
> 17. there were two, an upper and a lower shoal [Rudyard Kipling, *The Second Jungle Book*, 1897]
> 18. anxiety recognizes a better and a worse alternative [Thomas Hardy, *Far from the Madding Crowd*, 1906 (1874)]

Actually, any singular determiner prevents the noun it modifies from bearing plural marking if the determiner occurs in the last adjective phrase before the head noun.

> 19. The blue, the red, and a green ribbon need trimming.
> 20. The deciduous and this coniferous tree grow fast.
> 21. The blue and each gold stripe need touching up.
> 22. All the striped and one spotted rug are new.
> 23. Those warm and the one cold beaker need rinsing.

(We will not discuss the occurrence of the singular verb in sentences with distributive quantifiers, such as "Every zebra and giraffe has its own feeding schedule.")

Also, the singular determiner directly modifies the head noun and not a constituent of the adjective phrase:

> 24. A one-foot, two-foot, and three-foot fir tree are growing near the fence.

But consider:

> 25. A thousand accordion players are performing in the Los Angeles Coliseum tonight.

In (25) *thousand* modifies the head noun, but the indefinite article does not. In (24) *one, two,* and *three* do not modify the head noun, but the indefinite article does, though here in surface form the *a* is deleted optionally before the last adjective phrase.

It is not, however, just a singular determiner that prevents surface pluralization of the head noun. Curme says, "The verb is in the plural where there is an article or other limiting adjective before each of the descriptive adjectives to indicate that two . . . things are described. . . . Similarly, the verb is in the plural after a singular noun modified by two possessive adjectives referring to different persons: *Your and my wife* (or more commonly *your wife and mine*) *are good friends*" (59). Of course, Curme is not completely correct here. The "two possessive adjectives referring to different persons" do not decide number:

26. His and my spouse are colleagues.
27. *His and my fishing rod are in the car.

We would not say (27) but rather:

28. His and my fishing rod is in the car.
29. His and my fishing rods are in the car.

depending on whether we are talking about one or more fishing rods. In (26) part of the definition of spouse is the non-linguistic, legal restriction that in our society a person may have only one spouse. Presumably, in a polygamous or polyandrous society where ambiguity might exist, (30) might be well formed:

30. His and my spouses are colleagues.

It would be comfortable to ignore sentences like (26) because we could account for the unmarked plural noun in other sentences by a phrase structure rule:

In English, a surface head noun that is plural in reference is not marked as plural when it is preceded by a singular determiner modifying the head noun and no non-singular determiner modifying the noun occurs between the singular determiner and the noun.

Sentence (26), however, shows us that semantic reference, too, not just syntactic structure, affects an unmarked plural noun modified by compound adjective phrases.

We sometimes think we have three separate disciplines in semantics, syntax, and morphology; that is to say, meaning, sentence structure, and word formation are discrete linguistic entities. The structures we have been looking at show us that these subfields of linguistics are inseparable. We know the head noun is not marked as plural; that is to say, its morphology is not what we expect, given the rule of English that a regular, countable noun that is plural in reference is marked as plural; *tree* is about as regular and as countable an English noun as we find and yet is certainly not marked as plural in sentences such as (20) and (24). The semantics of (20) and (24), however, tell us that the subject of the sentence is plural; hence, the morphology of the main verb is plural. It is in the syntax of these structures, the restricting influence of a singular determiner, that we find the cause of the anomalous occurrence of a singular noun serving as the subject of a plural verb; it is in the semantics of these structures, too, that we find that the meaning of a noun can result in the same anomalous lack of agreement between subject and verb.

26. Is *between you and I* Good English?

RICHARD K. REDFERN
Clarion University of Pennsylvania, emeritus

Whatever is in general use in a language is for that very reason grammatically correct. [Henry Sweet, *New English Grammar*]

Like *ain't* and the double negative, *between you and I* is considered poor English, though it is used by millions of native speakers of the language. In discussing *ain't,* Dwight Bolinger calls "the proscription against it . . . unreasonable" (55). In discussing the double negative, Thomas Pyles and John Algeo say that "we lost a useful device for emphasis when it was arbitrarily outlawed" (22). Is it too late to recognize that *between you and I* is an established idiom that does not deserve condemnation? After eight years of collecting oral and written instances of the "wrong" pronoun in coordinate phrases, it seems to me that *between you and I* should be accepted as good English.

To mention first the most common occurrence, I have 125 examples of prepositional phrases in which *I* occurs instead of the *me* that school grammar calls for.[1] Here are three:

There is a brother between Mark and I. [a Grinnell College senior whose father is an American ambassador]

It was so nice for Nancy and I to go off together. [a woman with a bachelor's degree from Mount Holyoke and a master's degree from Yale][2]

The next step is for Jud, Jack, and I to talk it over. [a college English teacher with a bachelor's degree from the University of Illinois and a master's and PhD from Cornell—i.e., the author]

In addition, I have collected a dozen sentences involving other pronouns—for example:

People like you and we might vote for Anderson. [a woman with a bachelor's degree in German and a master's in library science]

In coordinate phrases which can be classified as direct objects, subjective case pronouns (almost always *I*) often occur as the second element in the coordination. Here are two of the 67 examples I have collected:

I want you and he to discuss it. [an English professor and Fulbright recipient who has served as department chairman in a college and a university]

... and it would let you and I and other people know where to go to register. [then President Jimmy Carter in a nationally broadcast radio address]

The six examples above are from speech, but I also have some from writing: "Thank you so much for taking care of Anne and I while we were in Clarion" (a Harvard junior in a thank-you note).

A coordinate phrase that functions as an indirect object is rare, but I have collected 11 in which the second element is a subject case pronoun—for example:

They denied my wife and I an enjoyable visit. [former Senator Barry Goldwater]

If my observations are correct, native speakers of English—whether British or American, whether well or poorly educated—say *between you and I* and the like unless they have been schoolmastered into using *me* instead of *I*. A professor of English, in a letter to me about this matter, referred to "the frequent occurrence of *I* where I have been trained to use *me*."[3] This tendency to use *I* unless we have been told to use *me* suggests an idiomatic quality about *I* which may be more significant than the "rule" of grammar which is cited to prove that *me* is correct. The *I* is idiomatic because it comes from our sprachgefuehl (the feeling that we have for our native language).

Almost all handbooks and grammars, however, say that *between you and I* is, as Frederick Crews puts it, "a mistake for '*between you and me*'" (408). As might be expected, many books offer an explanation for this "mistake." Overcorrection is the most widely accepted theory, and Henry Sweet's explanation in 1891 is probably one of the earliest:

As such expressions as *it is me* are still denounced as incorrect by the grammars, many people try to avoid them in speech as well as writing. The result of this reaction is that the *me* in such constructions as *between you and me, he saw John and me* sounds vulgar and ungrammatical, and is consequently corrected into *I* occasionally in speech, but oftenest in writing. [*New English Grammar*, 341]

Margaret Nicholson, who is unconscionably severe in using "illiterate" to describe "between you and I," writes that the *I* "perhaps results from a hazy remembrance of hearing *you and me* corrected in the subjective" (55). W. Nelson Francis and many others also subscribe to the overcorrection theory (*The English Language* 248). W. P. Lehmann's explanation resembles Sweet's: "Having been taught to substitute *I* for *me* in sentences like 'It wasn't me,' we go on to say 'with Mary and I'" (228).

A variant of this explanation has been suggested by several friends. After being corrected for mentioning themselves first, as in "Me and John are going outside," children switch to "John and I," even in the object position. This theory is supported by a conversation between a nine-year-old girl and her biology professor-father, a friend of mine who takes pride in remembering the rules of politeness he learned in school or at home. The conversation refers to a rubber ball:

Nine-year-old: Give it to me and Cindy.
Father: What?
Nine-year-old: Give it to me and Cindy.
Father (sternly): What?
Nine-year-old: Give it to Cindy and I.
Father: That's better.

Although Simeon Potter also cites overcorrection as a cause, he has an analysis that may be more attractive. After mentioning the frequency of *between you and I,* he says that the *I* occurs because our "feeling that the preposition *between* governs the objective case in the pronoun has grown so feeble that it cannot stand the slight shock of separation imparted by *you and* intervening." Potter also points out that, in Modern English, unlike Old English, there is "a weakening of the feeling for government or regimen . . . in the relation-axis construction" such as "between you and *I/me*" (118–19).

A different kind of explanation was offered in 1870 by E. A. Abbott. Referring to "irregularities" in Shakespeare's use of personal pronouns—e.g., *I* for *me*, as in "Here's none but thee and I" (*2 Henry VI;* I, ii, 69)—he said: "It is perhaps impossible to trace a law in these irregularities." In the next sentence, however, he offered his own suggestion, that the *I* in these phrases may be chosen rather than the *me* because euphony and emphasis win out over grammar (139).

Many books say or imply that *I* is wrong because *between* (or another preposition, or a verb) governs the case of the personal pronoun occurring after the coordinating conjunction. I question the validity of this analysis. In particular, I object to the familiar "proof": we don't say "Give it to I"; therefore, we can't say "Give it to George and I." Because it analyzes a coordination as if it were not a coordination, this is no proof at all.

Other explanations may be more plausible since they are not based on the idea that a preposition or verb governs the case of all pronouns in a coordinate phrase. Among British scholars, Sir Ernest Gowers says, in his revision of Fowler's *Modern English Usage*, that the *and I* behaves as if it were "a suffix to the preceding word, forming a composite whole not admitting of inflexion" (258). Sweet had written earlier that *you and I* had been "so frequently joined together as nominatives . . . that the three words formed a sort of group-compound, whose last element became invariable" in constructions such as *between you and I* (340–41). Eric Partridge takes a similar position when he writes that *you and I* in *between you and I* and *Bill, Harry, Mary and I* in *He actively dislikes Bill, Harry, Mary and I* are "apprehended as units, or, at worst, as physical pluralities serving as psychological units" (*A Charm of Words*, 34). Randolph Quirk and his co-authors, after suggesting that the *I* may result from overcorrection, add: "Another reason is that *you and I* is felt to be a unit, which can remain unchanged, particularly with the distance between the preposition and *I*" (*A Grammar of* 210–11).

An American scholar, J. J. Lamberts, referring to expressions like *Jane and I* or *him and me*, observes: "Whether we approve or not, the language often operates with such unanalyzed units, moving them intact to either subject or object position, especially if the first member of the unit happens to be a proper noun or other expression" (165).

These explanations are perceptive, and there are others. Otto Jespersen suggested that the subjective case pronouns may be chosen because of "the feeling that a word was virtually the subject (of a latent verb)." From standard authors, mostly British—for example, Fielding, Dickens, and Meredith—he cites some two dozen sentences containing coordinate phrases in which a subject pronoun, usually *I*, occurs instead of the object pronoun "which traditional grammar requires" (VII: 236). One of Jespersen's examples comes from Rose Macaulay's *Keeping Up Appearances* (1928): "it made Dad and I laugh" (VII: 237–38).

Jespersen uses the term "notional subject" for his conjecture about the pronoun being the subject of a latent verb. In contrast, there are many sentences in which a verb in plain sight might appear to have as its subject a coordinate phrase which is in object position. For example, the coordinate phrase in a sentence cited earlier ("People like you and we might vote for Anderson") can be thought of not only as the object of the preposition *like* but also as a new subject, as if "you and we" were the only subject of "might vote for Anderson," replacing or cancelling out "People like" in that split-second operation that the brain performs in choosing words.

Considerably different is an analysis by Samuel J. Keyser and Paul M. Postal. In referring to sentences such as "Marsha spoke to Harry and I," they say,

> *I* with a conjoined NP [noun phrase] is not subject to the *subject* condition. The conjoined NP containing *I* does not have to be a subject (though it can be one). ... For many speakers, the occurrence of *me* and *I* in coordinated NPs does not follow the rules for independent *me* and *I* but is subject to peculiar rules of its own. [17]

Thus, considerable thought has been given to accounting for the *I* in these phrases whose age and frequency are well established. *The Oxford English Dictionary* (second edition) gives eleven examples, the first of which, dated 1596, is a line from Shakespeare's *Merchant of Venice*: "All debts are cleerd betweene you and I" (591). *'Tween you and I,* according to Abbott, "seems to have been a regular Elizabethan idiom" (139). Jespersen says that "the combination *between you and I* has been frequent from ElE [Elizabethan English] to the present day" (273). H. C. Wyld, who gives four examples from the seventeenth and eighteenth centuries that are not in the *OED*, writes: "It is not uncommon at the present time to hear *I* used instead of *me* after a Verb or Preposition, as though the speaker wished to avoid the latter form" (331). Sterling A. Leonard cites an eighteenth-century work, *Lexiphanes*, in which *between you and I* was considered ungrammatical even though it was "almost universally used in familiar conversation, and sometimes by our best comic writers: see Wycherley's *Plain Dealer*" (188).

Other books confirm the frequency of the usage in the twentieth century. G. H. Vallins says that "'between you and I' has become standardized in modern usage" (61), and an American handbook uses the term "set phrase" for *between you and I* (Emery et al., 76). Robert C. Pooley says: "Every observer of cultivated usage is aware of the popular preference for the phrase *you and I* regardless of case" (V. McDavid 57).

Probably only a well-planned survey can establish beyond doubt that most native speakers of English, unless they have been schooled to do otherwise, use *I* or another subject pronoun after a coordinator in phrases in object position. Meanwhile, the explanations and suggestions by students of grammar and usage in England and the United States are worth further study: the explanation by Sweet, Gowers (H. W. Fowler), and others about *and I* as a noninflected suffix, Jespersen's suggestion about the notional subject, Abbott's suggestion that euphony and emphasis produce *and I,* Lamberts' observation about "unanalyzed units," and Keyser and Postal's statement about the "peculiar rules" which affect *I* and *me* in coordinate phrases.[4]

The important question is not whether one and only one of these explanations is correct but whether it is time to challenge the axiom or rule that a preposition or verb governs the case of all personal pronouns in a coordinate phrase in object position. That rule is not immutable truth, and it should be challenged because it requires native speakers to use personal pronouns in an unidiomatic way. Challenges will arise, however, only if there is greater recognition of sprachgefuehl, the principle that underlies the explanations mentioned above. Sprachgefuehl or language-feeling is a term similar to "linguistic sense," Sweet's phrase meaning "the faculty by which we instinctively know whether a certain form or construction is in accordance with the genius of the language or not."[5] To put the idea in another way, the desire to obey a rule—specifically, the rule that only the objective form of the pronoun is correct in phrases like *between you and I/me*—is so strong that the idiomatic use of *I,* based on our sprachgefuehl, is assumed to be wrong, despite its frequency in the speech of people of all social classes.

The conflict between prescriptive grammar and idiom shows up occasionally in the speech of those with considerable formal education, people who have trained themselves to use the objective form of the pronoun after the conjunction in these phrases. On at least four occasions I have heard a well-educated speaker use *I,* as in "He has asked Ed and I to visit his classes" (said by a college dean who was formerly an English professor), only to change *I* to *me* immediately. It is probably a misuse of the verb *correct* to say that such a speaker is correcting his speech because as Leonard Bloomfield wrote long ago

> the only danger that threatens the native speaker of a standard language is artificiality; if he is snobbish, priggish, or timid, he may fill his speech (at least, when he is on his good behavior) with spelling-pronunciations and grotesque "correct" forms. The speaker to whom the standard language is native, will hardly ever find good reason for replacing a form that is natural to him. [498]

It is time for all of us to accept a suggestion made by the authors of a British study of usage:

> If we can live comfortably—as we seem to do—with alternative spellings of words like *judg(e)ment* or *realise/realize* and with rival pronunciations of words like *controversy*, why should we not tolerate equally *averse to/averse from, under* or *in the circumstances, different from, to* or even *than, between you and me* or *I*, and so on. [Mittins et al, 114]

It is time to recognize that *between you and I* is good English.

Notes

1. In this article I consider only coordinate phrases in object position in which a subject pronoun occurs *after* the coordinator. My collection also includes examples of subjective case pronouns *before* the coordinator such as "for he and his wife" (said by an English teacher with a master's degree).

2. Those interested in the Queen's and King's English can compare sentences uttered by Queen Elizabeth II, "It is a wonderful moment for my husband and I" (Foster 219), and her father, King George VI, "for either you or I" (Pyles 255).

3. Letter dated 9 Dec. 1977.

4. More than one linguist has questioned the assumption that distinctive case forms in the personal pronouns are eternal verities. In speaking of personal pronouns, Edward Sapir says: "It does not follow that the case distinction as such is still vital" (166).

5. Quoted by R. A. Close (15).

27. *Absent* 'without':
A New American English Preposition

ALAN R. SLOTKIN
Tennessee Technological University

In the summer of 1983, I encountered a front-page article in the *St. Louis Post Dispatch* (22 Aug. 1983) that included the following quotation attributed to Joseph M. Kelly, assistant to the vice president of the Communication Workers, District 6: "Absent any unexpected developments, we should be in a posture of agreement by 11:59 Wednesday night." An informal survey of my colleagues at the start of the academic year showed, as I expected, that many English instructors considered the quoted construction either awkward, stilted, or jargon. While the appearance of *absent* in this and like constructions may have been neither very new nor unexpected, its usage had both relatively uncertain status and relatively uncertain origin. For these reasons, perhaps, *absent* has failed to gain inclusion in the listed prepositions of any current handbook of grammar that I have found.

Historically, *absent* has functioned primarily as an adjective synonymous with *missing* or, with stress shift, a reflexive transitive verb with the meaning of 'be away.' These two standard uses are amply demonstrated and attested to by most modern dictionaries and glossaries of usage. Indeed, of thirty-three dictionaries and manuals that I examined in 1983, thirty-one listed these—and only these—uses for *absent*. Contrary to the traditional verbal and adjectival usages indicated by most current and standardly used dictionaries, both the 1961 *Webster's Third New International Dictionary* (W3) and the then just-published 1983 *Webster's Ninth New Collegiate Dictionary* (WC9) listed an additional meaning for *absent*: as a preposition meaning 'in the absence of, without'—hence Mr. Kelly's "absent any unexpected developments." Interestingly, the *OED2* (the newly revised *OED*) does half-heartedly acknowledge *absent*'s prepositional usage, defining the term as 'in absence of, without,' but labels it as a "quasi-preposition" and relegates it to United States usage "chiefly Law." The citations in support of quasi-prepositional *absent* range in date from 1948 to 1983 and all are in such legal contexts as the following:

We think it clear that under this definition, *absent* any other facts, there arises. . . .
[*Rep. Supreme Court S. Dak.* (1948) LXX, 191]

Although certainly less prestigious than the *OED*, Harry Shaw's *Dictionary of Problem Words and Expressions* not only acknowledges the prepositional use of *absent* but also suggests, as my earlier article (Slotkin "*Absent* 'Without'") does, that one possible source of this shifted use may well be the ellipsis of phrases or clauses in which *absent* functioned as a participle. Shaw (55) states,

This word has taken on a relatively new meaning. As a preposition it is now frequently used to mean "lacking" or "without": "*Absent* certain details the coroner refused to render a verdict." The same general use is apparent in *granted* ("admitted") and in *given* (meaning "with"): "*Granted* I owe you the money, I can't repay you now." "*Given* the rate of inflation, my salary is really shrinking." Each such use involves ellipsis (something left out but understood): "if these plans are absent," "if it be granted," "if we are given the present state of affairs."

Millward (*Handbook* 274) reinforces the idea of shifted usage not only by commenting on both the increasing number of prepositions in Present-Day English and their unstable meanings and usage, but also by noting that these "new prepositions have developed primarily from participial forms of verbs (*pending, granted*) and from noun phrases that include older prepositions (*in return for, on the basis of,* [*in the absence of*])." The newest American unabridged dictionary, the *Random House,* Second Edition (*RH2*), does give both adjectival and prepositional labels to *absent* and cites as context for prepositional *absent* 'in the absence of; without' a sentence with less legal than socio-economic substance: "Absent some catastrophe, stock market prices should soon improve."

Does *absent* truly function in English now as a preposition? Or is that prepositional label simply a misinterpretation of an inverted absolute construction with deleted copula? Or, finally, is the latter label misapplied to a form that, through semantic similarity, has achieved participial status for some speakers? Each interpretation has some degree of plausibility, yet each has its problem. While most early, legal-political jargon uses of prepositional *absent* can be explained as inverted absolute constructions, the subsequent extension of prepositional use to more generalized contexts involves surface structures that do not seem to be transformations of absolutes. Moreover, the semantic overlapping of *missing, lacking, absent,* and true prepositional *without* and the functional overlapping of verbal and adjectival *missing* and *lacking* may have contributed to *absent*'s designation as a preposition by some standard dictionaries in recognition of apparent analogic shifting of the form's use.

In response to my inquiry concerning the basis for the *W3* and *WC9* designation of *absent* as a preposition, Frederick C. Mish, Editorial Director for Merriam-Webster Inc., kindly provided fifteen citations ranging in date from 1945 to 1980 (letter to the author, 23 Mar. 1984). Of these, the first eleven appear in legal or quasi-legal contexts and for which the following examples will establish the general pattern:

> 1. We think it clear, continued the Supreme Court, that under this definition, absent any other facts, there arises an implied contract that the patient will pay. [*Journal of the American Medical Association*, 24 Feb. 1945, 483]
> 2. Absent such a reservation, only the Court of Claims has jurisdiction to hear. [*Bare v. U.S.*, 107 F. Supp. 551, 17 Nov. 1952]
> 3. He's got the right, absent any specific statutory prohibition. [Unnamed lawyer, quoted in *The New York Times*, 17 Apr. 1976, 23A]

Given such contexts, Mish noted that my hypothesis that prepositional *absent* could well have developed from an absolute construction seems probable; however, Mish also stated an important caveat:

> I would feel surer of this if the standard law dictionaries recorded a lot of Latin phrases beginning with *absente*. They do not, in fact; *absente reo* is the only one. Still, a person who had the mental habit of rendering this as "absent the defendant" instead of "the defendant being absent" or "in the absence of the defendant" or "since [or while] the defendant is absent" might easily extend the use of *absent* in the belief that it was a neat, concise (even elegant?) turn of phrase.

Additional investigation of standard law dictionaries, including *Words and Phrases* (1964) and *Corpus Juris Secundum* (1936), only served to reinforce the picture of *absent* as verb or adjective along the same lines noted in most conventional dictionaries. Moreover, David Mellinkoff, Professor of Law at UCLA and author of *The Language of Law*, comments only that the prepositional usage noted in *W3* is "a commonplace in a legal usage . . . , [lawyers being] apt to say, e.g. 'Absent malice there can be no recovery,' 'Absent fraud,' etc." (letter to the author, 9 Apr. 1984).

Absent in all of the quasi-legal, legal, and governmental contexts supplied by Mish and reinforced by Mellinkoff can clearly be interpreted as the result of the inversion of an absolute construction with concurrent copula deletion. One can easily transform "absent such a reservation" back to *such a reservation being absent* with no loss of sense (or, to use Shaw's pattern of ellipsis and inversion, *if such a reservation were absent*). In such contexts, to call *absent* a true preposition seems to ignore the realities of stylistic transformations. Mish, however, also supplied four examples that seemed to indicate that an extended contextual domain for *absent* was developing during the late 1970s:

> 4. In a world absent politics and biology, they'd be chasing Tammy Mercer to do Kool-Aid commercials in a couple of years. [Jonathan Even Maslow, *Saturday Review*, 26 Nov. 1977, 50]
> 5. But absent that prickly pair, bad luck and bad management, almost all of the problems will be dealt with reasonably satisfactorily. ["Front Runners," *Saturday Review*, 7 July 1979, 8]
> 6. Absent strong pressures from society or religion to stay tied, we must exert ourselves. [Carl Tucker, "The Back Door: Special Delivery," *Saturday Review*, 1 Sept. 1979, 56]
> 7. Absent the regulations, it's another generation of kids down the drain. [Gerald F. Seib, *The Wall Street Journal*, 9 Oct. 1980, 28]

While quotations 5–7 lack the quasilegal element of the earliest citations provided by Mish, the same use of the inverted absolute seems the most probable interpretation for the usage of *absent*. Quotation 4, however, presents a more complex situation, not only because of the more generalized use of the form in relation to social changes, but also because, as Mish's letter notes, the phrase "has lost all color of the absolute construction. It is neither an introductory phrase nor an interrupter; it is an ordinary adjective prepositional phrase modifying *world*." Indeed, unlike the other contexts, it is difficult to take the phrasing of "In a world absent politics and biology, they'd be chasing" and transform it with added copula into a form that is reasonably natural. *Politics and biology being absent in a world, they'd be chasing* appears too awkward to be an accurate rendition of the underlying structure of a transformed absolute. In this one instance, then, *absent* does appear to have achieved true prepositional status. Such a development is particularly significant, since Greenbaum (*A College Grammar* 104) continues to place prepositions among the closed classes of English words, those classes which "rarely admit new words," and since most dictionaries, glossaries, and handbooks appear loath to allow new prepositions to have more than marginal status.

If this change in usage for *absent* is indeed change in progress, it appears to stem, moreover, from two possible grammatical analogies based on semantic similarity. In most usual adverbial clauses and phrases of condition, again, one expects to find either the present participle of a verb, as in *Excluding any unexpected developments*, or a preposition, as in *Without any unexpected developments*, functioning in the position of Mr. Kelly's *absent* in the quotation which began my investigation. An additional possibility, however, is for the adverbial phrase or clause to be the inversion of an absolute construction, as in the following: *Any unexpected developments being missing* → *missing any unexpected developments*; or, *Any unexpected developments being absent* → *absent any unexpected developments*.

Clearly, Mr. Kelly's sentence follows a standard introductory adverbial phrase pattern in which either (a) a preposition or a present participle of a verb appears as the introductory element or (b) an inverted absolute appears as the introductory element. Thus the sentence introducer might, depending on interpretation, be described in any of the following three ways: (1) preposition + determiner + adjective + noun; (2) present participle + determiner + adjective + noun; or (3) determiner + adjective + noun + *be* + *ing* + adjective → adjective + determiner + adjective + noun. In the instance of a single-word preposition as first element, the phrasal structure of the original sentence would allow the following sample list of introductory prepositional elements, but of which only *without* and its French loan-equivalent *sans* do not alter the sense of the quotation: *without, after, against, before, sans, notwithstanding, despite*. In the instance of a participial opener, the structure would allow, among many others, the following: *avoiding, contravening, excepting, eliminating, examining, ignoring, overcoming, lacking, missing*. In the instance of an inverted absolute as introductory element, only those adjectives which are semantically possible and which can be placed in the context after *being* are plausible. Thus the list would include the participles and plain adjectives *lacking, missing, absent,* but would similarly exclude *avoiding, contravening, excepting, eliminating, examining, ignoring, overcoming*—which clearly cannot occur in that context, since these are present participles of verbs for which the past participle functions as the adjectival element in absolute constructions.

The apparent shift in the use of *absent* to a preposition in general American English probably stems from the semantic similarity and overlapping of *absent, missing/lacking,* and *without.* The standard dictionary definitions alone show that a considerable degree of semantic compatibility exists for these forms. *Without* is normally defined as a preposition meaning 'not with; lacking.' Similarly, *lacking* is defined as 'being missing' or 'being without.' *Missing,* moveover, is defined both as an adjective meaning 'absent' or 'lacking' and, based on the definitions for the verb *to miss,* as a participle meaning 'failing to encounter.' Finally, *absent* denotes 'not present' or 'lacking.' The obvious problem of the semantic boundaries of these forms, combined with, in the case of *missing,* an identity of surface spellings for two underlyingly differing semantic forms, may have caused the transference of *absent* from adjective to preposition. Since surface similarity and/or semantic compatibility are frequent causes for analogic change, it is highly probable that many speakers would interpret the overlapping boundaries of *absent, missing/lacking,* and *without* as ample justification for an analogic shift of *absent* from adjective to preposition. The identical argument for analogic shifting of use exists for *absent*'s being interpreted as a participial form substituting for semantically compatible participles in absolute constructions.

Clearly, then, the semantic overlapping that exists for adjectival *absent* and prepositional *without* on the one hand, and for adjectival *absent* and for participial/adjectival *lacking/missing* on the other, demonstrates that the addition of *absent* to a standard list of English prepositions is not unlikely considering the prepositional designation already granted *absent* by *W3, WC9, OED2,* and *RH2.* Additionally, the continual appearance of prepositional *absent* in various media can only serve to expand the acceptability of the form and make it less of a linguistic fad. On 17 August 1987, for example, I fortuitously encountered three separate uses of the form in three different media. First, on ABC's "World News this Morning," White House Chief of Staff Howard Baker, in reference to the lack of freedom and civil rights in Nicaragua, said "absent those things. . . ." Next, in the "Periscope" section of that date's *Newsweek* (6), in the second paragraph of an article entitled "A Free-for-All in '88," Howard Fineman notes that "Colorado Rep. Pat Shroeder's candidacy would be based in part on her enlarged state leadership role absent Gary Hart." Finally, in a notice (dated August 10, 1987) for a stockholder's meeting of the Daily Cash Accumulation Fund, Inc. (4), one learns that "British & Commonwealth has informed OMC that it would not proceed with the acquisition absent arrangements satisfactory to British & Commonwealth." More recently still, I have seen the usage spread even to college students. When I asked one of my students during the Spring Quarter of 1989 how he had injured his leg, he responded that he had fallen during a baseball game and that he feared his fraternity's intramural team would be "absent my wondrous abilities" for a week or two.

Whether the prepositional usage label granted *absent* by *W3*, *WC9*, *RH2*, and Shaw or the quasi-prepositional status of the *OED2* is an accurate assessment of its current status may remain uncertain, although its use does seem to have gone beyond those contexts in which it could equally be interpreted as an element in an absolute construction. This is especially apparent in a recent citation from the *Palo Alto Weekly* (30 Aug. 1989, 14) provided by Dwight Bolinger: "While the study certainly documents Menlo Park's traffic burdens, it is absent the kind of detailed analysis that we hope and assume will be forthcoming in an environmental impact report." Clearly, in such a predicative use, *absent* can be interpreted as having prepositional status if one uses semantically overlapping boundaries as a basis for analogizing *absent* to prepositional *without*. Such conversions to prepositions of other parts of speech are, furthermore, not without precedent in the development of English as the developments of "*along* (from an OE adjective), *among* (from the OE prepositional phrase *on gemong* 'in a crowd'), and *behind* and *beneath* from OE adverbs" (Millward *Biography* 152) show. Just as clearly, *absent* can be interpreted as functioning in most of the above-listed citations as the adjective element in an absolute construction, which function may ultimately lead to its being interpreted as a present participial form equated with *missing* or *lacking*. Yet this, too, could augment the movement of *absent* from adjective to dual use as adjective-preposition, since some analyses of English grammar already include some present participial forms, for example, *concerning*, *considering*, and *regarding*, among the existing single-word prepositions of standard American English (see, for example, Francis *The Structure*, 307).

Quirk et al. (*A Comprehensive Grammar* 665–71) also include the present participial form *pending* among simple prepositions and mention a number of *marginal prepositions* which have "affinities with other word classes such as verbs or adjectives" (667). These include Shaw's (54) *granted*, but also include forms that touch more closely on the semantic overlapping of *absent* with other adjectival/participial forms indicating 'lack of,' 'being without,' etc.: *excepting, excluding, failing, wanting, minus*. Although *lacking* and *missing* are strangely absent from this list, one might certainly include many of them as preposition-like forms considering their near synonymity and acceptability when substituted for the preposition *without* in the following context:

> *Without* any snags, we began our trip.

Many native speakers would accept at least some of the following in this context: *absent, excepting, excluding, failing, wanting, minus, lacking*, and perhaps *missing*. Although one or more of these proposed substitutes may strike some readers as stilted, the inclusion of all within the semantic domain of <non-presence> may have contributed to the apparent analogic shifting of *absent* so that it shares both the prepositional status of *without* and the marginal prepositional status of *minus* (Quirk et al. 667), the only two other non-*ing* members of the list.

Not only is the inclusion of marginal prepositions a necessary extension of the category of preposition to encompass forms which function analogously, even though their primary functions may be as adjectives or participles, but also the inclusion of *absent* as such a form seems even more justifiable when one considers Quirk et al.'s (658–69) negative tests for prepositions: they cannot have *that*-clauses, infinitive clauses, or subjective case personal pronouns as complements. Since probably no native speaker of English would unequivocally accept *Absent that he should go, we went instead*, or *Absent to go, we stayed*, or *Absent he, we left* as acceptable English constructions, *absent* seems to fulfill these negative requirements for prepositional status. Moreover, all three types of characteristic prepositional complements listed by Quirk et al. (657) seem possible with *absent* even in non-legal contexts:

> Absent engineering problems, the engine proved successful. (noun phrase)
> Absent what the engineers had feared, the engine functioned well. (nominal *wh*-clause)
> Absent just failing to perform, the engine will be a success. (nominal *-ing* clause)

While the final verdict that comes with a new usage's elimination or survival is, of course, in the offing, *absent* does seem to have achieved at least marginal prepositional status in American English as it has moved from purely legalistic into more generalized contexts. Perhaps the next generation of handbooks and grammars of English will include *absent* within its inventory of true and/or marginal prepositional forms.

Note

Portions of this material have appeared in the two articles in *American Speech* that appear in my list of references. I wish to express my thanks to the University of Alabama Press for allowing that material to be used here.

LIST OF ABBREVIATIONS

ACD	*American College Dictionary.* 1937.
AHD1	*American Heritage Dictionary of the English Language.* 1969.
AHD2Coll	*American Heritage . . .* 1982.
AHD3	*American Heritage Dictionary of the English Language.* 1992.
AHD3Coll	*American Heritage College Dictionary.* 1993.
AP	*Associated Press Stylebook and Libel Manual.* 1984.
Chi	*Chicago Manual of Style.* 1982.
DARE	*Dictionary of American Regional English.* 1985– .
DD	*The Doubleday Dictionary.* 1975.
IEU	*International English Usage.* 1986.
NYT	*The New York Times Everyday Dictionary.* 1982.
OAD	*Oxford American Dictionary.* 1980.
OED1	*Oxford English Dictionary.* 1933.
OED2	*Oxford English Dictionary.* 1989.
OEDSupp	*A Supplement to the Oxford English Dictionary.* 1972–86.
RH1	*Random House Dictionary of the English Language.* 1966.
RH1Coll	*The Random House College Dictionary.* 1968.
RH2	*Random House Dictionary of the English Language.* 1987.
RH2Coll	*The Random House College Dictionary.* 1979.
RHWColl	*Random House Webster's College Dictionary.* 1991.
S-B	*The Scribner-Bantam English Dictionary.* 1977.
SCD	*Standard College Dictionary.* 1963.
W2	*Webster's New International Dictionary.* 1934.
W3	*Webster's Third New International Dictionary.* 1961.
WC7	*Webster's Seventh New Collegiate Dictionary.* 1963.
WC8	*Webster's New Collegiate Dictionary.* 1973.
WC9	*Webster's Ninth New Collegiate Dictionary.* 1983.
WC10	*Merriam-Webster's Collegiate Dictionary.* 1993.
WDEU	*Webster's Dictionary of English Usage.* 1989.
WII	*Webster's II New Riverside University Dictionary.* 1984.
WNW1Coll	*Webster's New World Dictionary.* 1953.
WNW2Coll	*Webster's New World Dictionary.* 1972.
WNW3Coll	*Webster's New World Dictionary.* 1988.

REFERENCES

Abbott, E. A. 1870. *A Shakespearian Grammar: An Attempt to Illustrate Some of the Differences between Elizabethian and Modern English.* 3rd ed. Rpt. London: Macmillan, 1929.
Acronyms, Initialisms & Abbreviations Dictionary. 1986. Detroit: Gale.
Algeo, John. 1973. *On Defining the Proper Name.* Gainesville: U of Florida P.
———. 1977. "Grammatical Shibboleths." *James B. McMillan: Essays in Linguistics by His Friends and Colleagues.* Ed. James Raymond and I. Willis Russell. University: U of Alabama P, 53–72.
———. 1983. "Usage." *Needed Research in American English.* Publication of the American Dialect Society 71. University: U of Alabama P, 36–53.
Allen, Robert G. 1983. *Creating Wealth.* New York: Simon.
American College Dictionary. 1966. Ed. C. L. Barnhart. New York: Random.
American Heritage College Dictionary. 1993. Ed. Robert B. Costello. 3rd ed. Boston: Houghton.
American Heritage Dictionary of the English Language. 1969. Ed. William Morris. Boston: Houghton.
American Heritage Dictionary of the English Language. 1982. Ed. Margarie S. Berube. 2nd college ed. Boston: Houghton.
American Heritage Dictionary of the English Language. 1992. Ed. Anne H. Soukhanov. 3rd ed. Boston: Houghton.
American Psychological Association. 1974. *Publication Manual of the American Psychological Association.* 2nd ed. Washington, DC: APA.
———. 1977. "Guidelines for Nonsexist Language in APA Journals: Change Sheet 2." Washington, DC: APA.
———. 1983. *Publication Manual of the American Psychological Association.* 3rd ed. Washington, DC: APA.
American Psychological Association Task Force on Issues of Sex Bias in Graduate Education. 1975. "Guidelines for the Nonsexist Use of Language." *American Psychologist* 30: 682–84.
Anderson, Richard. 1989. *Writing that Works.* New York: McGraw.
Associated Press Stylebook and Libel Manual. 1984. Ed. Christopher W. French, Eileen Alt Powell, and Howard Angione. New York: AP.
Atwood, E. Bagby. 1962. *The Regional Vocabulary of Texas.* Austin: U of Texas P.
Austin, Thomas, ed. 1888. *Two Fifteenth-Century Cookery-Books.* Early English Text Society 91. London: Trubner.
Baehr, Ann Ediger. 1964. "An Evaluation of the 1952 and 1962 Editions of the Thorndike Barnhart Beginning Dictionary." *Elementary English* 41.4: 413–19.
Bailey, Richard W. 1992. "The First North American Dialect Survey." *Old English and New: Studies in Language and Linguistics in Honor of Frederic G. Cassidy.* Ed. Joan H. Hall, Nick Doane, and Dick Ringler. New York: Garland, 305–26.

Bain, Alexander. 1904. *Higher English Grammar.* Rev. ed. London: Longmans.
Baker, Russell. 1982. *Growing Up.* New York: Congdon.
Baker, Sheridan. 1976. *The Complete Stylist and Handbook.* 3rd ed. New York: Crowell.
———. 1982. *The Practical Stylist: with Readings.* 5th ed. New York: Harper.
———. 1990. *The Practical Stylist.* 7th ed. New York: Harper.
Barber, Charles. 1964. *Linguistic Change in Present-Day English.* University: U of Alabama P.
———. 1981. *Early Modern English.* London: Deutsch.
Barnet, Sylvan, and Marcia Stubbs. 1980. *Practical Guide to Writing.* 3rd ed. Boston: Little.
———. 1986. *Practical Guide to Writing.* 5th ed. Boston: Little.
Baron, Dennis. 1982. *Grammar and Good Taste.* New Haven: Yale UP.
———. 1986. *Grammar and Gender.* New Haven: Yale UP.
Baron, Naomi S. 1984. "Computer Mediated Communication as a Force in Language Change." *Visible Language* 18.2: 118–41.
Barrère, Albert, and Charles G. Leland, eds. 1889–90. *A Dictionary of Slang, Jargon, and Cant Embracing English, American, and Anglo-Indian Slang, Pidgin English, Tinkers' Jargon and Other Irregular Phraseology.* [London]: Ballantyne. Rpt. Detroit: Gale Research, 1967.
Bate, Barbara. 1978. "Nonsexist Language Use in Transition." *Journal of Communication* 28: 139–49.
Baugh, L. S. 1987. *Essentials of English Grammar.* Lincolnwood, IL: Passport.
Beale, Walter H., Karen Meyers, and Laurie L. White. 1982. *Real Writing with Stylistic Options.* Glenview, IL: Scott.
Bell, James K., and Adrian A. Cohn. 1981. *Handbook of Grammar, Style, and Usage.* 3rd ed. New York: Macmillan.
Berlin, James. 1984. *Writing Instruction in Nineteenth-Century American Colleges.* Carbondale: Southern Illinois UP.
Bernstein, Theodore M. 1965. *The Careful Writer.* New York: Atheneum.
Biber, Douglas. 1988. *Variation Across Speech and Writing.* Cambridge: Cambridge UP.
Bigelow, Marshall T. 1885. *Punctuation and Other Typographical Matters for the Use of Printers, Authors, Teachers, and Scholars.* 8th ed. Boston: Lee.
Billington, R. A. 1964. *The Protestant Crusade, 1800–1860: A Study of the Origins of American Nativism.* Chicago: Quadrangle.
Blaubergs, Maija S. 1980. "An Analysis of Classic Arguments against Changing Sexist Language." *Women's Studies International Quarterly* 3: 135–47.
Bloomfield, Leonard. 1933. *Language.* New York: Holt.
Bodine, Ann. 1975. "Androcentrism in Prescriptive Grammar: Singular 'They', Sex-indefinite 'He', and 'He or She'." *Language in Society* 4: 129–46.

Bolinger, Dwight. 1980. *Language—The Loaded Weapon: The Use and Abuse of Language Today.* London: Longman.

Boyd, Ruth. 1985. "The Use of Sex- and Number-neutral 'They' in Standard English." Master's thesis, U of Florida.

Brown, Gillian, and George Yule. 1983. *Discourse Analysis.* Cambridge: Cambridge UP.

Bryant, Margaret M., ed. 1962. *Current American Usage.* New York: Funk.

Burgess, Walton. 1856. *Five Hundred Mistakes of Daily Occurrence in Speaking, Pronouncing, and Writing the English Language, Corrected.* New York: Burgess.

Cannon, Garland. 1987. *Historical Change and English Word-Formation.* New York: Lang.

———. 1989. "Abbreviations and Acronyms in English Word-Formation." *American Speech* 64: 99–127.

Carey, G. V. 1957. *Punctuation.* Cambridge Authors' and Printers' Guides 6. Cambridge: Cambridge UP.

Carter, Bonnie, and Craig Skates. 1988. *The Rinehart Handbook for Writers.* New York: Holt.

———. 1990. *The Rinehart Handbook for Writers.* 2nd ed. Fort Worth, TX: Holt.

Chambers 20th Century Dictionary. 1983. New ed. Edinburgh: Chambers.

Chicago Manual of Style. 1982. 13th ed. Chicago: U of Chicago P.

Close, R. A. 1962. *English as a Foreign Language.* London: Allen.

The Concise Oxford Dictionary of Current English. 1982. 7th ed. Oxford: Oxford UP.

Cooper, Robert. 1979. "Language Planning, Language Spread, and Language Change." *Language in Public Life.* Georgetown University Roundtable on Languages and Linguistics 30. Ed. James E. Alatis and G. Richard Tucker. Washington: Georgetown UP, 23–50.

———. 1984. "The Avoidance of Androcentric Generics." *International Journal of the Sociology of Language* 50: 5–20.

———. 1989. *Language Planning and Social Change.* Cambridge: Cambridge UP.

Copperud, Roy H. 1980. *American Usage and Style: The Consensus.* New York: Reinhold.

Corder, Jim W., and John J. Ruszkiewicz. 1985. *Handbook of Current English.* 7th ed. Glenview, IL: Scott.

Council of Biology Editors. 1978. *Style Manual: A Guide for Authors, Editors, and Publishers in the Biological Sciences.* 4th ed. Arlington, VA: American Institute of Biological Sciences.

Creswell, Thomas J. 1975. *Usage in Dictionaries and Dictionaries of Usage.* Publication of the American Dialect Society 63–64. University: U of Alabama P.

———. 1985. "The Great Vowel Shift in Chicago." *Papers of the North Central Names Institute* 5: 176–89.

Crews, Frederick. 1977. *The Random House Handbook.* 2nd ed. New York: Random.
Crews, Frederick, and Sandra Schor. 1989. *The Borzoi Handbook for Writers.* 2nd ed. New York: Knopf. First ed. 1985.
Crittenden, Charlotte. 1987. "A Study of Six Pronoun Usages for Practical Purposes." Diss., U of Georgia.
Crystal, David. 1985. *A Dictionary of Linguistics and Phonetics.* 2nd ed. Oxford: Blackwell.
Curme, George O. 1931. *Syntax.* Boston: Heath.
———. 1947. *English Grammar.* New York: Harper.
de Sola, R. 1986. *Abbreviations Dictionary.* New York: Elsevier.
DeWolf, Gaelan Dodds. 1990. "Social and Regional Differences in Canadian English: Ottawa and Vancouver." *American Speech* 65.1: 3–32.
A Dictionary of American English on Historical Principles. 1944. Ed. William Craigie et al. 4 vols. Chicago: U of Chicago P.
Dictionary of American Regional English. 1985– . Ed. Frederic G. Cassidy and Joan Houston Hall. 2 vols. to date. Cambridge, MA: Harvard UP.
A Dictionary of American Slang. 1975. Ed. Harold Wentworth and Stuart Berg Flexner. 2nd supplemented ed. New York: Crowell.
A Dictionary of Americanisms on Historical Principles. 1951. Ed. Mitford M. Mathews. Chicago: U of Chicago P.
A Dictionary of Slang and Unconventional English. 1970. Ed. Eric Partridge. 7th ed. New York: Macmillan.
A Dictionary of Slang and Unconventional English. 1984. Ed. Paul Beale. 8th ed. New York: Macmillan.
Dietrich, Julia, and Marjorie M. Kaiser. 1986. *Writing: Self-Expression and Communication.* New York: Harcourt.
Dornan, Edward A., and Charles W. Dawe. 1987. *The Brief English Handbook.* 2nd ed. Boston: Little.
The Doubleday Dictionary. 1975. Ed. Sidney I. Landau. New York: Doubleday.
Dressman, Michael R. 1974. "Walt Whitman's Study of the English Language." Diss., U of North Carolina at Chapel Hill.
Dryden, John. 1957. "Defence of the Epilogue." *Three Plays.* New York: Hill, 163–74.
Dubois, Marguerite-Marie, et al., eds. 1955. *Larousse's French-English English-French Dictionary.* 2 vols. in one. New York: Washington Square.
Dunbar, Georgia, and Clement Dunbar. 1989. *A Handbook for Exposition.* New York: Harper.
Eble, Connie C. 1985. "Slang: Variations in Dictionary Labeling Practices." *The Eleventh LACUS Forum 1984.* Ed. Robert A. Hall, Jr. Columbia, SC: Hornbeam, 294–302.
Ehrlich, Eugene. 1986. *Bantam Concise Handbook of English.* New York: Bantam.
Eichler, Lillian. 1926. *Well-bred English.* Garden City, NY: Doubleday.

Elsbree, Langdon, and Gerald P. Mulderig. 1986. *The Heath Handbook*. 11th ed. Lexington, MA: Heath.

Emery, Donald W., John M. Kierzek, and Peter Lindblom. 1978. *Handbook of English Fundamentals*. New York: Macmillan.

The English Handbook of Grammar, Style and Composition. 1988. Piscataway, NJ: Research & Education Assoc.

Evans, Bergen, and Cornelia Evans. 1957. *A Dictionary of Contemporary American Usage*. New York: Random.

Farmer, John S., and William Ernest Henley. 1890–1909. *Slang and Its Analogues*. Rpt. New York: Kraus, 1965.

Fasold, Ralph W. and Walter W. Wolfram. 1970. "Some Linguistic Features of Negro Dialect." *Contemporary English: Change and Variation*. Ed. David L. Shores. Philadelphia: Lippincott, 53–85.

Fergenson, Laraine. 1989. *Writing with Style*. Fort Worth, TX: Holt.

Finegan, Edward. 1980. *Attitudes toward English Usage*. New York: Teachers College P.

Fishman, Joshua. 1973. "Language Modernization and Planning in Comparison with Other Types of National Modernization and Planning." *Language in Society* 2: 23–43.

Flesch, Rudolph and A. H. Lass. 1947. *A New Guide to Better Writing*. New York: Warner, 1975.

Flexner, Stuart Berg. 1976. *I Hear America Talking*. New York: Touchstone.

Flynn, James, and Joseph Glaser. 1984. *Writer's Handbook*. New York: Macmillan.

Follett, Ken. 1983. *On Wings of Eagles*. New York: Morrow.

Follett, Wilson. 1966. *Modern American Usage: A Guide*. Ed. and completed by Jacques Barzun et al. New York: Grosset. New York: Hill and Wang.

———. 1970. *Modern American Usage: A Guide*. Ed. and completed by Jacques Barzun et al. New York: Grosset.

Foster, Brian. 1968. *The Changing English Language*. New York: St. Martin's. Rpt. 1969.

Fowler, H. Ramsey. 1980. *The Little, Brown Handbook*. Boston: Little.

Fowler, H. Ramsey, Jane E. Aaron, and Kay Limburg. 1992. *The Little, Brown Handbook*. 5th ed. New York: Harper.

Fowler, H. W. 1965. *Dictionary of Modern English Usage*. Ed. Sir Ernest Gowers. 2nd ed. Oxford: Clarendon.

Francis, W. Nelson. 1958. *The Structure of American English*. New York: Ronald.

———. 1965. *The English Language: An Introduction*. New York: Norton.

———. 1979. "A Tagged Corpus: Problems and Prospects." *Studies in English Linguistics for Randolph Quirk*. Eds. Sidney Greenbaum, Geoffrey Leech, and Jan Svartvik. London: Longman, 192–209.

———. 1986. "Proximity Concord in English." *Journal of English Linguistics* 19: 309–17.

Francis, W. Nelson, and Henry Kučera. 1982. *Frequency Analysis of English Usage: Lexicon and Grammar.* Boston: Houghton.

Frank, Francine. 1989. "Language Planning, Language Reform, and Language Change: A Review of Guidelines for Nonsexist Usage." Frank and Treichler 105–33.

Frank, Francine Wattman, and Paula A. Treichler. 1989. *Language, Gender, and Professional Writing: Theoretical Approaches and Guidelines for Nonsexist Usage.* New York: MLA.

Friedman, Sonya. 1983. *Men Are Just Desserts.* New York: Warner.

Fries, Charles Carpenter. 1925. "The Periphrastic Future with *Shall* and *Will* in Modern English," *PMLA* 40: 963–1024.

Funk and Wagnalls' Standard Dictionary. 1967. Intl. ed. New York: Funk.

Garner, Bryan A. 1987. *A Dictionary of Modern Legal Usage.* New York: Oxford UP.

———. 1990. "The Missing Common Law Words." *The State of the Language.* Ed. Christopher Ricks and Leonard Michaels. Berkeley: U of California P, 235–45.

Gefvert, Constance J. 1988. *The Confident Writer: A Norton Handbook.* 2nd ed. New York: Norton.

Gere, Anne Ruggles. 1992. *Writing and Learning.* 3rd. ed. New York: Macmillan.

Glass, Montagnue. 1911. *Potash and Perlmutter: Their Copartnership Ventures and Adventures.* New York: Grosset.

Good, Donald W., and Thomas L. Minnick. 1979. *Handbook.* New York: Macmillan.

Gordon, Karen Elizabeth. 1984. *The Transitive Vampire.* New York: Times.

Gordon, M., A. Singleton, and C. Rickards, eds. 1986. *Dictionary of New Information Technology Acronyms.* 2nd ed. London: Kogan Page.

Gorrell, Robert, Charlton Laird, and Margaret Urie. 1988. *Modern English Rhetoric and Handbook.* 7th ed. Englewood Cliffs, NJ: Prentice.

Grant, Donald L., and Mildred Bricker. 1975. "Some Notes on the Capital 'N'." *Phylon* 36: 435–43.

Green, William H. 1977. "Singular Pronouns and Sexual Politics." *College Composition and Communication* 18: 150–53.

Greenbaum, Sidney. 1988. "A Proposal for an International Computerized Corpus of English." *World Englishes* 7: 315.

———. 1989. *A College Grammar of English.* New York: Longman.

Guth, Hans P. 1977. *Concise English Handbook.* 4th ed. Belmont, CA: Wadsworth.

———. 1985. *New English Handbook.* 2nd ed. Belmont, CA: Wadsworth.

———. 1990. *New English Handbook.* 3rd ed. Belmont, CA: Wadsworth.

Hacker, Diana. 1988. *Rules for Writers: A Concise Handbook.* 2nd ed. New York: St. Martin's.

———. 1991. *The Bedford Handbook for Writers.* 3rd ed. Boston: St. Martin's.
Hairston, Maxine, and John J. Ruszkiewicz. 1988. *The Scott, Foresman Handbook for Writers.* Glenview, IL: Scott.
———. 1991. *The Scott, Foresman Handbook with Writing Guide.* New York: Harper.
Hall, J. Lesslie. 1917. *English Usage: Studies in the History and Uses of English Words and Phrases.* Chicago: Scott.
Halliday, M. A. K. 1985. *An Introduction to Functional Grammar.* London: Arnold.
Harper Dictionary of Contemporary Usage. 1985. 2nd ed. Ed. William Morris and Mary Morris. New York: Harper.
Harrison, James A. 1884. "Negro English." *Anglia* 7: 232–79.
Hart, H. C. 1983. *Rules for Compositors and Readers.* 39th ed. Oxford: Oxford UP.
Heffernan, James A. W., and John E. Lincoln. 1986. *Writing: A College Handbook.* 2nd ed. New York: Norton.
———. 1990. *Writing: A College Handbook.* 3rd ed. New York: Norton.
Henley, Nancy M. 1987. "This New Species that Seeks a New Language: On Sexism in Language and Language Change." Penfield 3–27.
———. 1989. "Molehill or Mountain? What We Know and Don't Know about Sex Bias in Language." *Gender and Thought: Psychological Perspectives.* Ed. Mary Crawford and Margaret Gentry. New York: Springer-Verlag, 59–78.
Henley, Nancy M., and D. Dragun. 1983. "A Survey of Attitudes toward Changing Sex-biased Language." American Psychological Association. Anaheim, CA, Aug.
Hiltz, Starr Rozanne, and Murray Turoff. 1978. *The Network Nation.* Reading, MA: Addison-Wesley.
Hodges, John C. and Mary E. Whitten. 1986. *Harbrace College Handbook.* 10th ed. San Diego: Harcourt.
Hodges, John C., Mary E. Whitten, Winifred B. Horner, Suzanne S. Webb, with Robert K. Miller. 1990. *Harbrace College Handbook.* 11th ed. San Diego: Harcourt.
Hofland, Knut, and Stig Johansson. 1982. *Word Frequencies in British and American English.* Bergen: Norwegian Computing Centre for the Humanities.
Hole, Judith, and Ellen Levine. 1973. "The First Feminists." *Radical Feminism.* Ed. Anne Koedt, Ellen Levine, and Anita Rapone. New York: Quadrangle, 3–16.
Hopper, Vincent, Cedric Gale, and Ronald C. Foote. 1982. Rev. by Benjamin W. Griffith. *Essentials of English Grammar.* 1961. New York: Barron's Educational Series.
Hornby, A. S. 1974. *Oxford Advanced Learner's Dictionary of Current English.* New York: Oxford UP.

Houghton, D. E. 1968. "Humor as a Factor in Language Change." *English Journal* (Nov.). Reprinted in *Aspects of American English*, 2nd ed. Eds. Elizabeth M. Kerr and Ralph M. Aderman. New York: Harcourt, 1971. 302–10.

Howell, James F., and Dean Memering. 1989. *Brief Handbook for Writers*. 2nd ed. Englewood Cliffs, NJ: Prentice.

Huddleston, Rodney. 1984. *Introduction to the Grammar of English*. Cambridge: Cambridge UP.

Hudson, R. A. 1980. *Sociolinguistics*. Cambridge: Cambridge UP.

Hughes, Langston. 1932. *The Dream Keeper*. New York: Knopf.

———. 1932. *The Negro Mother*. New York: Knopf.

———. 1959. *Selected Poems of Langston Hughes*. New York: Knopf.

Hunt, Douglas. 1991. *The Riverside Guide to Writing*. Boston: Houghton.

International English Usage. 1986. Ed. Loreto Todd and Ian Hancock. London: Croom Helm.

Interrante, C. F. and F. J. Heyman, eds. 1893. *Standardization of Technical Terminology, Principles and Practices*. Philadelphia: ASTM.

Irmscher, William F. 1981. *The Holt Guide to English*. 3rd ed. New York: Holt.

Jacobus, Lee A. 1989. *Writing as Thinking*. New York: Macmillan.

Jernudd, Bjorn, and Jyotirindra Das Gupta. 1971. "Towards a Theory of Language Planning." *Can Language be Planned? Sociolinguistic Theory and Practice for Developing Nations*. Ed. Joan Rubin and Bjorn H. Jernudd. Honolulu: UP of Hawaii, 195–215.

Jespersen, Otto. 1928. *Syntax*. Part VII of a *Modern English Grammar on Historical Principles*. London: Allen. Rpt. 1965.

———. 1938. *Growth and Structure of the English Language*. New York: Free. Rpt. 1968.

———. 1954. *Morphology*. Part VI of a *Modern English Grammar on Historical Principles*. London: Allen. Rpt. 1965.

Johansson, S. 1978. *Some Aspects of the Vocabulary of Learned and Scientific English*. Gothenburg: Acta Universitatis Gothoburgensis.

Johansson, S., and K. Hofland. 1987. "The Tagged LOB Corpus: Description and Analyses." *Corpus Linguistics and Beyond*. Ed. W. Meijs. Amsterdam: Rodopoi, 1–20.

———. 1989. *Frequency Analysis of English Vocabulary and Grammar*. Oxford: Oxford UP.

Johansson, S., and E. Norheim. 1988. "The Subjunctive in British and American English." *ICAME Journal* 12: 27–36.

Jones, R. 1987. "Accessing the Brown Corpus Using an IBM PC." *ICAME Journal* 11: 44–47.

Jonson, Ben. 1947. "The English Grammar." *Ben Jonson*. Ed. C. H. Herford, Percy Simpson, and Evelyn Simpson. Vol. 8. Oxford: Clarendon, 463–553.

Karls, John, and Ronald Szymanski. 1990. *The Writer's Handbook*. Chicago: National Textbook.

Katz, Elihu, Martin L. Levin, and Herbert Hamilton. 1963. "Traditions of Research on the Diffusion of Innovation." *American Sociological Review* 28: 61–78.

Kaye, G. 1989. "A Concordance Browser for Tagged Texts and Bilingual Texts." 10th Annual ICAME Conference. Bergen, Norway, June.

Kennedy, X. J., and Dorothy M. Kennedy. 1990. *The Bedford Guide for College Writers.* 2nd ed. Boston: St. Martin's.

Keyser, Samuel J., and Paul M. Postal. 1976. *A Beginning English Grammar.* New York: Harper.

Kiesler, Sara, Jane Siegel, and Timothy W. McGuire. 1984. "Social Psychological Aspects of Computer-Mediated Communication." *American Psychologist* 39: 1123–34.

Kiley, Dan. 1983. *The Peter Pan Syndrome.* New York: Dodd.

Kirkland, James W., and Collett B. Dilworth, Jr. 1985. *Concise English Handbook.* Lexington, MA: Heath.

———. 1990. *Concise English Handbook.* 2nd ed. Lexington, MA: Heath.

Kirszner, Laurie G., and Stephen R. Mandell. 1989. *The Holt Handbook.* 2nd ed. Fort Worth, TX: Holt.

———. 1992. *The Holt Handbook.* 3rd ed. Fort Worth, TX: Harbrace.

Klein, Ernest. 1966. *A Comprehensive Etymological Dictionary of the English Language.* New York: Elsevier.

Kolln, Martha. 1984. *Language and Composition: A Handbook and Rhetoric.* New York: Macmillan.

Krogvig, I., and S. Johansson. 1984. "*Shall* and *Will* in British and American English: a Frequency Study." *Studia Linguistica* 38: 70–87.

Kushner, Harold S. 1981. *When Bad Things Happen to Good People.* New York: Schocken.

Lamar, Nedra Newkirk. 1978. "Does a Finger Fing?" *Language Awareness.* 2nd ed. Eds. Paul Eschholz, Alfred Rosa, and Virginia Clark. New York: St. Martin's, 6–7.

Lamberts, J. J. 1972. *A Short Introduction to English Usage.* New York: McGraw.

Langendoen, D. Terence. 1970. *Essentials of English Grammar.* New York: Holt.

Lawson, Sarah. 1980. "Words and Women: A Transatlantic View." *American Speech* 55: 129–31.

Leech, Geoffrey, and Jan Svartvik. 1975. *A Communicative Grammar of English.* London: Longman.

Leggett, Glenn, C. David Mead, Melinda G. Kramer, with Richard S. Beal. 1988. *Prentice Hall Handbook for Writers.* 10th ed. Englewood Cliffs, NJ: Prentice.

Lehmann, Winfred P. 1962. *Historical Linguistics: An Introduction.* New York: Holt.

Leonard, Sterling Andrus. 1929. *The Doctrine of Correctness in English Usage 1700–1800.* New York: Russell. Rpt. 1962.

Lewis, Norman. 1948. *Better English.* New York: Dell. Rpt. 1956.

Librarie Larousse. 1960. *Larousse de Poche.* New York: Washington Square.
Lindberg, Stanley W., J. Martyn Walsh, and Anna Kathleen Walsh. 1980. *Van Nostrand's Plain English Handbook.* New York: Van Nostrand.
Linguistic Society of America. 1979. "LSA Style Sheet." *LSA Bulletin* 84: 46–48.
Little, Greta D. 1992. "Punctuation and Its Impact on Readers." *The Eighteenth LACUS Forum.* Ed. Ruth M. Brend. Lake Bluff, IL: LACUS, 464–73.
Little, Greta D., and Kimberly G. Johnson. 1988. "Punctuation in the Twentieth Century." *The Fourteenth LACUS Forum 1987.* Ed. Sheila Embleton. Lake Bluff, IL: LACUS, 289–98.
Logie, H. B. 1934. "Medical Nomenclature." *American Speech* 9: 17–24.
Longman Dictionary of the English Language. 1984. Harlow, Essex: Longman.
Longman Guide to English Usage. 1988. Ed. Sidney Greenbaum and Janet Whitcut. Harlow, Essex: Longman.
Longyear, Marie. 1989. *The McGraw Hill Style Manual.* New York: McGraw.
"LSA Guidelines for Nonsexist Usage." 1992. *LSA Bulletin* 135 (March): 8–9.
Luck, Martha. 1972. *Instant Secretary's Handbook.* New York: Dell.
Lumiansky, R. M. 1950. "New Orleans Slang in the 1880's." *American Speech* 25: 38.
Lunsford, Andrea, and Robert Connors. 1989. *The St. Martin's Handbook.* New York: St. Martin's.
———. 1992. *The St. Martin's Handbook.* 2nd ed. New York: St. Martin's.
McDavid, Raven I., Jr. 1958. "The Dialects of American English." Francis (1958) 480–543.
McDavid, Virginia, ed. 1969. *Language and Teaching: Essays in Honor of W. Wilbur Hatfield.* Chicago: Chicago State College.
McKernan, John. 1991. *The Writer's Handbook.* 2nd ed. New York: Holt.
MacKinnon, Catharine A. 1982. "Feminism, Marxism, and the State: An Agenda for Theory." *Signs* 7: 515–44.
McMahan, Elizabeth, and Susan Day. 1988. *The Writer's Rhetoric and Handbook.* 3rd ed. New York: McGraw.
Malinowski, B. 1923. "The Problem of Meaning in Primitive Languages." *The Meaning of Meaning.* C. K. Ogden and I. A. Richards. London: Routledge and Kegan Paul, 296–336.
Mallery, Richard. 1944. *Grammar, Rhetoric, and Composition.* New York: Barnes, 1967.
Malmstrom, Jean. 1977. *Grammar Basics: A Reading/Writing Approach.* Rev. 2nd ed. Rochelle Park, NJ: Hayden.
Manchester, William. 1983. *The Last Lion, Winston Spencer Churchill, Visions of Glory, 1874–1932.* Boston: Little.
Mandelik, Peter, and Stanley Schatt. 1975. *A Concordance to the Poetry of Langston Hughes.* Detroit: Gale.
Marckwardt, Albert H., and Fred Walcott. 1938. *Facts about Current English Usage.* New York: Appleton.

Marius, Richard, and Harvey S. Wiener. 1988. *McGraw-Hill College Handbook*. 2nd ed. New York: McGraw.
Martyna, Wendy. 1978. "What Does 'He' Mean?: Use of the Generic Masculine." *Journal of Communication* 28: 131–38.
———. 1980. "The Psychology of the Generic Masculine." *Women and Language in Literature and Society*. Ed. Sally McConnell-Ginet, Ruth Borker, and Nelly Furman. New York: Praeger, 36–78.
Memering, Dean, and Frank O'Hare. 1980. *The Writer's Work: Guide to Effective Composition*. Englewood Cliffs, NJ: Prentice.
Mencken, H. L. 1963. *The American Language*. One volume abridged edition of the 4th edition and 2 supplements. Ed. Raven I. McDavid, Jr., with David M. Maurer. New York: Knopf.
Merriam-Webster's Collegiate Dictionary. 1993. Ed. Frederick C. Mish. 10th ed. Springfield, MA: Merriam.
Meyer, Charles F. 1987a. "Apposition in English." *Journal of English Linguistics* 20.1: 101–21.
———. 1987b. *A Linguistic Study of American Punctuation*. New York: Lang.
———. 1989. "Restrictive Appositions: an Indeterminate Category." *English Studies* 70: 147–66.
———. 1992a. *Apposition in Contemporary English*. Cambridge: Cambridge UP.
Meyers, Miriam Watkins. 1989. "Adult Writers' Generic Pronoun Choices." *Beyond Boundaries: Sex and Gender Diversity in Communication*. Ed. Cynthia M. Lont and Sheryl A. Friedley. Fairfax, VA: George Mason U, 63–74.
———. 1990. "Current Generic Pronoun Usage: An Empirical Study." *American Speech* 65: 228–37.
———. 1993. "Forms of *they* with Singular Noun Phrase Antecedents." *Word* 44: 181–92.
Meyers, Walter E. 1972. "A Study of Usage Items Based on an Examination of the Brown Corpus." *College Composition and Communication* 23: 155–69.
Michael, Ian. 1970. *English Grammatical Categories and the Tradition to 1800*. Cambridge: Cambridge UP.
Miller, Casey, and Kate Swift. 1988. *The Handbook of Nonsexist Writing*. 2nd rev. ed. New York: Harper.
Millward, C. M. 1989. *A Biography of the English Language*. New York: Holt.
———. 1980. *Handbook for Writers*. New York: Holt.
Mittins, W. H., Mary Salu, Mary Edminson, and Sheila Coyne. 1970. *Attitudes to English Usage*. London: Oxford UP.
MLA Handbook for Writers of Research Papers, Theses, and Dissertations. 1977. New York: MLA.
Montgomery, Michael, and John Stratton. 1981. *The Writer's Hotline Handbook*. New York: New American Library.
Moon, William Least Heat. 1982. *A Journey into America, Blue Highways*. Boston: Little.
Naisbitt, John. 1982. *Megatrends*. New York: Warner.

National Council of Teachers of English. 1985. *Guidelines for Nonsexist Use of Language in NCTE Publications.* Rev. ed. Urbana, IL: NCTE.
Neeld, Elizabeth Cowan. 1986. *Writing.* 2nd ed. Glenview, IL: Scott.
Neman, Beth S. 1983. *Writing Effectively.* Columbus, OH: Merrill.
Neuleib, Janice, and Maurice Scharton. 1982. "Grammar Hotline." *College English* 44: 413–16.
New Century Dictionary of the English Language. 1942. New York: D. Appleton-Century.
Newmeyer, Frederick J. 1986. *Linguistic Theory in America.* 2nd ed. San Diego: Academic.
The New York Times Everyday Dictionary. 1982. Ed. Thomas M. Paikeday. New York: Times.
New York Times Manual of Style and Usage. 1976. Ed. Lewis Jordan. New York: Times Books.
Nichols, Patricia. 1980. "Planning for Language Change." *San Jose Studies* 6.2: 18–25.
Nicholson, Margaret. 1957. *A Dictionary of American-English Usage.* New York: Signet.
Nilsen, Alleen Pace. 1977. "Sexism in Children's Books and Elementary Teaching Materials." *Sexism and Language.* Ed. Alleen Pace Nilsen, Haig Bosmajian, H. Lee Gershuny, and Julia P. Stanley. Urbana, IL: NCTE, 160–79.
———. 1987. "Guidelines against Sexist Language: A Case History." Penfield 37–64.
"No 'Chicks,' 'Broads,' or 'Niggers' for *Old Mole.*" 1969. *Masculine/Feminine: Readings in Sexual Mythology and the Liberation of Women.* Ed. Betty Roszak and Theodore Roszak. New York: Harper Colophon, 291–93. Rpt. from *Nickel Review,* Syracuse, NY, 13 Apr. 1970.
Nunberg, Geoffrey. 1983. "The Decline of Grammar." *The Atlantic Monthly* Dec.: 31–46.
———. 1990. *The Linguistics of Punctuation.* Stanford: Center for the Study of Language and Information.
O'Hare, Frank. 1989. *The Modern Writer's Handbook.* 2nd ed. New York: Macmillan.
O'Hare, Frank, and Dean Memering. 1990. *The Writer's Work: Guide to Effective Composition.* 3rd ed. Englewood Cliffs, NJ: Prentice.
Onions, C. T., et al. 1966. *The Oxford Dictionary of English Etymology.* New York: Oxford UP.
Oxford American Dictionary. 1980. Ed. Eugene Ehrlich et al. New York: Oxford UP.
Oxford English Dictionary. 1933. Ed. James A. H. Murray et al. 13 vols. Oxford: Clarendon.
Oxford English Dictionary. 1989. Prepared by J. A. Simpson and E. S. C. Weiner. 2nd ed. 20 vols. Oxford: Clarendon.

Oxford Guide to the English Language. 1984. Ed. E. S. C. Weiner and J. M. Hawkins. Oxford: Oxford UP.

Packer, Nancy Huddleston, and John Timpane. 1989. *Writing Worth Reading: A Practical Guide.* 2nd ed. New York: St. Martin's.

Parsons, Elsie Clews. 1913. *The Old-Fashioned Woman: Primitive Fancies about the Sex.* New York: Putnam's.

Partridge, Eric. 1947. *Usage and Abusage.* New York: Harper. Rpt. New York: Viking Penguin, 1973.

———. 1958. *Origins: A Short Etymological Dictionary of Modern English.* New York: Macmillan.

———. 1960. *A Charm of Words.* New York: Macmillan.

Penfield, Joyce, ed. 1987. *Women and Language in Transition.* Albany: SUNY P.

Perrin, Porter. 1965. *An Index to English.* Chicago: Scott Foresman.

Perrin, Robert. 1990. *The Beacon Handbook.* 2nd ed. Boston: Houghton.

Phyfe, William Henry P. 1914. *Eighteen Thousand Words Often Mispronounced.* New York: Putnam's.

Picht, Herbert. 1985. *Terminology: An Introduction.* Guilford: U of Surrey, Dept. of Linguistics and Intl. Studies.

Portes, Alejandro. 1989. "'Hispanic' proves to be a false term." *Chicago Tribune* 2 Nov., sec. 1: 11.

Potter, Simeon. 1964. *Modern Linguistics.* New York: Norton.

Pyles, Thomas. 1971. *The Origins and Development of the English Language.* 2nd ed. New York: Harcourt.

Pyles, Thomas, and John Algeo. 1970. *English: An Introduction to Language.* New York: Harcourt.

Quirk, Randolph, and Sidney Greenbaum. 1975. *A Concise Grammar of Contemporary English.* New York: Harcourt.

Quirk, Randolph, and Jan Svartvik. 1980. *A Corpus of English Conversation.* Lund: GWK Gleerup.

Quirk, Randolph, Sidney Greenbaum, Geoffrey Leech, and Jan Svartvik. 1972. *A Grammar of Contemporary English.* New York: Seminar P.

———. 1985. *A Comprehensive Grammar of the English Language.* London: Longman.

Random House College Dictionary. 1968. Ed. Laurence Urdang. New York: Random.

Random House Dictionary of the English Language. 1966. Ed. Jess Stein. New York: Random.

Random House Dictionary of the English Language. 1987. Ed. Stuart Berg Flexner. 2nd ed. New York: Random.

Random House Webster's College Dictionary. 1991. Ed. Robert B. Costello. New York: Random.

Reid, Stephen. 1989. *Prentice-Hall Guide for College Writers.* Englewood Cliffs, NJ: Prentice.

———. 1992. *Prentice-Hall Guide for College Writers.* 2nd ed. Englewood Cliffs, NJ: Prentice.
Reinking, James A., and Andrew W. Hart. 1988. *Strategies for Successful Writing: A Rhetoric, Reader, and Handbook.* Englewood Cliffs, NJ: Prentice.
Richards, Jack, John Platt, and Heidi Weber. 1980. *Longman Dictionary of Applied Linguistics.* Essex: Longman.
Richmond, Virginia P., Joan Gorman, and Paula Dyba. 1985. "Generic and Non-generic Gender Referent Usage among Students in Grades 3–12." Eighth Annual Communication, Language, and Gender Conference, Lincoln, NE, 12 Oct.
The Right Word at the Right Time. 1985. London: Reader's Digest Assn.
Roberts, Paul. 1952. "Pronominal 'This': A Quantitative Analysis." *American Speech* 27: 170–78.
Rogers, Everett M., and F. Floyd Shoemaker. 1971. *Communication of Innovations: A Cross-cultural Approach.* 2nd ed. New York: Free.
Rosen, Leonard J., and Laurence Behrens. 1992. *The Allyn & Bacon Handbook.* Boston: Allyn.
Roy, Emil, and Sandra Roy. 1989. *Prentice Hall Guide to Basic Writing.* Englewood Cliffs, NJ: Prentice.
Russell, I. Willis, and Mary Gray Porter. 1981. "Among the New Words." *American Speech* 58: 111–17.
Sager, J. C., D. Dungworth, and P. F. McDonald. 1986. *English Special Languages.* Wiesbaden: Brandstetter.
Sapir, Edward. 1921. *Language.* Rpt. New York: Harvest, 1949.
Scargill, M. H. 1974. *Modern Canadian English Usage: Linguistic Change and Reconstruction.* Toronto: McClelland.
Schiffhorst, Gerald J., and John F. Schell. 1991. *The Short Handbook for Writers.* New York: McGraw.
Scott, Fred Newton. 1926. *The Standard of American Speech and Other Papers.* Boston: Allyn. (The title essay is abridged in Williamson and Burke 1971, 4–11.)
The Scribner-Bantam English Dictionary. 1977. Ed. Edwin B. Williams. New York: Scribner's Sons.
Semmelmeyer, Madeline, and Donald O. Bolander. 1965. *Instant English.* Mundelein, IL: Career.
Shastri, S. V. 1988. "The Kolhapur Corpus of Indian English and Work Done on Its Basis so Far." *ICAME Journal* 12: 15–26.
Shaw, Harry. 1981. *Harper Handbook of College Composition.* 5th ed. New York: Harper.
———. 1987. *Dictionary of Problem Words and Expressions.* Rev. ed. New York: McGraw.
Shertzer, Margaret. 1986. *The Elements of Grammar.* New York: Macmillan.
Sklar, Elizabeth S. 1988. "The Tribunal of Use: Agreement in Indefinite Constructions." *College Composition and Communication* 39: 410–22.

Skwire, David, and Francis Chitwood Beam. 1985. *Student's Book of College English*. 4th ed. New York: Macmillan.
Slotkin, Alan R. 1985. "*Absent* 'Without': Adjective, Participle, or Preposition." *American Speech* 60: 222–27.
———. 1989. "Response: Prepositional *Absent*: An Afterword." *American Speech* 64: 167–68.
Sorrels, Bobbye D. 1983. *The Nonsexist Communicator: Solving the Problem of Gender and Awkwardness in Modern English*. Englewood Cliffs, NJ: Prentice.
Spencer, Matthew Lyle. 1914. *Practical English Punctuation*. Menasha, WI: Banta.
Spitzer, Michael. 1986. "Writing Style in Computer Conferences." *IEEE Transactions on Professional Communication* 29.1: 19–22.
Staczek, John J. 1989. "'This here's your kitchen': Possessive adjectives as determiners." SECOL XL, Mar. 23–25.
Standard College Dictionary. 1963. Ed. Ramona R. Michaelis. New York: Funk.
Stanton, Elizabeth Cary. 1895. *The Woman's Bible*. New York. Rpt. as *The Original Feminist Attack on the Bible*. New York: Arno, 1974.
Stewart, Donald C. 1985. "Fred Newton Scott." *Traditions of Inquiry*. Ed. John Brereton. New York: Oxford UP, 26–49.
Stockwell, Robert P., Paul Schachter, and Barbara Hall Partee. 1973. *The Major Syntactic Structures of English*. New York: Holt.
Strehlow, Richard A. 1983. "The Varieties of Compound Terms and Their Treatment." *Standardization of Technical Terminology: Principles and Practices*. ASTM STP 806. Ed. C. G. Interrante and F. J. Hyman. Philadelphia: American Soc. for Testing and Materials.
Strunk, William, Jr., and E. B. White. 1979. *Elements of Style*. 3rd ed. Macmillan.
Success with Words: A Guide to the American Language. 1983. Pleasantville, NY: Reader's Digest.
Summey, George. 1949. *American Punctuation*. New York: Ronald.
A Supplement to the Oxford English Dictionary. 1972–86. Ed. Robert W. Burchfield. 4 vols. Oxford: Clarendon.
Sweet, Henry. 1891. *A New English Grammar*. Part I. Rpt. Oxford: Clarendon, 1960.
Sweet, Henry. 1953. *Anglo-Saxon Primer*. 9th ed. Rev. by Norman Davis. Oxford: Clarendon.
Teachers of English to Speakers of Other Languages. 1979. "TESOL Quarterly Stylesheet." *TESOL Quarterly* 13: 607–11.
Temple, Michael. 1982. *A Pocket Guide to Correct English*. New York: Barron's Educational Series.
Thomas, Henry. 1954. *Better English Made Easy*. Rpt. New York: Warner, 1983.

Towell, J., and H. Sheppard, eds. 1986. *Computer and Telecommunications Acronyms.* Detroit: Gale.

Traugott, Elizabeth Closs. 1972. *A History of English Syntax: A Transformational Approach to the History of English Sentence Structure.* New York: Holt.

Treichler, Paula, and Francine Wattman Frank. 1989. "Guidelines for Nonsexist Usage." Frank and Treichler 135–278.

Trimmer, Joselph F. 1992. *Writing with a Purpose.* 10th ed. Boston: Houghton.

Trimmer, Joseph F., and James M. McCrimmon. 1988. *Writing with a Purpose.* 9th ed. Boston: Houghton.

Troyka, Lynn Quitman. 1990. *Simon & Schuster Handbook for Writers.* Englewood Cliffs, NJ: Prentice.

———. 1993. *Simon & Schuster Handbook for Writers.* 3rd ed. Englewood Cliffs, NJ: Prentice.

Tyler, Lisa. 1989. "Nonsexist Language: Do People Really Use This in the 'Real World'?" Association for Business Communication Conference, Las Vegas, Nov.

US Government Printing Office. 1986. *Manual of Style.* New York: Gramercy.

Vallins, G. H. 1952. *Good English: How to Write It.* 2nd ed. London: Deutsch.

Visser, F. Th. 1972. *An Historical Syntax of the English Language.* Vol. 2. Leiden: Brill.

Walters, Keith. 1981. *Nonsexist Language: An Assessment of the Diffusion of a Communicative Innovation.* Thesis, U of South Carolina.

Watkins, Floyd C., and William B. Dillingham. 1986. *Practical English Handbook.* 7th ed. Boston: Houghton.

———. 1992. *Practical English Handbook.* 9th ed. Boston: Houghton.

Webster's Dictionary of English Usage. 1989. Ed. E. Ward Gilman. Springfield, MA: Merriam-Webster.

Webster's II New Riverside University Dictionary. 1984. Ed. Anne H. Soukhanov. Boston: Riverside.

Webster's New Collegiate Dictionary. 1973. Ed. Henry Bosley Woolf. 8th ed. Springfield, MA: Merriam.

Webster's New International Dictionary. 1934. Ed. William Allan Neilson. 2nd ed. Springfield, MA: Merriam.

Webster's New World Dictionary. 1953. Ed. Joseph H. Friend and David B. Guralnik. College ed. Cleveland: World.

Webster's New World Dictionary. 1976. Ed. David Guralnik. 2nd college ed. Cleveland: Collins.

Webster's New World Dictionary. 1988. Ed. Victoria Neufeldt. 3rd college ed. New York: Simon.

Webster's Ninth New Collegiate Dictionary. 1983. Ed. Frederick C. Mish. Springfield, MA: Merriam.

Webster's Seventh New Collegiate Dictionary. 1963. Ed. Philip B. Gove. Springfield, MA: Merriam.

Webster's Third New International Dictionary. 1961. Ed. Philip B. Gove. Springfield, MA: Merriam.

Weiner, E. S. C., and J. M. Hawkins. 1985. *The Oxford Guide to the English Language.* London: Oxford UP.

Wentworth, Harold. 1944. *American Dialect Dictionary.* New York: Crowell.

Wentworth, Harold, and Stuart Berg Flexner. 1975. *Dictionary of American Slang.* 2nd supplemented ed. New York: Crowell.

Wheeless, Virginia Eman, Cynthia Berryman-Fink, and Denise Serafini. 1982. "The Use of Gender-specific Pronouns in the 1980's." *Encoder* 9: 35–46.

White, Fred D. 1986. *The Writer's Art.* Belmont, CA: Wadsworth.

White, Richard Grant. 1880. *Every-Day English.* Boston: Houghton.

Whitehall, Harold. 1956. *Structural Essentials of English.* New York: Harcourt.

Whitley, M. Stanley. 1978. "Person and Number in the Use of We, You, and They." *American Speech* 53: 18–39.

Williamson, Juanita V., and Virginia M. Burke, eds. 1971. *A Various Language: Perspectives on American Dialects.* New York: Holt.

Willson, Robert F., Jr., John N. Kierzek, and W. Walker Gibson. 1982. *The Macmillan Handbook of English.* 7th ed. New York: Macmillan.

The Written Word II. 1983. New York: Houghton.

Wyld, H. C. 1956. *A History of Modern Colloquial English.* 3rd ed. with additions. Oxford: Blackwell.

INDEX OF WORDS CITED

a while, 131
a, an, 131, 184
about to, 127
above, 125
absent (prep.), 194
accept, 131
advice/advise, 131
advise, 126
affect, 132
Afro-American, 86
agenda, 126
aggravate, 131
aimed to, 21
ain't, 3, 24, 49, 132, 187
alibi, 128
all of which, 118
all ready, 131
all right, alright, 131
all that, 118, 127
all this, 118
all together, altogether, 131
allusion, 131
alone, leave or let, 105, 126
alot, 131
already, 131
among, 132
amount, 131
and, 58, 127
and etc., 131
and/or, 131
antenna, 69
anticipate, 125
any one, anyone, 131
any, of, 128
anymore, 2
anyone, 128
anyways, 131
anywheres, 131
apt, 131
aren't I, 2, 126
Aryan, 86
as, 131
as far as, 31
as long as, 106

as regards, 128
attorney, 104
awfully, 132
awhile, 131
bad/-ly, 128, 131
barf, 16
barrister, 104
BASIC, 13
BCS, 13
be (omit), 21
because, 132
beef, 16
behalf of, in or on, 128
being as, 132
being that, 131
beside/-s, 131
better, 127
between, 132
between you and I, 163, 187
Birmingham (pron.), 23
black, 81
blackamoor, 86
blue, 82
boarder (pron.), 21
booze, 18
border (pron.), 21
boss, 17
bread, 17
brother, 34
brown, 82
btw, 49, 51
bubblegum machine, 15
burgeon, 125
but, 58
but that/what, 132
can, 65, 68, 132
cannot but, 126
Caucasian, 87
caught (pron.), 5
celebrant, 126
censor, 131
censure, 131
center around, 131
certain, fairly, 126
Chicago (pron.), 5

Chicano/Chicana, 82, 90
chilly, 16
clap, 16
club, 38
cohort, 128
combine (pron.), 5
comple-/compliment, 132
complete, 126
comprise, 125
concerned, far as, 31
concerning, 200
considering, 200
contact (v.), 127
continual, continuous, 132
cot (pron.), 5
could of, 132
county mounty, 16
criteria, 131
crumbing, 15
data, 126, 128, 131
daughter, 34
dawn (pron.), 5
Dear Sir, 91
debut (v.), 127
delicious, 24
dent (pron.), 21
deprecate, 125
dew (pron.), 21, 26
different from/than, 132
dilemma, 125
dint (pron.), 21
discomfit, 125, 126
disinterested, 125, 131
diss, 15
dived, 29, 31, 139
don (pron.), 5
don't let's, 106
done, 126
doubt if/that/whether, 126, 128
dove (p.t.), 29, 31, 126, 139

223

down home, 25
dragged, 139
drug (p.t.), 139
drunk (adj.), 127
due to, 128, 131
each other, 126
-ee, 155
effect, 132
either . . . are, 127
enthuse, 131
etc., 131
ever, rarely, 127
except, 131
excepting, 201
excluding, 201
failing, 201
fairly certain, 126
family, 34
far as, 31
farther, 126, 131
father, 34
fault (v.), 126
federal, 67
fewer, 132
finalize, 128
five-finger discount, 15
flaming, 51
fortuitous, 125
French door, 86
French fries, 86
frog (pron.), 5
from whence, 128
further, 126, 131
garage (pron.), 22, 23
gear, 23
Gentlemen, 91
ghost, 51
gift (v.), 128
girl, old, 24
give (p.p.), 24
go for sushi, 16
gon, 21
gonna, 21, 50
good, 6, 131
gotta, 50
grandfather, 34
grandmother, 34
grandparents, 34

granted, 201
Gypsy, 82
hanged, 132
harrow, 27
harry, 27
hawk (pron.), 5
he, 91, 174
he or she, 174
head up, 125
headquarter (v.), 128
help but, 128
himself, 64
hock (pron.), 5
hog (pron.), 5
holly (pron.), 5
home, down or up, 25
hopefully, 69, 131
hot (pron.), 5
hug, 16
hung
hung (p.p.), 127, 132
I, 112, 187
I, it is, 109, 129
ice, 17
idle (v.), 126
if, 126, 128
illusion, 131
impact (v.), 91
imply, 131, 165
important/-ly, 126
in behalf of, 128
individual, 128
infer, 125, 131, 167
intrigue (v.), 126
irregardless, 131
is when, is where, 132
isolate (pron.), 5
it, 117
it is I/me, 109, 129
its, it's, 131
japscrap, 16
kind, 132
kind of, 132
knowed, 143
labeled/labelled, 102
labor/labour, 102
laboratory (pron.), 102
lack for, 128

lacking, 199
lacquer, 103
ladder, 103
ladybird, 103
laid back, 17
lame duck, 103
lamentable (pron.), 102
landward/-s, 103
larder, 103
lashings, 103
last, second or third, 106
lather (pron.), 102
launch (pron.), 102
lawman, 104
lay, 129, 132
lay a duck's egg, 103
lay-by, 103
layabout, 103
leaned/leant, 103
leaped/leapt, 103
learned/learnt, 103
leary/leery, 104
leave, 105, 131
leave alone, 105, 126
leeway, 104
leftward/-s, 103
legionary, legionnaire, 104
Legionnaire's disease, 11
legislature, 76
legpull, 103
leisure (pron.), 102
lend (n.), 105
lengthy, 104
less, 132
let, 105, 131
let alone, 105
let's, 106
leukaemia/leukemia, 102
levee, 104
leveled/levelled, 102
lever (pron.), 102
liable, 131
liaise, 106
libel, 104

INDEX

libeled/libelled, 102
licence/license, 102
lichen (pron.), 102
licorice/liquorice, 102
lido, 103
lie, 103, 129, 132
lie doggo, 103
lieutenant (pron.), 102
lift, 103
like (conj.), 69, 106, 126, 132
like for, 106
like to, 106
likely, 106, 127, 131
lint, 103
liqueur (pron.), 102
liquor, 104
litchi (pron.), 102
liter/litre, 102
livable/liveable, 102
liverish, 103
loan (v.), 105, 128
loath/loth, 102
local, 103
locate, 104
-log/-logue, 102
long as, 106
long-sighted, 104
loo, 104
look, look like, 106
loose, loosen, lose, 132
lorry, 104
lose, 132
loss (pron.), 102
lot (pron.), 102
loud hailer, 104
lounge suit, 104
louver/louvre, 102
love, 104
lovely, 24
lover, 104
lumber, 104
lumme! 104
lunchbox, 15
lurker, 51
luster/lustre, 102
luv, 104
man, 91

markedness, 2
marry (pron.), 21
materialize, 126, 128
may, 65, 68, 132
may be, maybe, 131
may can, 21
me, 112, 187
me, it is, 109, 129
media, 131
merry (pron.), 21
might could, 21
might of, 131
minus, 201
missing, 199
more complete, 126
most, 128, 131
mother, 34
myself, 64
native, 82
Native American, 81
nauseous, 125
Negro, 82
new (pron.), 21, 26
no, 163
noon (pron.), 26
nope, 51
not too, 128
number, 131
of, 131, 163, 169
of any, 128
off of, 131
OIC, 51
ok, o.k., okay, 131
old girl, 24
on behalf of, 128
one, 177
one . . . is, 126
-oneself, 128, 130
only, 128
OTOH, 51
our, 71
parents, 34
passed away, 2
paunch (pron.), 102
pen (pron.), 21
pending, 201
personality, 128
pin (pron.), 21

PITA, 51
pleaded, 29
pled, 29
pond (pron.), 5
posslq, 104
power (pron.), 21
practically, 128
predicate (v.), 126
premiere (v.), 128
presently, 126
president, 67, 169
principal, principle, 131
proven (p.p.), 128
providing, 128
providing, 66
quote (n.), 127
raise, 127, 131
ralph, 17
rarely ever, 127
re, 51
real, 131
real good, 6
reason is because, 132
reason why, 128
red, 82
Red Indian, 85
red man, 85
regarding, 128, 201
rehi, 51
responsible, 126
right smart, 25
rip off, 16
rise, 131
rouge (pron.), 22
sandwich, 86
savings, a, 128
saw (p.p.), 24
saw (p.t.), 29, 141
schmo, 17
screaming, 51
second last, 106
-self, 64, 128, 130, 131
seen (p.t.), 29, 141, 163
set, 132
shall, 68, 126, 129, 132
should like, 106
should of, 131
Sir, 91

sister, 34
sit, 132
slander, 104
slang, 17
sleaze-factor, 16
slow, 65
smart, a right, 25
snail-mail, 51
sneaked, 144
snuck, 144
so, 128, 131
solicitor, 104
sometime, 128
son, 34
sort, 132
sort of, 132
speak, 65
stalk (pron.), 5
state, 67
stock (pron.), 5
stomp, 128
suppose to, 131
sure (adv.), 131
sushi, go for, 16
swam, 141
swum (p.t.), 141
tackle, 23
talk, 65
tend, 128
than, 131
that, 65, 115, 126, 128, 131, 132
theirself, -selves, 132

then, 131
there, their, they're, 131
they, 174
they're, 131
third last, 106
this, 115
thusly, 128, 132
thy, 78
to, too, two, 131
toke, 17
too, 131
too, not, 128
toot (pron.), 26
towel (pron.), 21
tower (pron.), 21
toxic waste dump, 15
transpire, 128
trim, 23
try and, 127, 131
TSR, 51
tube, 16
Tuesday (pron.), 26
tune (pron.), 21
two, 131
type, 127
uninterested, 131
unique, 125, 132
up home, 25
usage, 1
use to, 131
various of, 127
veg out, 16
venetian blind, 86

via, 51
vice president of, 169
waiter, 35
wanting, 201
well, 131
when, 132
whence, from, 128
where, 132
where's the beef?, 16
whether, 126
which, 65, 115, 131, 132
white, 82
who, 64, 66, 132
who's, 131
whom, 66
whose, 131
why, reason, 128
will, 68, 126, 129, 132
wimp, 16
-wise, 127
without, 198
would like, 106
would of, 132
WYSIWYG, 51
ye, 25
yellow, 82
yep, 51
you and I, 187
you 'uns, 25
your, 71
yours, 107
yourself, 64